Poguemahone

Poguemahone

Patrick McCabe

unbound

First published in 2022

Unbound
Level 1, Devonshire House, One Mayfair Place, London W1J 8AJ
www.unbound.com

© Patrick McCabe, 2022

Typesetting by Christian Brett, Bracketpress

A CIP record for this book is available from the British Library

ISBN 978-1-80018-111-3 (hardback)
ISBN 978-1-80018-185-4 (trade paperback)
ISBN 978-1-80018-112-0 (ebook)

Printed in Great Britain by CPI Group (UK)

1 3 5 7 9 8 6 4 2

With special thanks to Paddy Goodwin

In loving memory of Paschal Quinn, Longford

NOTE:
pogue (Gaelic) = kiss
tóin = arse
pog mo thóin, *Eng trans*: poguemahone = kiss my arse

Oh yes, that's what they'll tell you
that the women are worse than the
men by far
&
whether or not that's true
I am sorry I have to say
that I do not know
but I'll tell you this
yes, this one thing I'll tell you
that it certainly is
when it comes to
our Una –
for this
longtime past
she has been
literally putting me
astray in the head,
with no matter where you go
it's Dan
Dan
Dan
yes, Dan this
Dan that
& Dan the other
every hour of the blooming…

ah, she's not the worst of them
all the same
not by a long shot
with some of the spakes
she comes out with

making you howl
with the laughter.
Get out of my way!
she crows
& away off with her then
swinging around the corner,
don't talk to me about
The New Caledonia and
funky inner cosmonauts
she calls back, hesitating,
dismissing me with an impatient
wave: now don't be annoying me
for I'm off on my travels
to get myself a cup of tea.
Yes, a sweet wee tasty cuppa
so let me be hearing no more
about it!

Oi – get over here, you!
she says the other day
yes, get you the frig on over,
do you hear?
Is it true that only just this morning
you were up in London?
yes it is, I says
what of it anyway
as she turns &
lets out this
outlandish yelp
making a swipe at a
crock of flowers,
causing a near riot in the lobby
as staff, from all angles,
come running
out of breath
are you trying to ruin
our reputation
one of them says,
with a bit of a nervous
laugh.

But for all our disagreements
I didn't ever think that we'd
end up where we did,
that is to say
beyond in Limehouse
Basin
tossing canvas bags
over the parapet of a bridge
shivering there together
in the cold East London dawn,
with the pair of us
awestruck
petrified beneath the red sky
spanning Jerusalem,
watching leopards with
the wings of eagles
gliding into land
over a body of water
already on fire.

I mean, you wouldn't, would
you?

But somehow that's how
it always tends to be
with our Una
that's how it always
seems to end up.

Anyhow, I was telling you
– after the two of us had
had yet another set-to,
in the exact same place,
the front hall where she'd chucked
the flowers,
I decided, once and for all,
that enough was enough
and so away I went, the very
second I got the chance,

off out the
automatic doors –
with nothing, only
a toothbrush &
a couple of shirts
flung inside a case,
down to the station
where I boarded the train
& headed on up to
London,
off once more in the direction of
good old 'Killiburn',
as Paddy Conway
the landlord of
The Bedford Arms
used to call it
in the old days.

& a right old trip
I had of it,
I have to say,
not having been anywhere
near the place
for God knows how long –
close on forty years, I'd say.

But all the same,
I'm glad that I did it
yes, went out of my way
to make the effort
because now that I'm back
all, at last, seems peaceful once more.
With a lovely sense of calm
miraculously having been
restored
(at least until this morning
when I heard her at it again).
I'll give you
Creedence Clearwater Revival!
she bawls at Todd the American.
Yes, what would you know
about music or anything else, she says.

Because me, I bloody well knew
Ian Hunter, yes and all the
rest of Mott the Hoople!

Not giving the poor fellow
so much as a chance to
open his mouth.

Causing a right kerfuffle and no mistake.

Which was not,
to be honest,
all that surprising
because she always gets like
that
whenever Hollywood
Awards Season once again
comes around
announcing to anyone
who can be bothered their
backside to listen
that she thinks Jane Fonda
will scoop the gold for *Klute*
& that Saoirse Ronan
– the 'poor child' – she doesn't
have so much as
a prayer
whether for *Mary Queen of Scots*,
Little Women
or any of her other
stupid films
which you have to laugh at
I mean, how could you not.
When you think of poor old Hanoi Jane
– Fonda, that is,
and her not having so much as
made a movie in years
never mind
running around
winning
Oscars
for
them.

With the next thing you know the Yankee, Todd, is ambling over –
dabbing away at the scratches she's inflicted, giving out about Richard
Nixon and the whole bloody motherfucking no-good bunch!
Don't talk to me about Tricky Dicky, he says, because I'm one hundred
per cent up to speed with just exactly what is going on there.
&, without so much as another word, he's away off down the corridor
again, complaining and disputing as he swings and rotates his plump
chunky fists in the air.

But apart from all that, it's a grand old spot,
with very few complaints, all told, these days.
Not now that Una's back in business
with her amateur dramatic
shenanigans,
making sure she's keeping the rest of us on our toes.
The Cliftonville Capers, she calls her most recent
foray,
swearing it's going to be the best show ever.
Although she hasn't, not for certain, entirely made up
her mind
Regarding the precise format
she intends it to take.

I'm actually at my wit's end,
she admits, shredding a tissue as she
shifts from one end of the window seat
to the other.

Sometimes in the night, you can hear her getting up
& moving around
slippering along the tiles of the corridor
or just sometimes sitting there alone in the library,
sobbing fitfully.
All the young dudes, she says to herself,
all the old decrepit wretches, more like,
carrying the news here, there &
everywhere,

                                                  all

              over

the

              accursed, blasted place.

Only the other day she put a fish in the laundry.

Hanoi Jane, to be honest,
she isn't all that bad,
but as far as movies and films go
I've always preferred the
old black-and-whites.

There's always matinees,
any amount,
just as soon as you've
enjoyed your tasty yum-yums,
courtesy Cliftonville à la carte.

The maitre d'
is a dead ringer
for Margaret Rutherford – that
you maybe remember
from a lifetime of playing
all these bossy spinsters on bicycles
with her spaniel jowls
& bulky frame
not to mention her formidable
no-nonsense manner,
like she's headmistress
of a girls' public school.

Ah, good old Margaret,
she's always somewhere
nosing around
to see what it is she might
be able to see.

They say that the women
are worse than the men
riteful, titeful titty folday.

I was just in the middle of humming
a couple of verses away to myself
when out of the blue arrives Una who
declares, smacking her fist: 'This time, Dan,
I definitely have it!'

& stands there, poised,
waiting for me to answer
arms folded, beside the potted plant
but before I can manage to
so much as open my mouth
she exclaims:
'The show I've decided
I'm going to put on
the name of it is:
Green For Danger!'

& starts picking at the
threads of her jumper
all breathless
elaborating as to how
whole streets in her mind
seem to have
disappeared –
yes, taken
away in seconds
completely
& utterly
obliterated
she says,
without so much as a
by-your-leave
with you just standing
there, minding your own business
when – whee! – you hear
this rocket

it's a V-1
& then you hear nothing
until down it comes
& another wall
or gable-end tumbles
gone, as so many memories
before
reduced to rubble forever.

I'm glad she's made the decision
all the same
although I wouldn't thank you
for the likes of Trevor Howard
who was actually in the film
she was talking about
Green For Danger
with all his big talk about being
this fearless and courageous
night-time commando
going on all these missions
when all the time
he's sitting at home
reading the *Daily Express*
& chomping *hmmph hmmph*
on his briar
for fuck's sake
I mean, I ask you.

Una's latest recruit
for her Cliftonville Capers
All-Star Repertory Troupe
is Butley Henderson
who must be over eighty
if he's a day
& is under the impression
that he's God's gift to music.

Although I have to admit he's a
dab hand on the cornet:
Miles Davis
Kind of Blue –
you name it.

Although you wouldn't think it
to look at him
with those great big specs
and a big roundy bonce like
it's been carved out of lard.
Still not over what my sister
got it into her head
to do to him only just
the other day
convinced it was him
who'd started this business
of calling her names
& whispering to everyone
that she's the spit of *Ho Chi Minh*
with all the weight she's
been losing since coming in here
toasted good & brown from sitting
in her wheelchair out among the roses.

Yes, here he comes, it's Ho Chi Minh!
she swears she overheard him saying
except that I know
it was Todd Creedence & his buddies who
christened her that
but o boys, I swear,
I really did have to laugh
because Una, God love her
she really can be hilarious
whenever she gets something
into her head
grabbing the brass instrument as poor
old Butley, he just snoozes away
in a rattan chair on the verandah
with his paws on his paunch
as – PARP! – right into his ear
doesn't she blast it
scaring the bejasus out of
the poor old divil

'*O, mother mercy!*' he squeals
like someone you'd hear
in the village
back in Ireland long ago.
'*Yes, Currabawn!*' she squeals
as she lifts it up
and blows it again
into his poor old other
ear this time

& then goes off with her two sides
splitting,
tossing the instrument away with disdain
as she shouts to all and sundry
Damn and blast yiz English no-good
Sassenachs
Una Fogarty she'll fart in your face!

Before slumping across the sofa
in the foyer
& starting up this falsetto whistle
an impromptu rendition of an
old showband tune
one we used to dance to in the
Killiburn National long ago
about some poor old idiot who left
his village in Co. Galway
& went off to America
with his brown-paper parcel
underneath his arm
& before he knew it
had found himself conscripted
& shoved in the back of a Chinook,
heading straight for Saigon
and the battleground of South East Asia.
'The Blazing Star of Athenry'
it was called,
as off he went to get himself
riddled.

&, as God is my judge,
never in my life have I seen my sister
laughing
not like that
with her two legs splayed as
the tears rolled down her face
thinking about the poor old conscript
getting himself dumped away out
there in Vietnam.
Poor wee Athenry! she squeals,
before slinging a cushion and
hitting another elderly resident
in the face.
'Boo hoo!' the woman bawls, wagging
her finger at the unrepentant Una,
who by now is turning cartwheels,
spry as any young thing
having lost four stone,
a veritable human twig
in fact
& just about as far as you might
possibly imagine
from what was once the humungous
'Fudge' Fogarty
in good old Killiburn, North London,
long ago.

Now a nut-brown stick
at the tender age of 70 yrs.

O, man alive,
but some of the crack
you can have in here!

Because that *loodramawn* Trump,
he was back on the television
again this morning.

'Motherfucker!' shouts Todd Creedence
shaking his fist at the screen
because he, really and truly,
absolutely *loathes* the
orange-headed goon
& was about to go over
and knock the power off
when, fortunately,
David Attenborough appeared
introducing a segment about this plucky
little iguana
outwitting all these snakes
in the desert
'Motherfucking gooks!' bawls Todd
as the wee lizard scuttles
and away with him then to the
relative safety of the higher ground.

But what's this I was saying
yes, I was telling you
wasn't I, about
The Bedford Arms
the pub up in Killiburn where
we all used to drink.
All the old gang
in the good times,
Elephants Quigley and Mike Ned
& Tom McGlone from the townland
of Moondice –
well, damn it anyhow
haven't I gone and
forgotten the whole bloody thing again.

But look, don't worry,
for it'll come back
by & by,
like
            a gopher
                              poking its snout
                                        above a crater.

Le cúnamh Dé, as
Auntie Nano used to say.

Yes, with the help of God
what you're thinking of
it'll come back –
but not always,
with it arriving
sometimes
almost as if to taunt you
standing poised
there in front of you
before taking off
& haring away off down the
boreen
before you can even so much
as catch a grip of
it
when, out of nowhere,
you hear that familiar whistle
going *whee*
& then *whee* again
as you lift your head
with your mouth
hanging open
& realise that it's already
too late,
for now that the whistling's ceased
here it is
yes, it's coming
coming
coming
coming
out of the sky
the noiseless destroyer
V
V
V

& there you are
like an *ommadawn*
standing in rags
trembling right there
in the middle
of the road.

With the only problem being
that there isn't any road –
no, not any longer
nothing, only bomb-gap
with what had once
been a street of buildings
now completely vanished
& already tangled weeds
growing in and out
of the decimated roofs.

But, anyway,
where was I
yes, the pub up in London
The Bedford Arms
wasn't I telling you
where, to my surprise,
on my recent journey
up Killiburn way
instead of Paddy Conway
who did I discover,
standing there behind
the counter
only this brand-new Nigerian barman
who you wouldn't have
expected in a million years
to know the slightest little bit
about
clurichauns or
leprechauns
or anything to do
with the old tales and stories
of Currabawn,
or, for that matter, Ireland –
but, as I was soon to discover,
in fact, there was very little
that he *didn't* know
about the subject
everything, indeed,
to do with them
making these precise little sketches

on a beermat with the sharpened point
of a pencil
as the pair of us
sat there
chatting away

this is what he looks
like, he said,
what would be
our equivalent in Nigeria.
There are those who would insist
Mr Exu is the devil, he told me,
but that is not true, because mostly
he is a person like us. You will
see, for example, that he does not have
horns.
Indeed, his principal symbol, his
one essential and necessary attribute
being the erect phallus
which is, of course, the sign of life
& constant vitality
that makes *Exu* the embodiment of
energy, of *axe*.

With him sliding the
drawing across the counter
as he gave me a smile
& I had to laugh
when I saw this
particular detail that he'd
pencilled in
namely a great big monstrosity of
an extended, anglewise prick
which looked so funny
set against the tall grinning
figure's flaring swallowtail
coat.

'Yes, Mr Exu!' he laughed,
that's what they call
him in the little village I come from
in Africa
in the place where I was born,

that devious mythical trickster,
poet of melancholy,
weird user of words
watching them tumble wild in his head
as they take his fancy,
one minute there smiling
without so much as a care
in the world
& then the next thing you know
the world framed in the living
pearl of his eye
where you see yourself standing
looking back out at yourself
for he brings them free as any
bird of the air
every single story as ever there was
slipping with ease across
the frontiers of language
whether blackbird
or robin
perhaps even creatures that cannot be named
or seen
he is the one
who comes for us when it's time,
whether it be the thirties
or the forties
or the seventies
the one that in your culture
you tell me is called
the *gruagach*.

No, you genuinely
wouldn't have expected
a twenty-four-year-old African barman
to know the first thing about
any of that
all that ancient old folklore stuff
the very same
as Auntie Nano used to love
to tell us all about
when we were small
the fairy *Shee* and

the magic of the hawthorn
yes, ghosts and all the rest of
that type of thing.

But that is exactly what he drew
the one and only *Mr Exu*.
& who,
with that smashing great ponytail
& high-polished white loafers,
really did cut the most handsome
& dashing figure all told,
especially with that neat little
trança
a twirly wee braid curling elegantly
backward
more commonly found, or so my
Nigerian friend informed me,
in the carved Yoruba images of Exu.

But anyhow, back to London
and the old times and the way
that, in modern days, things
would appear to have gone.
It's difficult to credit the extent to which
'Auld Killiburn', as they used to call it,
how it has transformed over the years.
With very few of the old-stagers in evidence now
&
the few that are in a sorry-looking state
exhibiting no end of strokes & limps
& the Lord knows what.
But I'm still very glad I took the trouble
to make the trip.

Here in Cliftonville Chateau
I'm sure you'll be pleased to know
there's a rescue dog called Murphy
an Afghan with these two big panda eyes
& everyone is stone-mad cracked
about him,
with that huge pink lolling tongue

as he watches the telly
alongside Todd, who dotes on him.

Go, iguana! is all you can hear.

Auntie Nano used to have a *madra* too.
A dog, I mean.
With the very same black-rimmed eyes and
huge stilt-legs.
And who bit the arse off a fellow
in her club one night,
Mike Ned Hurley, as I recall.
Not that poor old Mike,
God rest him,
not that he merits much sympathy
in hindsight
for it was his own bloody fault
never sober a day in his life
&, even yet, I can see him,
standing at the top of the stairs
at the entrance to Nano's club
& under his arm
a manhole cover
warning everyone about
what it was he was going to do
yes, once and for all,
show everyone
just what it was that 'Mike Ned' thought
yes, thought of so-called
'great' fucking Britain of 1974
ha ha, he whooped, look at it now
not quite so quick to tell us all what to do
the laughing stock of the world
so you are
with your oil crisis
& your three-day week
power shortages
& even the Queen of England
having to brush her teeth in the dark
well don't worry Ma'am

for I'll very quick fix that
for you, says Mike
aye, & for everyone else that needs
it down there.
Anyone dumb enough
to get in the way of a man from Mayo
are you listening, you scutbags
are youse attending to the words
of Mike Ned Hurley?
I'm a rambling man, a gambling man
All ten of youse I'll batter
And if you must the rozzers call
To me it will not matter.

Yes, he would give it to them,
he vowed repeatedly
every single Oxbridge layabout
and no-good limey Sassenach
who made it their habit to
frequent the world-famous
premises of the one and only
Nano Fogarty.

Grr! he snarled again
elevating the weighty steel
discus good and high above his head
Watch out, you lot, they
heard him snarl,
for here it comes
to do some damage
to every last one of you
yes, every single
bully boy
psychopath
he shouted
every man-jack, swank
&
crank
each drunken reporter
communist
waster
or
big-mouth lout

Mike Ned is the man
he is the one to sort you
out
once and for all
yes
once and for *fughing all*
let there be no mistake about that,
Nano Fogarty, he snarls,
as
up goes the circular cast-iron
weapon of destruction
as he releases a final unmerciful howl
&

bump
bump
bump
down it goes
the heavy cast-iron plate
clunking
& clanging
for all it's worth
before landing with a wallop
right in the middle of a
plate of steaming brown stew
belonging to a hod-carrier
I knew from the town of Attymass,
coincidentally in County Mayo too.

So that's the sort of thing
you'd have to learn to expect
if you wanted to frequent Auntie Nano's
famous club
in the heart of London City
directly underneath
the Piccadilly Line

No other comes close! blinked the neon sign
above the door.
With pretty much every specimen of
social outcast
poet, Trotskyist, neo-Trotskyist
to be found holding court

along with no end of union
leaders, anarchists, hippies, yippies,
glue-sniffers
&
a significant complement of out-of-work actors
& directors
not to mention
policemen
sacked and otherwise
security guards
neo-fascists
crypto-pinkos
rear admirals
queer admirals
neo-loyalist tub-thumpers
and every other kind of crony imaginable
sooner or later ending up in
Nano's famous club
underneath the station
in the heart of
Piccadilly.

With pretty much anything likely to happen
when you got there
such as Brendan Behan threatening Harold
Pinter with a 'cough-softening blue fucking
Jaysus of a walloping' one night
&
then ending up with the pair of them singing
together onstage.

In its time, it was one of the most
sought-after late-night West End establishments
a subterranean wonderland located slap bang
in the heart of Piccadilly
from the outside more like a public toilet
than a than a *demi-monde* cavern
where every manner of temptation was
purportedly available.

But then in those days the spell of the
drinking club was still extremely powerful
& not just late or in the early hours either

but, even more so perhaps,
around midday & into the early afternoon
with the lights still turned down
&
everyone sipping their expensive
poison, gossiping away like there was no tomorrow,
it possessed the allure of profoundly embargoed
fruit.
So small wonder Brendan Behan would
drop by whenever he was in town,
on one occasion taking a piss
on top of the tropical fish
& Nano
swearing blind
that he'd never get back in.
No, I'm afraid
I'm afraid
not this time
not on this occasion,
a chairde,
my friends,
not a chance.
HE IS BARRED!

Then the next thing you'd go in
& the two of them would be
horsing glasses of the rawest
whiskey down their throats
knocking back lashings
of porter and hard *uisquebaugh*
like they reckoned there
was no tomorrow
& performing every ballad
&
poem
under the sun
including, as it happened,
one of my own particular favourites,
'The Killiburn Brae'.

Which goes: they say that the
women are worse than the men
riteful-titeful-titty-folday!

& is all about
this woman
driving the devil completely demented
so much so
that he brings her back
on his shoulders all the way
from hell,
as Nano went, *whoop!*
and hoisted her heavy tweed
skirt way above her knees –
you ought
to have seen the faces
of the visitors,
those curious tourists
you would get in there,
on safari assessing the oddballs –
as the bowld Nano Fogarty
what did she do,
kicked off her slippers
as Brendan Behan gave a roar
before taking the proprietress
by the hand &,
gazing sympathetically
into her eyes,
began rotating her small hand
hypnotically, like a spinner turning
her wheel,
now near, now distant
then kicking his heels & full-throating
with *brio*:
Yes, there was an auld man down by Killiburn Brae
Riteful, titeful, titty folday
There was an auld man down by Killiburn Brae
Had a curse of a wife with him most of his days
  With me foldoarol dol, titty fol ol
  Foldol dol dolda dolder olday

The divil he says I have come for your wife
Riteful titeful titty folday
The divil he says I have come for your wife
For I hear she's the curse and the bane of your life
  With me foldoarol dol, titty fol ol
  Foldol dol dolda dolder olday

O, man alive,
as they used to always say,
you never heard better
than the auld balladry that night
as Nano, God bless her
doesn't she take a flying *lep*
and land right in front of
this astonished American.

They say that the women
are worse than the men,
you could hear her screech then,
even louder than Behan,
as the American
what does he go and do then
he vanishes underneath her voluminous
homespun tweeds
yes, swallowed by the tent
of her homespun, billowing *sciorta*

& disappears, God
help him
somewhere in
there among the folds of
Nano's petticoats
as she sings away
&, up on the rostrum,
Behan The Laughing Boy sings
his heart out,
even worse than before.
Yee-hoo, he cheers,
give the woman
    in

      the

         bed

           more

             porter!

Ah, now, but they were grand times surely
in good old London and Killiburn
long ago,
may God forgive me should I play you false.

It was 'as good as a play'
you would often
hear them comment
in Nano's Famous Club
& which I must concede
it most definitely was that
the night Joe Meek from Holloway
came wandering in
the dark and troubled
but extremely gifted record producer
with the long jaw and gleaming, lathered quiff
in his single-breasted charcoal suit and black tie
& who eventually, later on,
succeeded in shooting
first his landlady
& then himself
& who, on this particular night
had been discoursing at length
on the subject of the 'little people',
or 'the grogueys' as he called them
confiding to anyone
he could find who was
prepared to listen that
he knew, and always had
that, just by looking at Nano,
gazing into those eyes of emerald green
that she was
'one of them'
yes, their own flesh and blood,
that *groguey* breed and kin.

You can believe Joe Meek,
he repeated, emphatically
before starting off again into lost
airmen and their ghosts

and the howls you could sometimes hear
after midnight in the cemetery
in the graveyard opposite his flat
on the Holloway Road
where he recorded the nocturnal
pleas of the souls of
seriously unquiet vampires
along with the plaintive appeals of
many lonely 'grogueys' adrift in the dawn
what, it hardly needs stating,
with chat the like of that
it came as absolutely no surprise at all
to any of the customers
when they opened the paper
and saw his chalk-pale face looking back at them
Joe Meek, as it turns out, not so meek
& who had turned the pistol on himself
as his landlady lay there dying at his feet.

But, like all the eccentrics
for whom our Nano's had
provided a kind of home from home,
everyone agreed he'd be sorely missed
'God bless you, Joe, me auld
segocia – may you rest in everlasting
peace!'
someone shouted as they
raised a glass
'It'll be all quiet in North London
now!'
'To Seosamh O'Ceansa!' everyone cheered,
'God speed to you, Joe, for there's not a one
in Nano's as'd ever utter a cruel word against ya!'

With one man making the sign of the Cross
as a signal mark of respect for 'Mr Meek'
& his unique
understanding of all
those other strange &
unearthly other worlds
far beyond this one that we know,
or think we do.

As peace once again
being seen to reign
in Nano's,
or so it seemed –
because you were never
quite sure
no, never what you might call
one hundred per cent certain
with that unpredictable
giddygoat atmosphere
where you knew that anything
practically anything at all
it could happen at any moment
with the atmosphere
enhanced
by the dim electric's shine
on the potted plants
and Nano's own specially appointed
colour scheme of lurid 'Irish' green and gold.
Which had the effect of making you feel
right from the minute you sat down
that you were not unlike the unfortunate
fish that Behan had pissed on
swimming aimlessly
among the artificial reeds,
mindless in warm water.

There were also supposed to be spies
in & out
from time to time
although I couldn't
vouch for that claim's
authenticity either.
Kim Philby, they said
was one of them
one night, along with
Noël Coward.

Yes, suave as you like, apparently,
in the warm red glow of the
alcove, chatting away to Nano herself
& smoking through an elegant holder.
Ian Fleming will be dropping by

later on,
I remember her whispering behind her hand
that night.
Although, in fact, he didn't –
at any rate, not while I was there.

But then, like all of us Fogarty
Auntie Nano
didn't she have a reputation
for being something of an exaggerator,
you might say.
Yes, a dewy-eyed gilder of the lily,
perhaps.
A bit like myself, as my sister Una is
always saying whenever she wants to get
a dig in.
Yes, more self-indulgent *raiméis*
coming out of my brother's mouth
a lot of old balderdash
courtesy of our man Dan.

Not that I care what she says
for, as I'm sure you'll agree,
there's no one more contrary
when it comes to it than our Una,
God love her.

So, whenever I see she intends
to be like that
I just walk away & go on with
my story
whether it happens to be
about life that we lived
on the building sites
long ago or the fun and games
we had in Nano's.
Like the night, for example,
she introduced me to 'the delightful
Peter Sarstedt'.

Where
do

you
go
to
my
lovely
was the song that he'd had some
success with at the time
I think it may actually
have reached number one.
O Peter! Nano moaned,
with those emerald-green
peepers twinkling
Peter my sweetheart,
my
very
own
lovely
boy
Peter
my asthoreen
grá
my own dashing
fear
óg
lán
de
draíocht
– why, goodness,
that dear boy,
he is absolutely *dripping*
with charm!

Peter Sarstedt was born in Delhi, India, in the year 1941,
where his parents were civil servants – part of the old
established Raj, the British administration.
Both parents were classical musicians.
He went to the boarding school in Kurseong in the Darjeeling
district of West Bengal.
I think it was his bushy black staple-shaped moustache that
Nano felt most attracted to – I mean, I have to admit, it was
really impressive.
Is maith an wonderboy, soitheach an-álainn e!
Yes, he really is quite a dish, she used to always say,

in his stylish black knitted polo.
Little did she ever dream that he'd end up featuring in
mine & Una's story,
with those same plaintive triplets of a French
waltz rendered on an accordion,
swelling at the feet of a bleeding, crucified
Christ
beneath a copper sunset on a hill above Jerusalem.
As a leopard with the spread wings of an eagle came
gliding in to land
on the surface of a river
already on fire
but never mind about any of that for the moment
because we can talk all we like about that later on.

Anyway, didn't I happen to be sitting at the bar this evening,
with Nano just having popped out for a moment, when I
look up and see who's falling in the door – only curly-haired
Brendan Behan, the notorious rebel hellraising writer, with
his shirt unbuttoned and the eyes rolling in his head, tripping
over his unlaced, mud-spattered shoes.
With it not being
long before he threatened to
lay out the whole 'fughing' band
of us, getting a hold of the jazzman Johnny
Dankworth
who happened to be laying out
cables on the rostrum
& swinging him back & forth
by the collar & announcing that
although he didn't come to London so
much anymore
because those 'shagging fughers', the rozzers,
were after him,
that before he left, he was going
to give every 'shagging tom-tit bastard in
London' a hiding
they weren't very likely to forget in a hurry
before stumbling & falling on top
of the cymbals as Mr Dankworth,
one of the city's best-known celebrities,
shook his head in exasperation
before giving a wry grin and carrying on

rehearsing with his group
picking up where they'd left off
with Behan – miraculously, in key! – snoring
his heart out like a baby
somewhere away there at the back
underneath the crowded stage.

I remember that occasion
particularly well
being as it happened to be
the night of the
Queen's Coronation & the fellow
whose company I'd been enjoying
most of the day
what's this his name was
oh no, here they come
those whistling, interfering,
sky-piercing bastards
those accursed doodlebugs
always arriving when
you least expect
& there being not so much
as a single thing you can do
as they hang there suspended
just for that teeth-clenching moment
stall
in a glacial silence
& then
down
down
down
yes, down
they
come
V
V
V
one after the other
& then, sure enough,
the name of the poor old
bastard you've been drinking
with
has been blown to pieces
as has the memory

of everyone else who'd
existed that day.
So, welcome, ladies and gentlemen,
to yet another patch
of obliterated, scorched ground
entire streets of houses
pubs
& factories
erased in silence
without so much
as a
  by
    your
      leave.

What I *do* remember, though
is one of the songs that that old comrade
whoever he was
had been singing when
we'd been roistering – I think
in a bar somewhere
along The Strand,
a boisterous tune
about McAlpine
the builder.

Which was one, in actual fact,
made famous by none other
than Behan himself,
made famous
on the first night of his
play, *The Hostage*.

The bells of hell go ting-a-ling-a-ling, he sang,
snapped by every pressman in London.

Mr Behan, sadly, died in 1964.
Una says she was glad to see the back of him
because all he ever was
was a no-good bowsy
& braggart
yes, to hell with the selfish ignorant, good-for-

nothing
she says
& then starts crying & picking fights with
everyone around her
but that's only when she's feeling upset
and experiencing yet another bout
of the dreaded, what we call the *imní*.
Which'd be another word for anxiety or depression,
in Gaelic.
Describing what it's like
when the V-1s have appeared
hanging there in silence
glacially frozen in the air
just above your head
getting ready to come in
to come right down,
going:
V
V
V
before whaddayouknow
another whole street or
a factory has gone
pouf.

Yes, it's a hard old station,
make no mistake –
& let there be no two ways
about it.

As God is my judge
till the day I drop
out of my standing
I do not think
I will ever forget
that
      very
            first
                  day
when I set off for the

great big city
'allo, Lahndin!
to commence what was for me
a whole new way of life.
What, another one,
do I hear you ask?
Or, at any rate, any of them as knows
me,
or even the smallest bit about me
but it's not a question I could
accurately, properly
answer
not being *sartin sure*,
as they say,
whether it's the second, third or
maybe even the fifty-hundredth
version of one's 'starts' – *ha ha!* –
as they used to call it on the building
sites.
Where I worked so hard
in my time, aye knuckles to the bone –
dig
dig
dig
& more digging,
for Wimpey, McAlpine & John Laing.
But anyhow, there I was
off yet again
in my seven-league boots
wandering anew
on my extensive world travels
now having landed
on the shores of majestic 'Albin'
or the UK as
it is known
now this would be long ago
when all of the world
as we knew it
was young
&
there was divil the talk of
computers or Brexit
barely even the 'Common Market'
with nothing much to be seen

about the streets
only
maybe a pack of rats,
watching intently from an alley
as feral a gang as ever
you clapped eyes on
crouching, huddled in the shadows,
saying to themselves
I wonder will we do him
aye, that'd be a good idea
let's roll the Paddy
in this time
of civil unease
industrial unrest
& power cuts
& strikes
every five minutes
with everyone blaming
not only Paddy & Biddy
& the Irish with their bombs
but poor old Mr Patel as well
smiling while he's picking
your pocket, they insisted,
getting ready
to get his hands on your job,
establishing corner shop
after corner shop
yes, that's what the skinheads
& bovver boys
wanted to stop
aye, put an end to
& Enoch Powell too
swearing that soon there'd
be rivers of blood
as Mott the Hoople
the latest greatest rock band
in the world
fronted by Ian Hunter
they took to the stage
with David Bowie's
'All The Young Dudes'
the tune he's written
especially for
all those fans

                    crowding to the front of
                    the stage
                    so abjectly adoring
                    each one of them
                    reflected in the mirrors
                    of Ian Hunter's aviator shades
                    as he grimaced behind the microphone
                    with that great big
                    blonde Afro frizz
                    & iron cross
                    commencing his performance
                    hey you
out there
                    hey

                                        hey

                                                            my pretty ones
                    hey

                    are you out there

all

        of you   inner
                        young

cosmonauts
                        can you hear me

                    freaks

                            where are

        you

                    yes &
                    everyone blaming
                    poor Pat
                    & the economy

permissiveness
riots
&
strikes
strikes
strikes.

So there you
are, that was the way of it,
back in the days
that were long before these
so is it any wonder
that no matter how I try
God bless & keep me
that I never will be able to
forget
that very first time
aye, God knows, the very first day
I clapped eyes on a skinhead
for you didn't have them much

not in our wee homestead
no, scarce few bovver gangs in
the quiet little village of Currabawn
with its streams & mountains
& humble stone cabins
& the Civic Guard on a bicycle
once a week
pedalling past the pump
in the square
& him whistling away
lie-dee-til-dee-die
& sorra the word
about 'ceann-gans' at all,
which of course
is the ancient Irish term
for skinheads
going back centuries
except that it doesn't,
entirely concocted by
my own good self,
ha ha.

One of whose formidable breed
was now engaging with me
very intently indeed, I have to say –
on a street corner
close by John Lewis
staring fiercely
just staring
with his thumb hooked
in his denims
a close-cropped
narrow-eyed blondie
with gleaming silver
Union Jack braces
& not a hint of
a bristle between his ears,
beaming as he raised his steel toe-capped
boot
aye, radiant as he elevated
those impressively polished Doc Martens
& bang bang umph!

So that wasn't so good
as down I went
bidunk on the floor
how do you like that Paddy he says
not much, I'll wager
& no, not one bit
I have to say
I didn't take to it
at all
or what came next
as he flailed
& thudded
& crunched
& kicked
braying take that, Mr Turf-Ears
& how do you like
them apples Mr Paddy with
his parcel
underneath his arm
with your bashed-in hat
& your old tramp's coat
take that, motherfucker

& that
& that
& that
'cos you got no right
coming over 'ere!

& such a crack of bone
as the two of us heard then
with it only being as I happened
to have the wit & the grace of God
about me
that I managed to roll under
a skip and take some refuge
before re-emerging just that
little piece more composed
& says to him
Skinny oho Skinny
I say there, Skinny Mr Skinhead sorr
Lord Hooligan of Hooligan
how about this
you wiry stubble-headed
dead-eyed
little fucker
&
before you know it

   *   *   !   *
     *   *   !   *   *
   *   ! *   *   !   ✳ !
    * !   *
      *   *   * *   !   !
           !
✳   * ! * **!**   !   *   *!✳*

ker-clunk! and he's down!
& now who is it's doing
all the dancing
yes, who is the Lord of the Dance
now I wonder
aye, and whistling too
tootle tootly!
as is my wont:

Pat he may be foolish and sometimes very wrong.
Paddy's got a temper, but it won't last very long,
Pat is fond of jollity and everybody knows

there never was a coward where the three-leaf
shamrock grows!

Come on, Paddy *agus*
pogue
      ma
            hone –
yes, kiss my emerald-green,
unrepentant arse!
I cheered as I hopped
for all the world
like a giddy wee
songster –
a triumphant ickle avian,
a blackbird, maybe,
a little *londubh deas* –
advancing, don't you know,
with little hopperty mincing steps,
trilling quavers to beat the band.

Which is the very same as always,
whenever I happen
to get excited
laughing my heart out
for that's just the way
of peripatetic Daniel Fogarty
both now, and in the future,
not to mention all those
occasions
in the far distant past,
where, in the mists of time,
out of force of habit
I was seen to do the very same thing
falsetto-rejoice in one's irrefutable
triumph.

For, before you know it,
having been taken, really quite
utterly by surprise,
the misfortunate poor little
stubby-headed bastard

he's lying there moaning
& imploring me, please,
Mother Of God, to desist –
just the same as the hobo
that he and his mates
had rolled the week
before
in an underpass somewhere
close by Elephant & Castle
& which all the newspapers said
had been prompted by *A Clockwork
Orange*,
& which
whether it is true
or not
I do not know
all I can say is
that in the case of my *ceann-gan*
adversary
it absolutely & one hundred
per cent was
for as I concluded my whistling
rubbed my hands &
shook myself down
there wasn't so much as a peep
out of that poor old beaten-down
skinhead *craythur*
lying there rolling
in his pumping,
thick black blood
with the echo of my
trilling still ringing in his ears
yes, that same one of old
as you'd be inclined to describe
as one's signature tune
never far away
when Dan 'The Rambler'
Fogarty happens to be in town.
At first soft & low
almost as if it isn't there at all
before rending the heavens
in a razor-sharp crescendo
a whistling fierce fair set
to rattle the world.

So, there you are,
that was a nice thing to
have happen to you, wasn't it?
On the very first day of
one's introduction to England
or should I, perhaps, more precisely say
that ancient, magisterial dominion
known as
Albin.

It often makes me laugh looking back now on those old
times, for
such a *ruaille buaille* did he make
that poor chap
Lord o Lord bless us, the yowls and hollerings whenever I
think of them
but then, of course, that was the way that things were in them
times, yes the way that they certainly seemed to be going
not that it was going to put me off
in the slightest
o no no no

          *SKOL
*WRIGLEYS
              *NON-STOP   *BRYLCREEM

*MAX FACTOR   *EL PARADISE

          *CLOCKWORK NYMPHO   *CHERI

      *CHAMPAGNE SHOWER   !!!!!!!!!!!

*PIGALLE   *BLUE COCKATOO   *SEXTET

*FUJI   *SCHWEPPES   *TWA
                                        *CLUB PANAMA
      *BOVRIL

              *WIMPY

    *MARY MILLINGTON   *ALFRED MARKS BUREAU

      *JOHN MENZIES   *CINZANO

*NEW PICCADILLY   *LOVECRAFT   *XXXX

*JESUS CHRIST SUPERSTAR

yes, this was the place for me
I said
&
before very long
in the land of Ziggy Stardust
Enoch Powell & Mike Yarwood
I soon was ensconced in
my humble new lodgings
a discreet tenant
one might say
of No. 45 Brondesbury Gardens
up in Killiburn, NW6
also known as 'The Temple' in those days
Ashram Of Love
anarchy & revolution
as well, of course,
of inner cosmic travelling
where my sister Una had somehow
managed to end up – at the tender age
of twenty-three.
& now, you can believe it
was to be found lying prostrate
underneath that
long lanky miserable Scottish seagull
& Ian Hunter lookalike

who went by the name of
Troy McClory
who never missed a chance
to say
I
love
you

yes sweet lovely
vulnerable
Una

[44]

Fogarty, sister of Dan –
I
love
you
oh
oh
oh
so
much

& if any of youse
out there you think that is good
maybe 'sweet' & 'tender'
or, even better, uplifting
then you ought to have
heard the lumps of poetry
that the Scottish bard he started
reading her then,
yes, all those moving chunks of
verse
some of which he wrote himself
in ring-bound notebooks &
scattered bits of paper
because Troy was a poet
oh yes
baring his soul every hour
of the day, using
all these words

broken

       up

                 in

     pieces

floating around

     here
                &   there
like birdies

          yes

             for all

the world

    like

        little birdies

or, in Gaelic, *éiníní*

        fragmented the very same

as this
       but

              not because

Troy

              was old
      or anywhere near to
becoming elderly

     like my poor sister

     or finding
           it

increasingly more difficult

        to join up all the

dots

      & circuits

    to

        link

   them together
   so as to make
   some kind of sense.

   No, not that,
   it wasn't due to that at all
   but simply because the poems

they tended to read
in those days
that was the way
they were
although, as Una often says,
they didn't have to worry
for time, inevitably, would
do its work
&, before they knew it,
the words would soon
be flying around like
confetti
yes, all by themselves,
in places such as Cliftonville-Sur-Mer,
completely independent
of anything any of us might
need or
   want
     them
       to
         do.

But, back then, of course,
when you're young and in your
twenties
you don't think that, no
no one does,
not when Mike Yarwood &
David Bowie also are young,
yes, almost the very same age as you
& the handsome Scottish student
that you love
is standing up again on the kitchen table
with those mirror shades shining
as he opens his notebook & enquires of
his acolytes, squatting beneath him cross-legged
on the carpet
with their number
including my sister
agog, venerating him
as back goes his hair
& up he ascends again
with some verse by
e. e. cummings,

with there not
being so much
as a sound
as, in his eloquent,
articulate Edinburgh burr
he
read aloud for his adoring fans:

buffalo bill
now there was a handsome man
a man who could break
one
two
three
four
pigeons
& so what I want
to know right now is,
friends
yes, what I want to know
from you is, friend...

how do you
like
your
blue-eyed boy now
Mr Death?

But poetry wasn't all
Troy McClory was good at
laughing his head off
as he scooped up his
invisible pretend-microphone
& once more commenced his
London Palladium
impressions
with his whole body shaking
windmill-waving his arms
as he launched into a flurry
a melange of disparate voices
in colloquial Gaelic dialect
with which he couldn't, possibly,
have been familiar.

Now how did that happen?
Because Lord save us and bless us if he
doesn't look like a fellow *faoi gheasa* –
yes, like all of a sudden he's been
cast beneath a spell
as he snaps his fingers
and starts into this story
about a fellow from Ireland
the old country do you see
about this funny little man
a wee roving rascal
who used to ferry his drink
around in a jar
a crockery pot of golden *uisquebaugh*
from which he quaffed liberally
all his days
before ending up on the streets
of Killiburn
living hand to mouth
like a *gruagach*, explained Troy,
a stray of the streets
who might well have died
without not so much as a one
to care for him
only for Breslin The Carpenter
who, out of pity, being a fellow
countryman, took him in
– for all the thanks he was set to receive,
God help him,
when, in the course of a dispute over
his new tenant's behaviour,
a belt from a lump-hammer took
out most of his brains
& left him there, groaning, without so much as
a by-your-leave
on the floorboards,
& he set about rifling the pockets of the soon-to
be-deceased
and then away he marched, off out on the road
once more
(wasted that night, on account of
the amount of drink he had consumed
with his pouch of rifled monies)

[49]

yes, the divil & terror that was known as
Dan 'The Rambler' Fogarty,
formerly of Currabawn.

I'll give you the honour of
the Fogartys!
he had bawled, right into the
astonished Malachy
Breslin's face.
Yes, right into the phizzog of his former landlord,
as a matter of fact, I'll break your fucking head!
he announced,
before taking a wild swing
with the lump-hammer he was clutching
take that, you tight-fisted, lowborn
twister! he cried
as poor old Mal, God love him, was felled,
in a state of utter incomprehension and perplexity.
& Dan The Rambling Man
flung the bloodied instrument from him
and without further ado
made himself scarce.
Heading, determinedly,
along the River Thames
where, by dint of further stealth –
although he himself might well
have claimed the status of 'destiny' for
such developments –
he found himself the tiniest, compact
but, most of all, extremely discreet
compartment
at the summit, one might say, of a house
in Brondesbury Road, NW6
which, inadvertently,
coincidentally, in those exact same chambers,
Dan's mother
God rest her
had died by her very own hand
so very many long years ago,
God be good to her sweet blessed
soul.
So here I am, mused Dan Fogarty
to himself, in the place all along

where I was meant to be
with me travelling, surely, for a long time,
done
& all me efforts now concentrated
on keeping an eye on my kith & kin
&, in the process, ensuring
their good name
never again, in my presence,
is slighted.

But I was telling you, anyway,
about Troy McClory,
and what he did next
and him filled to the gills
with every class of stimulant –
cast adrift in his mind
in a world of freshness and greenness
unsurpassable
never before having noticed roses
seeming so vivid
the willowherb so riotous
the meadowsweet so odorous
& all-pervading.
He started flapping his arms
as his eyes began to roll
turning around in circles
first this way, then that –
like he's under a spotlight,
standing there centre-stage.
O! Tie A Yellow Ribbon Around The Old
Oak Tree, he carolled,
wiping his eyes and relating
another new story
about this other particular *gruagach*
& his ribbon
& how some farmer had tried to claim
his buttery crock
yes, get his hands on his pot of gleaming
gold
by tying a little coloured ribbon marking the
spot of its location in the middle of a field

fixing it onto a tall swaying stalk
and then returning home for to get himself
a spade.

Well, such a surprise as he got!
exclaimed Troy,
upon his return when he saw, to
his amazement,
an entire field filled with stalks
and to every one, tied a fluttering coloured hankie
Tie A Coloured Ribbon? Somehow, I don't
motherfucking think so!
the young Scotsman hollered, stumbling
across four or five chairs
before collapsing in a heap.

Moaning and groaning
as he lay there
half asleep
laughing about the presence
that was rumoured
to be attached
to this very house!
Yes, hidden somewhere,
although
who the hell knew where,
but there had been, for sure,
long before they'd ever come
near the place
or seen sight nor sign of it
talk of something,
although the devil God only knew
what,
certainly not a gruagach
for there were few who would
have known or ever heard of such
a foolish thing
that is to say,
a rascal who had no end

of powers
it being
within his gift
to make sheep break out
see cattle die
o yes
turn milk completely sour overnight
prevent the hens from laying
should he want to,
cast a dread disease upon
the household
if such a thought should
enter his head
but, with all of that said,
equally, no better man has there ever
been to pipe a tune
or play a melodeon
not to mention
on occasion
do a good turn
indeed, at times
being so eager to please
he can just as easy
become a pest about the house
running about as he does
small chores
often creating more mess than
he clears
tripping up the housewife
as she goes about her work
aye, unaccountably as she
goes about her business
tending to her chores
but that's not the half of it
pelting individuals with stones
rocks and other objects
as they walk around their property
making burning peat fall out
from the fireplace
but most of all
singing bawdy songs
at all hours of the day and night
disclosing scandalous things
concerning the visitors and occupants

of the house
from secret locations around
the rooms
and talk about drink?
no end of it, from cask or keg
or barrel
you can be sure of that
for it is here the mortal needs
to be wary
with the gruagach's capacity
for alcohol far outstripping
that of any human being
& him still regaling the company
with no end of yarns

& then away off with him
ag béicil and bheith ag roaring
trick-acting, hopping and whoring
throughout the night along
with his wicked, diminutive
clann or his *chairde*
yes, his friends
opening, maybe, a gate
for the purpose of releasing
the farmer's cattle
overturning hayricks
or committing no end of
other such rogueries
before settling down by
the light of the moon.

& such a hoarse cry as was
dramatically
released by Troy McClory
with no one rightly knowing
what to do
as he gave an unmerciful
flying leap, landing
right in the middle of his audience:
IT'S NEARLY AS BAD AS
DARBY O' GILL AND THE LITTLE
PEOPLE! he shouted.

Before rolling around on the
bare carpet in front of the fire
& lying there among a pile of beer cans
fit to burst & lighting more joints
& then afterwards claiming
not to remember
a single word of what
it was had been going through his
mind as he'd lain there
or what it was
he was supposed to have said.

'Man, that night, it really was weird – whatever
kinda shit that was we were smoking!'

A hundred yellow ribbons?
I mean, what the fuck?
He hadn't even seen *Darby*
O'Gill – the film,
he disclosed
& knew sweet motherfucking fuck
all about it.
'Wherever all of that came from,' he said,
blearily handing yet another
smouldering joint to
his neighbour.

Then someone, when he said that,
would laugh a bit nervously
before changing the subject as quickly
as they could
because, in a world of 'weirds', experiencing
Troy convincingly impersonating
Mike Yarwood
impersonating the politician Denis Healey,
going: Oo! Silly-billy, silly-billy! –
it was just that little bit too 'far out',
as Tanith Kaplinski had remarked
under her breath.
'Not to mention all that raving
about strange music & such
coming from behind the skirting board.'

But it did end OK
– thanks be to *God*, someone might
have said
if they had believed in such a thing
as a gruagach,
that is,
instead of Krishna or perhaps
Meher Baba.

But, anyhow, didn't Big Peter Hanlon
arrive in carrying a full ounce of hash
with everyone
acting out Cheech & Chong
impressions
before Peter began talking about
the night he knew he had seen 'him'
or 'it', motherfucker, whatever you
want to call him

&, boy, did he give a vivid description
waving the jay as he opened and closed
his tired, squinting eyes
I know you are never gonna believe it
he said
but I know what I saw
right over there by the skirting
when all of you guys were gone
for the weekend
it was a deformed, gnome-like thing
a sort of a clumsy caricature of
a human being
more, to be honest, like
a six-week-old foetus
grey and no bigger, I ain't
shittin' you, than a gooseberry
hey Big Peter, hey my man
I remember him saying
giving me this wave
the man he didn't even have a face
no face, man?
No, he didn't even have a face
but still he kept on saying

hey Big Peter
get on over
come on over here
he beckoned
& then said it again
in what I think
must have been Gaelic
& what did you say to him, Peter?
they asked
yeah, what did you say to the little guy
& it was at that that the room
fell about, just exploded
as Big Peter snorted with his face all
creased up
and sank right down into the
centre of a bowl of chilli
Bless your pointed little head, brother! I
said,
that's what I told him, man – I couldn't help it.
& then when I looked again, he was gone!

Far out, said Joanne
Too much, they all agreed
as Peter scooped another spoonful
and whooped: bless your little motherfucking
pointed head!
collapsing into another fit of convulsions.

When all the laughter had subsided
after that there followed a light smattering of applause
as Troy got up
taking our Una by the hand
come on in here my Lady Ocean
he said
because that, of course, was what he always
called her, you see
my sister
with no one so much as batting
an eyelid
as he had his way, once more, with her
inside on some cushions

o making an unholy *ruaille buaille*
so they were
because that was the way
he was, Troy McClory,
anything he wanted
he used to fucking
get
it
but what someone
should have told him is
them as ill-rated
us Fogartys never throve
yes, someone ought to have
informed him of that
& just how innocent
my beautiful sister was
in those days
& still is
here in Cliftonville
in spite of all our
unfortunate disagreements.

It makes me sick, even yet
just to think of it
with his pale pimpled *tóin*
– pronounced 'hone',
as in poguemahone,
in otherwords, 'kiss my arse',
hoisted in the air as he threshed
with abandon
'O my sweet fucking Lady Ocean!'
he kept on groaning,
before collapsing in a heap
having enjoyed his glorious
three minutes of *marcaíocht*
or 'mickey-jump-jubbling'
as Nano used to call it.

& of which, in her club, there had
never been any shortage.

No end of which I had witnessed
myself,
having been present whenever a Maltese
fellow got stabbed
– over a woman, of course,
what else,
one particularly rowdy
Saturday night.
Not that it seemed
to unduly bother Nano
'Not a gentleman!' was all
she had to say about that
as I sat sipping a cocktail
lost in contemplation
not long after the Laughing Boy
died, the pet name that she'd
put on Brendan Behan
we'll never see his likes again
that was all she had to say
as off she went, up to greet
Al Martino
if you ever heard of him
even better than our own Matt Monro
Nano always said.
Maybe that's why
Una is always humming his
most famous tunes.

Yes, sitting by the library
doing her knitting
or going through her notes
& bits & pieces of the script
for her forthcoming opus with
her Cliftonville Capers troupe
& which really does seem
to be doing the trick.
As Margaret Rutherford says
'providing her with a focus'.

Yes, that's it
with the net result being
that I can safely say
how never before have I seen
her look so good
but not just good in a healthy
kind of way
but almost gloriously radiant
at times
& which
considering what the two of us
have been through down over
the years
& not just Troy
plenty of other things too
any amount.
Yes, it really is a great thing to
be able to say.
Because I know she still
thinks
or at least part of her does
that all I ever wanted to do
was cause trouble & raise
indulgent mischief

& that whatever initial impulse
there might have been towards
protecting her
that, very soon, it took a back seat.
It simply isn't true, however
although I do understand
why it was she might have thought that
because one thing is for sure
whatever else about
Una Fogarty
she did love Troy.
Yes, genuinely & truly did love
Troy 'The Jockey' McClory.
In a manner that was really quite
hopeless, really.
So it's not like I'm trying to deny that
or anything – or am in any way jealous.

I just wanted to look after her, that's all
so I'm terribly sorry
if there happens to be
something
          wrong
                with
                          that
because, you see,
I
      don't
            think
                  there
                        is

                              ok?

there's a thing I was wondering
just now
does anyone know
what the Gaelic word might be
for 'defenestration'?
Because I, I'm afraid, unfortunately, do not.
All the same, though, it really is regrettable
what happened in The Temple
at 45 Brondesbury
that day,
I mean talk about gloomy Sunday
because, of course, as usual
it was raining
but no matter how bad things
had become in the flat
no one really could have expected
that, someone throwing themselves
from a fourth-storey window.
Which is what the occupant of
the landing room did
Tanith Kaplinski
without so much as a word
to anyone
after thinking she's seen a unicorn

looking up from the courtyard
and saying
come on down
when everyone knows
there's no such thing
as a unicorn, I mean
– yes, come on down
it urged as she laughed
& then just swan-dived, *ker-plunk*
out into the open
crashing down
through the overhanging glass canopy
onto the glistening cobbles of the courtyard
an occurrence which, I suppose
if they had actually been able to
be honest about it, signalled
the beginning of
the end of
the dream of a new society
that had sustained The Temple
all through the summer
& indeed well before
yes
No. 45
Brondesbury Gardens
aka
The Mahvishnu Temple
slán leat
good luck now
and to those good old times
of a future that never came
no, never arrived
in spite of all the people who said it
would
including
Abbie Hoffmann,
Eldridge Cleaver,
Bobby Seale
&
Mr Tune-in
Turn-on
Drop-Out
High Priest
Timothy Leary

not to mention
Syd Barrett,
Pink Floyd
& The Third Ear Band
as day turned into night
around the table of revolution
in the front room of The Temple
as Ian Hunter & Mott the Hoople sang
'All the Young Dudes'
& Mike Oldfield's eerily repetitive piano motif
introduced the record

T
U
B
U
L
A
R

B
E
L
L
S

which some people
were already holding responsible for it all
with its sub-currents and resonant chimes having
already been availed of in *The Exorcist*.
& with everyone who was asked
insisting that no
of course it wasn't cursed
that, at least, was what they said
in the beginning
& why they kept playing it
over
&
over.
With Troy, especially, thinking it
all a great old laugh,
putting on a blanket and
dragging it right over his head

as he started to growl and put on this
demon-gurgle saying I am Pazuzu
& I've come from the desert so watch out
man 'cos this for sure it could really be a bummer
& which it was
except no one, initially, even opted
to pass so much as a casual comment
on the noise that Tanith had insisted she'd
heard coming from somewhere behind
the skirting
groaning, she said,
and then pots & pans
banging
as Troy went on laughing, amusing Una
with his Wrangler boots up on the chair
spare a penny for a poor altar boy Faddah
pretending to be the priest from the film ha ha
rustling noise said Big Peter no way
I didn't hear or see nothing, lady
but then I guess I was stoned right out
of my box
spare a penny for a poor altar boy Faddah
said Troy again
& he could really do it good
it was a great old laugh

when they did eventually hear it
o it must have been weeks after
Tanith had first mentioned it
no one thought to link it
with that which might be made
by *gruagachs* in the old times
or clurichauns
or anything else,
more like what you might
hear coming from grasshoppers
& certainly not a wandering soul
who had fashioned a cubbyhole
a snug little secret room
where he kept himself
quiet, enjoying his own
company
always making sure to keep
one eye open for Una

& just what the Scotsman and the
rest of them might be up to
but which of course
was only a back-of-the-pub
rumour
with no one even knowing, like
many of the whispered contentions
regarding Dan
if Malachy Breslin
had ever even existed,
never mind killed to death by a belt
from a lump-hammer or anything else.
It was supposed to have happened in the
late forties or early fifties.
With the attic where he was supposed
to be domiciled, at least according to
himself
now, for many a long year sealed up,
with the only thing, mebbe, fit to
be billeted there being a robin, aye
an spideog,
or, if not him, his little air-slicing
comrade among the clouds,
that equally tireless voyager,
an londubh –
aye, the blackbird.

Anyway, as I was telling you,
not long after my arrival
here on the jolly shores of Albin
I took into what we do the best
us incorrigibly restless
ill-at-ease wanderers
those 'always on the move'
migrant labourers
with restless souls
like all the Fogartys
as never could be said
to have ever had a proper home
one as you could safely say
was your own.

In the course of our travellings
up & down the length of Albin
often finding ourselves, God be good to us
in the likes of a place
you often heard of called *The Spike*
a class of accommodations, you can be sure of it
where you would encounter a type
as'd make our auld skinhead
look the spit of Larry Grayson
a scaredy-cat
a knock-kneed auld lump of a softie is what I mean.
Well, anyway, in The Spike they often
used to chat far into the night
especially after a skinful
fellows as had been to the doors of hell
& back
with many a tale to tell
of their ramblings
up and down the length of Albin
did you ever hear of the unhappy gruagach?
I remember one fellow saying
a buck by the name of Hardy Jim from Kells
aye, well he'd be a bad one to
meet & you on the high road home
he said
o aye, he went on,
for he's
the unhappiest little fucker as
was ever known in Creation
o the black and bitter eye
& the downturned cruel mouth
but yet, all the while, the flash in
the twinkling orb
in the middle of the duskus dark, continued
Hardy Jim, when there wasn't so much
as a whimper across the world.
There was this fellow, you see
in the town that they call Kilcash
in the very dark deep and quiet part of
Ireland, in the south.
Aye, Kilcash.

& there was this fellow living there
do you see
who thought himself all the
big modern go-ahead
this would have been oh in 1923
when the pictures and the cinema
they were only just getting started
& when, after the civil war and all
that style of thing there, there wouldn't
have been the divil very much to be doing
in the neighbourhood of Kilcash
only maybe counting your spits
at the crossroads
or tugging on your *péist*
late at night under the covers
so, this lad by the name of Tom Twomey
didn't he get to thinking
sure, amn't I the sort who as aisy as
falling arse over tit off a log
could turn my hand to anything
that I please
so why not establish my own personal
pictiúrlann
my own private cinema, in otherwords
yes, here in Kilcash
where they're the double of husks walking
that seem to be dead already
for the want of a wee bit of
entertainin'
so off he went on the bus, aye to Cork
where he knew of a theatre and it the
wonder of the whole of the South Of Ireland
that in them times would have been
called The Alhambra, do you see
& it being an irresistible lure
to poor old Tom Twomey
who, as I say, liked the odd drink
& would often be known to scarper
away off with some cans of film
that had been left there for collection
aye, left there unattended
at the end of the hallway
& which he did again on this particular night
& him not long off the omnibus from old

Kilcash
yes, one two three four five aluminium cans
of film
of which he only took one, two no, three
Laurel & Hardy & one of his favourites
Harold Lloyd
ah sure how would they not love them
he said
as back he went to his old home town
& to Mattie McLarnon's granary
indeed
which, as far as being an *amharclann pictiúr*
goes
or Wonderland Emporium
of the moving image
it was a very long way indeed
from The Tivoli or The Luxor or indeed
The Alhambra
with the only means of access or exit
being the crockeddy old ladder
hanging down from the upper door
o what a show it was going to be
the play of the century
with Stan & Olly and, as well
as that, Harold Lloyd
& him shouting help me help me
for I think I'm going to fall off this
clock
well, what a sad and maybe foolish
idea it might seem to us all in these times
yes, in the days that are now
how close to madness it might seem
when you think of all the poor folks
squashed in there
with not one or two but
twenty
thirty
forty
fifty
yes, actually fifty-five people
paying for their ticket as they
wrung their hands in childish glee
one by one ascending the old
rickety ladder

which was then pulled up
& the door heavily bolted
because all this was highly illegal
you see
with no licence or nothing
& the cans of film stolen
not that that auld divil Tom
Twomey was going to mind
what with all the shillings
he was set to make

&
what a mistake that was
said Hardy Jim
especially when people were
allowed to be smoking
with no one, indeed, giving it so much
as a second thought
at least until a stray flaring match
it was tossed away without a care
& such a riot was going on
with everyone whooping, leaning
back on their chairs
as down
came
the
match
over
one
of
the
silver
aluminium
cans
&
sailed
right
into
the
middle
of
it.
With everyone knowing, or at least they do now,

the risks associated with cellulose nitrate film stock
& just how easily it can – yes just
how easily and how quickly it can…
& that's what it did.
Large, toxic quantities of poisonous gas
& literally sheets of hot, intense flame, explained Jim.
Those unfortunate people were all seen to perish in the ensuing
blaze, he went on,
prior to finding himself afflicted by what can only be described as
an appalling 'fit'.
Or what Nano used to call an 'a serious episode of The
Tremblings'.
Because Hardy Jim from Kells – he really had been shivering all
over as he concluded.
Describing, as best he could, the 'gnarled, wizened phizzog' that
had been witnessed by those who had scarcely survived the
conflagration.
Just on the point of death, they explained.
When we thought we were goners.
& do you know who that was? I remember Jim saying. Well do you
Dan Fogarty, I'm wondering to myself now as I sit here fornenst
you.
As I shook my head.
He who hasn't been right or proper born, he continued gravely,
that'd be the one who's called *the gruagach*.
How many died in the end? I asked.
Forty-seven, he said, might even have been closer to
fifty, for some remains were never discovered.
The gruagach, I murmured, he who hasn't been properly
born.
'Not the same as you or me.'
As Jim got up and said he had to be in Chester by morning, a
weathered hand running through grey wisps of thinning hair.
Boys o boys! he sighed, and then was gone.

I really had liked that old Hardy Jim from Kells.
I really and truly had.
Him and his story of the gruagach who
had never properly lived
because he hadn't
been

correctly
or
right-proper born.
The very same
as myself
God knows…
but look here
I'm wandering
yes, I'm going
&
forgetting myself again
because you see
I wanted to tell
you
yes, I wanted to tell you
all about my trip last month
back up to the old city
& tell you all about
how I got on
in London
after having yet another big bust-up
with you-know-who
worse than the men?
the men are fucking angels
believe me
compared to the likes of
Mrs Weasel Fogarty.
ah but, God love her
you know
she's not the worst
is what I was thinking
as I boarded the carriage in Margate station
&
left Una to her constant contrariness
and was off again rambling
racketty racketty, on the train.

So yes, there you have it
that was me
beep beep beep
& away off out the door
of Cliftonville Hotel-Sur-Mer
when nobody was looking
with a nice, tasty sambo
courtesy of Southeastern catering
& a hot, restorative cuppa
in front of me on the table
ar an traen
yes, sur le train
pulling out of Margate
with me just about having had it
thank you
with me auld sister's
crabbit complainings
– and after having a good old natter
with the new Nigerian barman
in the Bedford Arms on the Killiburn High Road
I made my goodbyes and set off at
once towards the top of
the Edgware Road
in the direction of *The Rambler's Rest*
motel, erected this long time now
on what once was the site of a certain
demolished late-Victorian house
regarded in its time
as the centre of anarchic freedom London
namely The Mahavishnu Temple
situated at No. 45
Brondesbury Gardens.
& with me hardly, I swear,
being in the place half an hour
before I found myself making friends
with the genial night porter
whose name was Andrew Hamilton
who must have been close on sixty or sixty-one
& who actually remembered Mike Yarwood
being a guest
or so he claimed.
But then, being a Celt
the same as myself
you could never quite be

one hundred per cent certain
but I was prepared to concede him
the benefit of the doubt
particularly since he accommodated me
handsomely, acquiring for me the
exact apartment I wanted
what is now No. 12
but used to be the room on the third-storey
landing
back in the days when old Mahavishnu
it was still in full swing
& which of course is now a fabulous
De Luxe walk-in condominium
complete with electronic curtains,
internet and all the rest.

We had a great old chat about
all that, me and him,
with his eyes misting over
when I told him about The Temple
and all the things that had gone
on
'Scarcely the throw of a stone
from where I'm sitting now!'
I said, 'Over there used to
be poor Tanith Kaplinski's room!'
Och I've seen a lot of changes
so I have over the years
I heard him saying then.
Although whether they're all
for the better I couldn't say
to tell ye the truth, he says, what
surprises me most when I think about the
period you're talking about
is just how contented I remember actually being
& that's in spite of all the strikes
& unrest & the devil knows what.
Because I know at the time
I never stopped complaining
I really & truly didn't, Dan Fogarty,
& that's a fact.

I couldn't for the life of me
say, at least with any accuracy, quite
how long the pair of us had been sitting
there sipping whiskey
by the imitation fire in the foyer
feeling good
real good
as a matter of fact
yakking away about Yarwood
& Bowie, Ian Hunter & all the rest
& trying to recall just how bad it was
what we called the Winter of Discontent.
With one thing leading to another
& me filling him in then
about all the fun and games that we once used
to have in Nano's
with him especially being amused
by the plight of the poor 'pissed-on' fish in
Brendan Behan's aquarium.
 Ah but, you know, Andy, I explained
just as me auld Auntie Nano used
to say, God be good to her, that old
Laughing Boy, he wasn't the worst of them
not by a long shot
& I'll tell you something else
I went on
loosening up my vocal cords
a fine man to sing whenever he
wasn't *ar meisce*.
I explained that meant 'drunk'.
& that's how the two of us ending
up humming 'The Coolin'
which, being Scottish, Andy knew
& was more than able to see it through
to the end
before, being pretty exhausted after my
travels up from Kent
not to mention the few little *deochanna*
I'd enjoyed already in The Bedford Arms
I decided at last it was time
to turn in.
How long do you propose to be staying
at The Rambler's Rest, Mr Fogarty?' asked Andy
pronouncing it 'Fuggherty',

more guttural than I'm used to
& which gave me a warm glow
like he figured I was some kind of
aristocratic rural Irish royalty
– all the way from Currabawn, Co. Tipperary.
Some hope, I'm sorry to have to say!

Although already I was beginning
to regret having been honest
& neglected to take the precaution
of supplying a false & convincing name
at least until I'd my business concluded
& was safely back in the arms of my sister
well maybe not exactly in her arms
but once again sound and secure in her company
because, whatever else, us old Fogartys
we really & truly do belong together –
no matter what that aggravating weasel
of a sister of mine might insist to the contrary.

Although that's not a very nice
thing to say
& I know it
considering the state
she was in when I got back
like now she didn't remember
anything at all
picking away at the threads
of her jumper
& saying as she stared off out
at the sea
what's that there
& then after that
did Matt Monro sing
with Mott the Hoople
I didn't know what to say
I was sick
because I know myself
what that *imní* can be like
or depression & anxiety
which is more how they tend
to describe it these days
Imní, yes

– what Nano, as I say, used to call
The Tremblings
or Trimmlins
as she preferred to pronounce it
& of which we've both had our share
Tá sin cinnte.
Yes, that much is certain
for they're never far
away
those late-night wakings,
the sounds
na fuaimeanna:
rustling
rustling
rustling
like giant grasshoppers
something you might see on David Attenborough
on some undiscovered tropical island
because if it's there
he will find it
The Planet Earth King
as Todd Creedence calls him.

Before he comes on, you'll always
have some other quack
who's no stranger to *imní*
or anxiety or depression either.
But believe you me,
it wasn't much better in the time
of Mike Yarwood
in fact, if I'm honest
it might even have been worse.
Or *worst*, as Ernie Gillespie from Norwich used to say.
Oh, that old Ernie
– every time I think of it.

We'd been given this job down in that country, do you
see
after I met this young spalpeen
in The Bedford Arms
a dacent whip of a youngster
all the same
Dan, he says,
will you be above on the Cricklewood Broadway

[76]

they're looking for men
will you be there at seven
At seven, I says
& so there I am
& away with the lot of us
in the belching transit.

With me, I declare, so fagged out
from drinking in The Bedford the
previous day
don't I sleep the whole danged
way from London
in spite of the carolling
from McFyber of Ballivor
and he pumping his
chest all the way along
the Great North Road
I'm Barney McFyber
I come from Ballivor
where I live with me mudder
she's grá gheal mo chroí!
with cries of whoop!
& Come on, Ballivor!
You never lost it
Barney you cur-dog
God save and bless you
whoop but you're a good 'un!
so you are
so you are
the devil take you

&
before we know it
isn't the poor auld
transit
with the door practically hanging off
isn't she pulling up outside a beat-up old
Nissen hut
of the sort that were everywhere
in them times
after the war.

You'll not be a-wanting for anything here
we were informed by our guide
a nice spring bed and mattress.
four nice blankets
a pilla
and a pilla slip
all at five bob a week
latrines to the left, breakfast at seven.
For while it was fine
o God aye
nothing not a damned hate
wrong with it at all
but then, for a few, cabin fever set in
three of the lads went into town and got drunk
and got into a fight with some locals
there was hell to pay in the canteen
the next morning.
You drunken blackguards! bawls the priest
becoming more and more furious,
you rotten lousy inebriated no-good blackguards
you ought to be ashamed of yourselves
waking up people in the middle of the night
rousing them from their Christian sleep
have you no respect for your country or yourselves?
But that wasn't the only *imní*-inducing aspect
you might say
for the canteen manager was a half-Sassenach
by the name of Ernie
Gillespie,
a workman who spent twenty years
of his life in England and hadn't
so much as a good word to
say about the Irish.
Bloody Paddies
spud and buttermilk merchants
the worst
the worst
the worst
coming over here to make trouble
for that's all they ever do
setting off bombs and the like.
Why don't they stop in their own bloody country
and not be taking the bread out of the mouths of
decent people?

Gillespie, I'm afraid, was disliked by virtually
everyone but most of all his own.
And, in common with a certain
Troy McClory, who did the very same to our
poor little innocent, credulous Una
some years later, I'm sorry to say,
made the fatal mistake of mocking
the appearance of a
quiet and shy, somewhat overweight
female who worked as a
waitress in the canteen.
She was a rosy, buxom, good-natured girl
who – her nose still red from crying –
ran out of the kitchen to tell her boyfriend
Hughie The Buck, a Kilkenny brickie
built like a couple of steel barrels
roped together
Hughie was a hot-tempered man
at the best of times
& now he throws down his shovel and marches
murderously in.
Is that what you'll do? responded
Ernie Gillespie defiantly to
consistent and repeated threats
brandishing a carving knife, is that what
you're telling me you'll do,
Mr Buttermilk?

Before proceeding to elaborate that if
any backwoods hillside savage
Irish cement-chucker ever dared to come next or near
him
that he'd carve out his gizzard, right there
& then
just see if he wouldn't.

With the *gist* of it being
that Ernie Gillespie he had this cat
this cat, you see, that he really and truly doted on
everywhere outside of the canteen that he went
this little pet he called Gracious went along with him.
So the next day Gracious what happens

[79]

she's disappeared
this large, sleek tabby upon which
was lavished all the affection
that Ernie Gillespie lacked for humanity
she just could not seem to be located
anywhere.
Gracious often went on hunting trips
during the day but always returned,
without fail, to the camp each night to be fed.
Initially, Ernie didn't pay much attention
to the fact, I mean, that the cat had not been seen
in the kitchen since morning
but grew more and more worried
as the evening wore on
& there was no sign of his beloved tabby.
The following morning, he does not say a word to
anyone but just goes about his work quietly
with a white, set face.
Later he phones the police to report that his tabby cat
Gracious
she has been stolen.

He does not go to bed at all
but is heard crying and searching with a storm lamp
in the elm woods surrounding the camp.
It was fated to be a very sad morning of imní
some hours later
when Gracious was found by a
labourer in a ditch
her head stove in by a spade.
When the body was brought in
Ernie Gillespie said nothing
just nodded his head and walked out of the kitchen
& was last seen heading for the train
& the following morning five hundred men
ate dry bread for breakfast.

Ah yes, there's no doubt about it
Níl aon amhras faoi, to use Nano's words
there's nothing worse than the onset of 'the
trimmlins'.
& its slow, grim, steady & exceedingly sly
invasion of the parts of you that
you don't know yourself

[80]

like uisce faoi thalamh
Nano used to say
water flowing noiselessly
underneath the ground
going hush
and then
hush again
exactly what Ernie Gillespie
happened to be thinking
as he sat in the drizzle
on the platform awaiting his train
hush he heard
is that you Ernie
only to look up
in the direction where the
voice was coming from
there to see, to his surprise
a little birdie
yes, a perky-looking fellow
sleek and black as it stood
there perched on a branch
the branch of a willow
regarding him with a black pearly
eye
unflinching
unyielding
Seo dhuit do chuid, he distinctly heard it call
yes, this is your lot
but then what else ought you to have expected, Mr
Gillespie?

He covered his face
& when he looked again
it was gone
there was just the twig
glazed over with rain,
vibrating just a little
before becoming still.
As, overwhelmed by *imní*,
Ernie plunged his sorrowful face
in his hands
in the exact same manner as a certain blonde-haired
Scottish adversary of my own was set
to do in the times that were coming.

Step forward, Troy 'The Hammer Man' fucking
McClory
assume your position and await the sombre
declaration of those vigilant plumed custodians

but

that wasn't the last time
Ernie Gillespie descried the *little birdie*
because late that night he happened to see it
again
in the corner of a window in the darkness of
a workman's shed
lit only by the moon
&, even though this time
it bore the face of a man
he still recognised it

& felt like laughing
because the countenance it showed
yes, that which it displayed
it might have been of someone
close on a hundred years old
& which is why
he felt like bheith ag gáire
yes, wanted to chuckle
yes, laugh quite a bit
go hee hee hee
ha ha ha look at that
I mean, did you ever?
Except that he didn't,
& which was probably, in the circumstances,
just as well
considering the look on his visitor's face
ar eagla na heagla was a phrase used by Nano
& which means: the very fear of fear itself

imní

anxiety

ar eagla na heagla

the worst possible outcome.

That is exactly what it means.

After that episode, until the day he died
Ernie Gillespie was never to breathe
a word about that particular experience
or the ones which were to succeed it
not to anyone.
I mean – how could he?
What could he possibly say, for heaven's sake?
'You'll never guess who arrived in my bedroom late last
night – say around three or four a.m. – a bloody dwarf, I ask
you, about the size of a four-year-old child.'
That would be a laugh all right.
So that was what
like so many others who came after him
down the years
& including poor old Troy McClory
Ernie from Norwich he made the decision
not to open his mouth
about it
or so much as say a single word
about *gruagachs*, *wee birdies* or anything else.
But that approach too
is freighted with inevitable drawbacks
& shortcomings
for, as we all know
if you tend to bottle something up
too much, you're leaving yourself open
to a dose of the trimmlins.
O but yes & indeed you are
& that is exactly what happened
in the case of poor old Gracious-less
Ernie Gillespie
who died of a Sunday afternoon,
when it was raining
just after, appropriately,
Songs of Praise had finished
in The Spike in Camden
as a matter of fact.

I had almost been on the point
that particular night in *The Rambler's Rest*
along with Andy Hamilton the night porter
of actually sharing that sad story with him
but in the end decided not to
being as we'd been having way way
too much fun
with all those old yarns
that he'd been telling me from the Shetlands
& then myself, in turn, going on to elaborate
about Nano's celebrated underground playground
which he couldn't get enough of
even if he'd never heard of it, he said
in spite of having lived in the city
all these years
och you're a great old character he said
telling me all about this eccentric
hostess relative of yours
as off I went, emboldened further
elaborating to beat the band about
what used to go on in the alcoves
of the club
with Nano in her sheath dress
meeting the punters out front
'Arrah, Musha McTitty!'
being her legendary catchphrase
applied to royalty & commoner alike.
'Arrah, Musha McTitty, there are you
to fuck!'
the 'present Miss Fogarty' would
bray by way of introduction
on her doorstep
releasing that great big whinny of a laugh
as she waved her cigarette
in its tortoiseshell holder
just like she had done on the night the famous
Movita arrived on the arm of Jack Doyle
the world-class Irish boxer and singer
known far and wide as *The Gorgeous Gael.*

Hello there Jack, she says, Musha McTitty
with her not being aware that –
although, given his reputation

perhaps she ought to have been –
the dinner-jacketed Corkman
unfortunately was
highly inebriated
but didn't touch her as they
all went trooping in
for he & Nano, they were
the very best of pals
but instead turns around and slugs Movita
yes, yes hits her a smack
right slap-bang in the puss
& sends her
flying across a tray of glasses
with the house band, Johnny Dankworth &
His Orchestra, carrying on as if nothing
at all had happened
ladies & gentlemen
may I have the pleasure of introducing
Miss Cleo Laine
doodle-doodle-doo-bop-bop-a boo-boo!
sang the curly-haired diva to appreciative applause
doobee-doot-en-doop-ee
please tell that you love me most
during this short time
this one season on the coast...

I think it was the same night Behan pissed on
the fish.
With Nano, impressively, electing to keep her counsel
regarding the entire affair.

With the very same approach being reserved
for President J. F. Kennedy
when, as an apprentice journalist
learning his craft in London,
the future American president
had arrived in unannounced
& enjoyed, as he told her later, a
refreshing glass of sparkling Coca-Cola.

An occurrence, as Andy had intimated to
me once or maybe twice that night,

that was, to some extent, taxing credibility
& acquiring the aspect of what Mrs
Margaret Rutherford here in Cliftonville
might be inclined to call
a little birdie of her own
a fib, in otherwords.
Which was the term she used
whenever she sensed any attempt
to hoodwink her, for
whatever reason.
But nonetheless it happened
& I should know
because I was there
scribbling away in the corner
o yes, sight unseen, in one of
those famous alcoves
Dan the vigilant, scratching observant
little squinty-eyed man.
Because, small or tall,
I'm never far away
beady-eyed, alert
noting all
without fuss
with little ceremony
in among the shadows.

However, what's this I was saying
to you a moment ago
just there now.
Yes, I was telling you, wasn't I
Andy & our late-night chat
in the motel up in Killiburn
making sure, however, to stop
short of explaining why exactly
it was I
had taken my leave at all
of Cliftonville
& travelled up on my own on the train
to London
back to the *scene of the crime*, you might say.
Why, do I hear you ask
did you bother doing that
why, Dan Fogarty

what was the reason?
Why, especially, after all this time,
nearly forty-five years, for heaven's sake
close on half a century
almost
well, the reason, to be honest,
is perfectly simple
I wanted to know if my *treasure trove* would
still be there
in the place I'd left it
stored it, for safety, all those many long
years before
wrapped in a little ball of tissue.
And, sure enough, when I searched
there it was
my priceless little oval shield
that radiant escutcheon
scarcely the size of a sixpenny coin
with only a few small inconsequential
scratches upon its surface.

As I brushed it lovingly with my sleeve
I had to laugh when I recalled
how the little medal, how much it
reminded me of the old Irish sixpence.
'You can't use that on here,' they used to say
whenever you'd get on the bus
before tossing it back in your face
& laughing.
Gazing down upon the face of
that silver shield – *or scáthán airgid*
it was like swimming in the strange wondrous
waters of history
parting the more you looked
down in there in that lovely polished mirror
of Time.
Which was the reason that I kept
on vigorously polishing the silver
medal with my sleeve
yes polishing
&
polishing
&
polishing

until I was near exhausted
with the sweat in streams
running down off my forehead
as I took out my wallet & safely
put away the little oval medallion
sky-blue with a durable silver
border
remaining still astounded that
in spite of this lengthy passage of time
I had succeeded in locating it exactly
where I had secreted it
carefully concealed behind the plaster
in two or three fleecy layers of pink-and-white
tissue paper
hidden so effectively hidden
that I'd actually had to prise it out with a pencil.
But, in spite of all my trimmlins,
and they were many
believe me, do,
I was buoyed by the knowledge that
my sister Una would be so overjoyed
whenever she heard
my wonderful news.

O Maria Concepta sine peccato qui ad te
confugimus!
O Mary conceived without sin
pray for us who have recourse to thee!
You found my miraculous medal! already I could hear
her excitedly exclaim,
clapping her hands as she jumped up & down.

Although, all the same, you could never
be a hundred per cent sure with Una.
No, never quite.

Nonetheless, I popped the wallet in my
inside pocket
&, entirely contented,
made my way inside to the bathroom
where I threw a goodly portion of *uisce*
yes, water
onto my face

brushing my teeth furiously
as I stood there, quite high
before running to the window
and directing my gaze all along
that familiar old thoroughfare
that beat-up but still beautiful boulevard
of thwarted ambitions and lost loves known
as the Killiburn High Road,
God bless it, now utterly changed
but somehow still exactly the same
in spite of
Vodafone
Costcutters
Primark
&
Sports Direct
with the building shuddering as another HGV went
rumbling by
past the betting shop where Biddy Mulligan's
traditional public house
used to be.
Many's the whiskey I enjoyed in there
I reflected
&
the odd pint too
ha ha
ha ha
o indeed & I did
troth and surely I did
for you just cannot beat that auld
uisquebaugh so you can't

& if you don't believe me
why not ask good old Troy
yes, ask my sister's boyfriend
Troy McClory
because I mean, after all
being a Scotsman
he would have to
know
fucking everything
although that's not something
I'd ever have said about the night porter
in The Rambler's Rest

yes, good old Andy
who I was sorry I didn't get a
chance to say goodbye to

as I waited out front in the rain
for a taxi
tapping my wallet
still secure in my inside pocket
I wondered just what might have become
of me and Una
if only fortune had been more in
favour of us Fogartys
back then
in the auld times in Killiburn
especially when we lived,
when we were residents in, The Mahavishnu
Anarchist Temple
ah well, I sighed
but then that's life
& I don't suppose, really, that we're
ever destined to know the truth about that,
Because everything changes
that's life & you must accept it
Ay, that's the way, Andy Hamilton
the night porter had ruefully sighed
at the conclusion of one of his stories
we all change, & poor auld Killiburn
it's no different
in many ways altered beyond recognition
even if, at first, you mightn't think it.
For you'd be hard pressed to find an Irish
labourer around here now
the life that you and me knew
it's over, Mr Fuggherty
now it's the turn of someone else
what with all this Instagram
YouTube & who knows what
& indeed there can be very little
doubt about it,
Snapchat or whatever
for who, can you tell me, has
ever heard of Mike Yarwood now?
Where did he even *go*?

Not to mention Mott the Hoople.
Although I have to say
there's a funny side to it too.

As Margaret Rutherford discovered
only just the other day
when she asked my sister what might be the name
of the presenter on *Planet Earth* being as
she'd momentarily forgotten it.
Our Una, quick as a flash, and with not
so much as a flicker of uncertainty, nodded
helpfully – and, with an authoritative snap of her
fingers, informed her: *Ian Hunter.*

Once I caught her sticking a stamp
on the heel of her sandal.

Yes, so there you are – that's the way everything's
set to go.
Everything has no choice but to change.
'O begod aye!' as Pop McRoarty,
used to say in The Spike, God rest him.
It does that,
it does that,
it does that surely,
dammit sowl
it sure does that.
It'll do that, Dan
me sound young chap.
Dammit sowl, it surely will.

That means 'damn your soul' in Gaelic.

A phrase that was common
in the old times
before computers
prior to the days of
Twitter & Tinder
Snapchat,
Grindr,
or fuck me till I'm blue
in the face

even though
I don't even know so much as your name
& when you're done
come on Mr turn me over
& do the mickey-jump-jubbly
as you *playze*
yes, do it again
&
again
&
again

Aye, *dammit sowl* –
that's what they
used to say
a poor auld colloquialism that no one
now knows about
or cares
as indeed why
should they?

Unless, as poor auld Nano
observed on one occasion,
they might be glad of it one day
when, like so many that have preceded them
they're prostrate, raving,
on sheets of sodden linen
imploring clemency
the same as poor old
once-upon-a-time handsome
Troy
yes
the sexy
sister-banging Hammer Man
would-be artist
all the way from bonnie Scotland

begging for a priest, or something
anyone
as might assuage his trimmlins
& dreadful
imní.

God between us and all harm
all I can say is
I only hope the like of it doesn't happen
to you, whoever you are, or any
that's close to you, your
dearly beloved
because that's generally what happens
you're walking along
& it's standing there before you
hello, my blue-eyed boy it says
or girl
&
there you are
cold and white
a great big block of
imní incarnate
whispering
imminent erasure!

just like
Troy used to conjure up
at his readings
in the Putney Arts Club
or sometimes on the table
in the front room of The Temple
as the place filled up with smoke
& everyone tapping their bongoes
or clinking their little
tinkling golden bells
as out he spread his arms
like a whopping great
misty-eyed, blonde-haired
Messiah
reading to them aloud
shaking his matted
hair free & in that great big
over-enunciated educated
Scottish voice
looked directly into the eyes of
our hopelessly adoring Una
his Lady Ocean
& began to boom & sonorously
declaim

Pablo Neruda.
or – more often,
Mr T. S. Eliot
if you
please
& how do you
like them now
your sweet
& good-looking
blue-eyed boys
yes how do you like
them now
Mr Death

ah
shut
your
fucking stupid Scottish mouth
think you know everything
yes, try closing
your
bloody bake
once and
for fucking all
& get on the magic fucking
bus
back
to
Auld Reekie
yes
back to your stupid
'auld' Scotland,
why don't you?

Because he did cause no end
no end of trouble
the fallout of which we are living with
even yet
& why every day I am still
worried about Una.

But nonetheless I'm still reassured by my trip
to London
because I know that that
little miraculous medal
it still means a great deal
to her
which is why she makes sure
to keep on wearing it
close to her chest
just like our mother God rest
her and keep her
that little oval shield
shining blindly out of the
fog of history
& which is why
now that I've made it in one
piece back to Cliftonville
I've decided to call a halt to all of
my complaining
& do my best, once and for all,
to look after my sister
who seems to be responding really
positively I have to say
I hope you won't be throwing this into a bag
I said to her yesterday when they gave us halibut for
tea
Mike Yarwood, she says
& I really had to laugh
as I tried to do my best to get her
back to the original subject
semolina is better than rice she says
as Rutherford goes past & taps Connie on
the shoulder
everything all right she says to the Brazilian
Princess
who doesn't, I think, even hear her
at all
in a bit of a daze herself, she is sometimes
but Margaret Rutherford doesn't
seem to mind all that much,
leaning across the table & fiddling
with her watch
chatting away to Butley & Roystone Oames

all about David Attenborough's
latest discovery underseas.

With after dinner
everything else seeming fine and dandy
with not so much as another word about semolina
not to mention once-celebrated comedians
from the seventies
& now all the chat being about
– well, of course! – the forthcoming show
directed by my sister
which is going to surpass anything
The London Palladium has seen in years.
She's so busy organising
that she's really got as thin as a whip, so she has.
God be with the old 'Days Of Fudge' when she
must have been tipping fifteen stone!

Sometimes she'll jump up &
for what seems to be absolutely
no reason whatsoever
emit this wail and go white as a sheet.
& which reminds me
although to be honest I wish it didn't
of one of the residents of The Temple
who used to carry on in
a similar fashion
it's Joanne Kaplan I'm talking about
who used to reside in the second-floor
apartment, next to Una.
With Joanne's chunky brown polo neck & shag-cut
hair, knee-length suede skirt and high brown
boots she looked
not at all unlike
the high-class escort
Bree Daniels in the film *Klute*
& was possessed of a style
and grace that was particularly comparable
I must concede

although not, perhaps,
in more recent times
no, not so much of late
certainly, where the exigencies of forbearance
& dignity were concerned
because all she kept saying
all she could seem to think of
repeating
after they'd been in the flat
six months
so here's another horrible thing that's
happened to me
why are all of these rotten awful things
occurring with such wrenching regularity in my life
please can you tell me the answer to that
just
what
in
heaven's
name
is
going
on –
does anyone know
because I'm afraid
I don't
No, I don't
I don't
I'm afraid
o Jesus
o God
I've got to
take something
I have no choice
I
have
got
to
take
something.

But, as might be expected,
what with the life they were living,
all of it,

it was all in her mind.

At least that's what everyone else in The Temple
kept saying.

Attributing these purported 'incidents' she had been
going on about
to the recent suicide of her flatmate.

After all, they reasoned, Tanith Kaplinski was your very best
friend, so it's going to be natural.

Handing her a joint or a glass of mulled wine.

They'd been having a beautiful time on the lawn this day,
enjoying a barbecue as little wisps of woodsmoke came
drifting languidly over the garden fence.

Not that their neighbours had given them any indication of
being in any way impressed.

'Drown the whole bally lot of them in the canal!' Roystone
Oames the accountant from No. 44 had sourly avowed,
'Bloody ragbag of smalltown outcasts, intellectuals and
would-be revolutionaries, downright slouchers who wouldn't
fit in anywhere, haven't done so much as a hand's turn in
their lives.'

But hadn't objected, all the same, when they'd done him the
favour of walking and looking after his dog, the golden
Labrador, which Joanne loved.

With the walking of the dog, as it happened, proving an
effective way of distracting Joanne Kaplan.

Who, as they all knew well, in recent times had been
experiencing such a degree of imní and tribulation that she
was likely as not to burst into tears at the slightest
provocation.

And now there was the business of 'the egg'.

'No!' she objected, 'I just *know* something threw it!' – and
they had to acknowledge that they themselves felt somewhat
sickened.

'I wouldn't mind,' they complained later, 'but when she
started bringing *The Exorcist* into it – well, I mean, come on!'
The Exorcist
they were talking about,
the film they meant,
the controversial feature
which was playing
at the time
& which she hadn't
in fact
shut up about

over
&
over
&
over
she went on
well, that was way too much
they said.

Although a great many people who had
seen the feature had subsequently found themselves
becoming affected
&
in all sorts of ways
that, at least,
was what Joanne Kaplan swore.
Even cursed! she repeated, you don't have to take my word
for it.
However, even my sister had scoffed at such a suggestion.
That is to say, 'Fudge' Fogarty, as they had taken to calling
her, privately, at the time.
With those great big flowery dresses and skirts, like
something you might have seen her in later on, participating
in one of her own *Cliftonville Capers* productions.
Playing a character from an amateur drama show, entitled
perhaps *At Home with the Fogartys* – with Una
commanding the role of the neurotic, overweight
mother.
Big Fat Fudge who looked the image of Mama Cass.
& which is something they wouldn't be
able to say about her now,
all these years later
the old skinny-ma-link.

But back then, in The Temple, it's true that she weighed a
ton.
Yes, definitely fifteen or sixteen stone,
our Una.
An absolute monstrosity, it's fair to say, she was.

However, I was telling you
wasn't I
about Joanne Kaplan, Miss 'Klute' herself.

And how, at breakfast the following day she'd kept on
insisting there'd been 'blood in the egg'.
That had, somehow, come flying right out of the
cupboard
entirely of its own volition.
It was after that they'd begun getting really worried.
You could tell by her eyes that she'd been up all night.

Composing lyrics, if you don't mind.

Yes, had taken it into her head
apparently
to concoct for herself a little
bit of a romantic ditty
a poem at 3 a.m.
or capitulate to the act of doing so
with it being
as she explained
more or less
written for her
as her pale white hand went
scuttling across the table & the
words began
with a speed and articulacy
that, I have to say, astonished her
as she gripped the pen
with a ferocity she feared might
see her break it
but all the same
she couldn't for the life
of her
seem to stop scribbling
what is wrong in this world
with us
she pleaded
where it's so easy to
find oneself lost
becoming invisible
reduced to a document
in a case file
a Polaroid photo
with no name
just a number

a rabbit's foot
maybe
a medal or a bracelet
some other memento
a letter
abandoned
with only that
to ground you
& make you feel real
in this world
without sunlight
where everyone is watching
from a distance
through peepholes
in closed, heavily bolted
doors.
What is the mystery of our identity?
she implored –
in this crowded world
so suffocating
& predatory
with sly, subtle,
deviant
forces always at work
in this long unfinished tunnel
this place which is warped
hopelessly disfigured
where I have a sense of being
trapped,
stammered Joanne Kaplan –
of being caught
in a huge, endless-seeming
subterranean studio room
but maybe I'm just imagining it,
she croaked
as she let the pen slip
yes, dropped the biro
now realising she was feeling
entirely exhausted
& just that little bit relieved
now that the
writing
it was all,
at last, complete

with the only consequence
being that she
wasn't in the least
expecting what happened next

nearly fainting right
there on the spot
when one of the eggs from the carton came
flying right at her through the door
of the cupboard which she had just
that very second opened
yes, hit her right smack dab
in the middle of her face
followed by another
1
2
3,
with the thick yolk running all down
the front of her sweater.
&, just the same as Una, certainly in more
recent times
it being just the last thing she wanted to do
to make fun of what had happened.
To tell the actual God's honest truth
doing her damnedest best to suppress her wails
but finding that she couldn't
as in rushed the others
reassuring her
giving her water
flapping around all
over the place.

But finding themselves somewhat consoled
later on, at the breakfast table
where Joanne Kaplan, more or less,
seemed to have come back to herself
at least before knocking over the small jug of milk
with her elbow
& Troy only managing to reach out & intercept it in
the nick of time
as all of the words from the poem she had
written the night before came racing

all at once to her lips
as those hypercautious eyes kept on darting
from one to the other
& she kept on
demanding
please will you try
& give me some answers
what is the reason for all these flaws
and compulsions?
Why must we remain disfigured in this icy blue
nightmare?
Chasing one another
into ever-darker shadows
over and over
not knowing why
as she laughed, somewhat giddily, and
went and knocked over the milk jug
again
only this time ignoring it
as it splintered in pieces
& continued to carry on talking
only faster this time
until they all made excuses
because they had to get away
from this, what Troy had called
the worst vibe ever –
but which was just the beginning, really.

With, after that, her deciding to stop
going into college altogether
preferring to potter around all day
in her dressing gown
in her bedroom
smoking cigarettes
skittering across to the window
to look out at the traffic passing on the High Road
reading out slogans
small print
from passing trucks
sly, she said, so *silent*
deviant
subtle
but watching,
always watching.

'For Christ's sake!' Troy McClory
had finally snapped one day,
'I don't reckon we can go on like this.
Something has got to be done!
You have got to get a grip, Miss Kaplan!'
& do you know what Miss Kaplan went & did
then?
Went over and struck him violently across the face.
Why, sometimes she could be even worse
than Una
at least in those very extreme moods.
'This house gleams with inhuman malevolence!' she
screeched, 'Banal malice – or don't you
understand? Don't you get it, you fucking Scottish
prick?'

So
whatever it is you might think of that
the net result was
that it proved to be the straw that broke the camel's
                              back.
With them putting it to a vote
& deciding, for definite,
that something had to be done.
It was Big Peter, quite by chance, who had spotted the advert
in *Time Out*, a radical magazine catering for the alternative
lifestyle.
Offering the services of 'Don Butterworth' – *not your
average exorcist* – but those amounting to what was
described as *a Complete & Comprehensive Spiritual
Decontamination Experience.*

After much discussion
everyone in the end
agreed to give it a go
with Joanne herself
declaring herself immensely relieved.
And that was how Phil Mitchell
happened to arrive in a bumpalong
little white Transit van into Killiburn

in the middle of the nineteen-seventies
long before the programme
EastEnders
(which Todd Creedence never misses
in Cliftonville – or Una, God love her,
come to that)
yes, a long ways before
it was ever conceived of
that was exactly who
Donnie Butterworth looked the spit of
swaggering along
swinging his bag
in a green knitted army sweater
sporting shiny elbow patches
smoking a cheroot
with a
big fat shaven bullet head
on his shoulders
& that scrawny little wife
running after him
chain-smoking fags
insisting on following him
wherever he went
Scottish too of course
aye Don och aye that's right
Miss Scrawny Bags keeps repeating
agreeing with every single word
he utters
& there was no shortage of them
I can assure you
no, no scarcity of blather at all
as around strolled Donnie with
his hands on his hips
sucking in a great big draught
of air
& mordantly shaking his head.
Two-up, two-down semis
that's where the battle against
evil is being fought out on the ground
these days!
he says, with authority.
No, you don't go to the London Dungeons
or the Tower Of London
you go wherever Mr and Mrs Bloggs live

lost souls may smell reasonably fragrant
but evil ones are putrid.
The pavements are full of the ghosts
of friends and neighbours
this whole city is congealed with them.
But remember there is only so much I can do
because evil is an elusive migrant
too wily and centrifugal ever to be totally
extinguished.
He looked right at McClory and started to deftly roll
a cigarette between his fingers.

Me and the queen here, you see
we just came over from Hoxton
all hell had been breaking loose
went unreported until one of the family
clean through a window she flung herself
only fourteen she was, poor girl
the woman was distraught, inconsolable
when I arrived with my kit
said she'd never seen anything like it
describing, like they often do
a drop in the temperature
a shape, like a blob of ectoplasm
her lodger, she used to call it
yes, I've been having quite a laugh
with my lodger, she said, kind of
hysterical till doll here got her a drink
of water
all summer
he's been up them stairs.
My lodger, yeah.
Her lodger, hmm.
Presenting as he had as a decent and responsible
unassuming fellow
before he got into his stride
good and proper
tearing not only her house but her mind apart
Now, what seems to be your particular problem? he says to
Troy, looking right at him.
& I had to laugh when I saw he was intimidated.
Troy, I mean.

As indeed were the entire raggle-taggle, dumbstruck
bunch.
Which comprised, although this list
is by no means exhaustive –
with 'heads', as they called them,
coming and going all the time.
In what was purported to be
the premier 'crash pad' in all
of North London, maybe even
south of the river too.
The 'family' included:
 1. Big Peter Hanlon
 2. Jenny Venus
 3. Joanne Kaplan
 4. Maddie Lynam
 5. Dessie McKeever, 'Lord Offaly
     Of Down'
 6. Frank 'The Blind Owl' Olson
&
all the rest of them
looking as if they hadn't slept in
a month.
Old Fudgy McFudge, of course,
our Una
she was the worst of the lot
being afraid to so much as
whimper a word
looking terrified in case he might single her out
hey you, fat fuck
but he didn't of course
o but of course not
because if anything, Phil Mitchell/Don
Butterworth
he was a gentleman.
Yes, had to hand it to that old Donnie –
because whenever it came to intimidating
overeducated Scotsmen & making big speeches about
the subject of the paranormal
well, I have to say
that there really didn't seem
to be anyone to touch him.
As he kept on walking up and down, flailing his arms &
kicking open doors
scattering around these fistfuls of powder.

And, in response to Joanne's question, making it clear that
yes, he had in fact seen the film, *The Exorcist*.
But that is just what you don't want to pay no attention to,
you understand? Because at the end of the day, that's just
fiction. And if that old *Captain Howdy* – if he happens to be
somewhere around here, present in some as yet undiscovered
part of this house – then, let you make no mistake, my friends
– you and me, we are going to find that sucker!
As he climbed the stairs, two at a time, demanding to be
admitted to the room 'where *it* had happened'.
Where Tanith Kaplinski had met her tragic end.
As they stood beside the window ledge and, all of a sudden,
Troy said: Tell him, Jo, about the egg.
'I see,' said Don. 'Egg, I see.'
As he waited for a moment, stroking his chin.
'Uh-huh,' he murmured, as his wife looked on
leaning over like an overeager clothes peg.
&, then in the heel of the hunt,
saying nothing.
Let me be clear, continued Don Butterworth, about just what it is
you're dealing with here. Every night London is placed under siege.
Every night, across this city, thousands of people are attacked and
maimed. Especially between midnight and two a.m., hours when
the human body is at its lowest ebb, and when sorrow gnaws most
viciously at the heart. That is when they are spotted. Those who see
them, or who start to suspect that the tantrums and mood swings of
their teenage daughters are signs of demonic possession, are too
scared to tell anyone. So they stay silent, going slowly out of their
minds with distress and confusion.

There wasn't a sound in the room as he spoke,
apart from the faint sobs of Joanne's suppressed weeping.

Sister Una was as red as a beetroot.
Still dreading, like she has always done, some form of
personalised, in-depth interrogation.
But which, fortunately, was never to materialise.
Then Joanne screamed, before running off and locking
herself in the bathroom.
As Don Butterworth smiled wryly, examining a long-spent
roach in a saucer.
You could hear the sound of a breakage in the
bathroom.
With it turning out Joanne had gone and smashed

a glass
in a hapless attempt to do what Tanith had succeeded
in doing.
You could see the blood oozing out underneath
the door.
But it turned out not to be serious
just a superficial wound is all.

Ah now – talk about old times
all the things that used to go on.
Although, when I think of it, there's damn
near as much animation and contrariness
in Cliftonville.

&, in this regard, I would have to nominate Butley Henderson
in particular.
On account of he never stops asking me and Una just why it
is we insist on lapsing into Gaelic – blathering away in a
language that no one else, apart from us, will ever have a
hope of understanding.

I wish I knew is the only answer I can give to that.
Maybe it's got something to do with ancestral memory.
Although, considering the way that we've been these days,
the pair of us – all I can say is God help the ancestors
with you never knowing when
the V-1s are lining up and getting ready
before it's *green for danger*
& all systems are go
as:
W
h
e
e!
& another whole streetful of houses
has the hell blown out of it.

Ah, all the same
to some extent
you do get used to it

& manage to laugh it off
which reminds me
all I can say is
it's just a pity that them
effing squealing doodlebugs
that they wouldn't target Trump.
Who never seems to have a problem
in this respect
or if he does
doesn't appear to have any trouble
disguising it
standing up there in the Oval Office
blabbering on about healthcare &
Obama
& Mexicans & walls
& who knows what the fuck he's going
to come out with next
all I know is he's not threatened by
any V-1 bombers
with the only pity being, as I say
that I wish he was.

They had him again
on Fox Rolling News this morning
& after watching his performance
I have to say that I genuinely do not know
which of the two of them is the worst
him or that other steely-eyed
óinseach
who goes by the name of
Putin, over in Russia.
A grand parcel of rogues to be coming on anyone's television,
if you ask me.
As Nano might say.

& all I can do is wonder
just what she & all her old-time cronies
yes, what the old gang
would have thought of it all
or anything else that's going on now
in the world of computers
& Sports Direct
filming your little 'bud'

aye, your wee mickey,
& sending it to strangers
not to mind
recording crashes &
live-streaming them as they happen
even killing yourself sometimes
in front of a camera
you can do that too
& say maybe now you'll love me
ha ha
yes, now you're sorry
yes, now you'll freaking love me
ha ha
take that!

o yes, they're quare old times
& that's for sure
but it's the way it is
& it's not going to change
night noon & morning
24/7 they'll tell you if you ask them
that's if you manage to catch their attention
& they're not watching

!   *   !   *   *   !   *
*   !   *

!*

!   *   *

    *   * !!   !

some new game or other
& which seems to have got worse
ever since Spudhead Central, that big fat
orange-faced *prata*, as Una calls him
managed to get himself into
The White House.

Any time she hears him she's over straight away
shaking her little bony fist at the screen
chewing her jumper
giving out about his policies
only sometimes then saying

things you mightn't expect
or approve of
such as
as a matter of fact
I think Donald is right about the Mexicans
send the whole frigging shower of them back
Enoch Powell's right
every last single one
into the wagon go the lot
back to the kippeens that they came from
haw haw, she says
how would they like that
& goes laughing away
scratching her backside
o now our Una
the things that she gets up to
so you see what I have to
tolerate
but what about us I says to her after that
did we not do the same
us Irish
in our time
yes Paddy & Biddy the so-called wandering Irish
we exiles
what about us our Una I says
& all the places that we settled
across this world
only to hear her saying
as she looks at me, tugging on her threads
yes, picking away at the strands of her cardigan
why was I ever born, our Dan
can you tell me that
cen fáth gur rugadh me?
Why did I have the fucking
misfortune to get born?

& to which what answer can I possibly
give except
at least you
Una
you were actually, *properly* born
which is a lot
fucking
more

than
can be
said
for
me,
poor old stray and
rootless
Dan
Fogarty.

It makes me glum, thinking back
on those times.
With the smoke coming drifting across the fence in that suburban
garden, a flute solo lilting through an open upstairs window
succeeded by a soft staccato of hand drums and a
mellifluous melange of Eastern strings
with Tanith Kaplinski preparing another great big pot of chilli in the
kitchen
& Big Peter Hanlon from Dundalk regaling everyone with tales of
his travels
among the hills of Afghanistan where he'd scored some more
amazing poppies
bringing them back to his homeland
the spiritual garden that was Mahavishnu.

Where had that day gone
yes, where had it disappeared to
&, indeed
where had we gone to, ourselves
for, in the aftermath of Don Butterworth's visit
one almighty fucking shadow
seemed to have fallen
yes, come out of nowhere to spread out across
the interior of
Brondesbury Gardens.

Where, once upon a time
under the guidance of Troy McClory
& Tanith Kaplinski
a unique collection of like-minded individuals

had come together to go on a never-before
travelled journey
yes, psychic cosmonaut souls
inner wanderers
intent on creating a whole new Nirvana.
With everything now
in the aftermath of Butterworth's elaborate speeches
appearing hell-bent on conspiring to thwart
every single laudable ambition
destroying in the process everyone's private
Hy-Brasil
as Dessie McKeever, aka Lord Offaly Of Down,
had once described it
in a memorable phrase.

With the neighbours banging on the doors
at all hours of the night
having had their sleep repeatedly
and constantly interrupted
or so they said
by all kinds of robust argumentation
& various episodes of profane behaviour.
These affronted community representatives
included Roystone Oames
who, along with Butley,
quite by coincidence,
arrived here in
Cliftonville

& which I have to say pleased me
reminding me as he did
of those good old Killiburn days.

'You've got a bloody nerve, you lot!' he
shouted up from the street
outside No. 45
one night in his dressing gown.
'When decent working people are trying
to get themselves some sleep
people who, more fool them,
fought for the likes of you in the last war!'

There had also been numerous telephone calls
to the police

with less-than-veiled imputations
of 'devil worship' being practised on the premises
of 45 Brondesbury Gardens
a consequence, probably, of Don Butterworth's
intervention
with his van, of course, being noted outside
along with Troy's insistence on playing
Black Sabbath records through the open window
at all hours.

Having been warned by the police to
'at the very least curb some of their
 unfortunate tendencies'
there ensued a period of relative tranquillity
at least until Troy, considerably
emboldened by a prodigious intake of amphetamines
one day, holding a book of poetry at arm's
length and attired
in a purple 'wizard's' cloak
clambered out onto the windowsill
and informed 'North London' to be prepared to
'be addressed'.
Which it was, as his hair flew around him
& he gestured with all the extravagance
of which only he was capable:
how many pigeons
do you think you can break today
my friend
                    not one

not two
                              no
no pigeons at all
                                        Mr Death
so attend to me
as I stand here tonight
speaking ha ha for the dignity

of man
& all those blue-eyed
boys
that you have threatened

for not
one fig
do we care for you
do you hear me

Mr Death
Can you hear me Mr Death?
Mr Death

can
          you
                              hear
me?

          I hope you
can

For not one fig do I care for you
you hear?
You hearing me
Mr fucking Imminent Erasure
for make no mistake
I fear you not!

& now
so he said
all was quiet
& everything was again
back to normal
because nothing
no 'Man'
no 'Fuzz'
no 'Death'
could ever begin
to threaten
the magnificent
unassailability
of the citadel of freedom
the Hy-Brasil of Possibility
that The Mahavishnu Temple
in spite of all the attempts to

undermine it
had so proudly become
'Ain't that right, lady?' he said to
his adoring Una
'Ain't that the case, my lady,
Lady Ocean?'
And did that great big ball of
fudge blush!
Right to the roots, I kid you not.
O how she loved him, that silly stupid
colleen!

In those leather trousers
& Ian Hunter-style shades
of late having begun modelling
himself on the front man of
Mott the Hoople
chewing the stem of his aviator
shades
talking about laying down some
more 'groovy' tracks
naming some of the other bands
that he 'dug'
such as Mom's Apple Pie
whose latest album
has just been banned
on account of it featuring
a 'chick's cunt!', he had laughed
as one's poor old sister
why, she flushed again
even worse this time
Lord if she didn't wish it
the ground to swallow her up
a *chick's cunt*, no less!

But, as Nano always says –
sin e an bhealach.
Yes, that, I'm afraid, is the way it has to be
when someone has the misfortune
to fall in, head over heels
& there's divil the bit
it would seem
we can do about it.

An mhaith leat an mickey-jump-jubbly?
he said to her then
sitting across from her at
the table
in otherwords, would you like to 'ball' –
is that what you'd maybe like to do
little colleen
or, should I say, Ireland's answer to
Ten Ton Tessie
And then away with the pair of them, up
to his room
where it's off with the leather
trousers & shades
galloping away to the sound of
another of his favourites
the band *King Crimson*
particularly the album
IN
THE
WAKE
OF
POSEIDON
And such a *ruaille buaille* as they made
I mean, what an absolute *thundering*
fucking racket.

Och ah dinnae know
where in the bloody hell
all those words came frae
tha' night!
the bold Troy had exclaimed
after more or less having wrecked
what few little pieces of furniture
they had, on the night
in question
hopping, I declare, about
like a kangaroo
making all these weird
faces
and flapping his arms
before finally seating himself at
the fireplace, in the chimney corner
speaking in tongues
like someone you might find

in a *bothán* by the very side
of the wild Atlantic
lighting bong after bong
speaking in verse and the
oddest version of Western Irish
speech, mountain-talk half
the time unintelligible
about all the dreams he'd been
having about The New Caledonia
which he and Una were going
to establish
just as soon as he got his degree
with the two of them deciding to leave
London forever
& across the bright blue sea
in a sailing ship
travel to what would become
their own personal Eden
Caledonia, strummed Troy,
o my Caledonia
beautiful mystic isle
of the imagination
where aglow in the chrism
of a mist-shrouded Arcadia
to that realm of bliss & sunshine
we are coming
& soon
our new republic will
be declared upon your
shores
our own special psychedelic
wonderland
oozing and throbbing with colour
populated by unicorns, angels
& white, cooing doves
freed from war
& the tyranny of
'The Man'

that phantom island
of which we've long dreamed
a revolutionary new society
which they said
could never be

but which, believe me,
very soon will
yes, against all the odds
will become a reality
that no one again will ever dispute
because Caledonia
– we're coming home!

As he hauled poor Una
out onto the floor
still laughing when he said
that, seeing as she looked like
Mama Cass
who better to sing
about California
except that, of course,
it wasn't that
but Caledonia he sang
in recognition of the coming new republic
a community designed to be
superior, even
to that of the much-envied Mahavishnu Temple
isn't that right Una
because this ain't no dream
no, no dream at all
Una Fogarty agreed
but a reality, cried Troy
a reality
m

     a

        a

           n!

as, all of a sudden,
her Scottish boyfriend began to
tremble and quiver
all over again
only this time even worse
with a line of froth on his lips
& Una Fogarty fell back onto the sofa
helpless
watching as the tears came rolling down his

face
& he committed himself to all
kind and manner of fits and eruptions
as his shoulders shook
& with wild eyes he regarded
them all
through a swaying curtain
of winding purple smoke
before they heard his voice change again
man, said Big Peter
this sure is good shit
as come here to me, Troy demanded
in the tones of an old woman
close on eighty years of age
as he *scraked* away
come here to me now, are you listening
to me, *craythurs*
quit your gabbin' and
be attendin' to me now
this instant
hee hee hee and ho ho ho
astonished as they were
having them in fits of hysterics
before he'd finished
o 'twas a wild and eerie
night, amn't I telling you
and me coming home
by the wild and lonesome glen
that skirted the edge of a deep ravine
known as Glounashee Pass
God bless the hearers as I
sit here before you this night
when up out of nowhere it's
not a word of a lie
I'm telling
for up it rose
the wickedest whirlwind
& there before my eyes
stood an fear beag liath
three foot high and he known
as the old grey man
declaring in tones
that might have been a
death-rattle

commingled with ancient
before Christ
lordly talk
aye, he rattled, I'm the old
grey man of the Fogartys
them that
was cast out of heaven by
an arrogant and vindictive
God
&, dacent man that I am,
I have come to warn you
be careful now, do you hear
what it is I'm saying
before climbing on the back
of the smallest of the little
cattle that were standing beside
us in the moonlit dark of the glen
'Good luck now!' he screeched,
'just be mindful of what I've
been telling you!'
& away with him then
rocks clattering along
the slope
waving his arms on the back
of a pudgy little Friesian
no bigger, as it ran, than the
average house cat

But such yelps!
O man! Troy McClory
screeched
like someone or something
was doing all this talking
for him
no end of it
until, at last,
he collapsed in a heap
with everyone thinking
even my darling Una
that it had been some kind
of 'epic poem'.

Yeah, motherfucker! That
sure was good fucking gear
that night! he would often
remark long after,
I must have rolled at
least a dozen bongs
Yeah, a dozen motherfucking
spliffs at least!
With everyone nodding
just like they'd done
at the thought of his random
story about the 'little
guy'
mounted on a cow, vanishing into
the mist before turning
into a white stranger
in the distance
releasing a burst of vengeful
indulgent laughter
whirling his stick
high above his head
calling back: 'Mr Exu!'

Then, when they looked again,
the stranger was gone,
just as if he'd never existed,
with his anglewise prick and white
shoes along with him.

Far out! murmured Dessie
McKeever
Lord Offaly Of Down
as Troy, doing his best to rig
the stereo up to the light socket
for reasons best known to him
suddenly let out an almighty roar
falling, head first, right
into the fireplace
before emerging, covered from
head to toe in ash
as Big Peter took another fit of the
giggles

Man! he cried excitedly, you look
like motherfucking Isaac Hayes!
& that was sure a laugh
as they all fell around
shoving down slugs of Jack
Daniels as they did so.

So, was it any wonder that Roystone & Butley
their neighbours from next door would decide,
eventually, that they had no choice but to lodge a
formal police complaint.

Yes.
With it being inevitable that, sooner or
later
The Motherfucking Pigs or The Fuzz
as the occupants of No. 45
liked to call them
would arrive up
not banging the door down or anything
but being quite civil, really
when they said: I think by now
we've had more than enough
of all this
don't you, ladies and gentlemen?

Statement Of Arresting Officer, dated Sept 30, 1974:

I had been to the premises at 45 Brondesbury Gardens on a number of previous occasions – having been summoned there by neighbours who had issued complaints of, variously, 'noise pollution' and 'strange occurrences in the night', squabbles etc.

The premises I found very rundown and off the beaten track. It would be fair to say that there is little in this strongly black and Irish quarter of Kilburn to attract property speculators – it is what I would describe as premier squatting territory. I have to say, if it is not inappropriate, that what I found greeting me when at last admitted was – to say the very least, quite off-putting. Indeed, it may be no exaggeration at all to suggest that there are those who might indeed have been horrified by my discovery. In place of a curtain there was an old worn blanket hanging limply from a piece of string, partially blocking out the daylight from the downstairs front room. It is distasteful even to note this, but what I found also was a deranged puppy, an Airedale, to whom someone had apparently administered LSD.

This come-and-go 'crash pad', alternately classified by its tenants as *The Mahavishnu Temple* and *The Kingdom Of Hy-Brasil*, was evidently a place where these young men – for although there was a female presence, it was distinctly in the minority – could enjoy the pleasures and freedoms of the big city, well away from parental constraints.

The girls, it seemed to me, were mostly local, especially glad to be off the leash and making up fast for what in many cases had been unhappy and repressed home lives.

Behind the makeshift curtain on the ground floor lay the previous night's debris: the ashes of an orange crate in the fireplace; stolen red workmen's lamps; the candles that they burned when they were tripping on LSD. And the remains of the food, most of which had been stolen by an Irish youth who gave his name as Desmond McKeever – an eccentric who dressed in a navy-blue hussar's jacket with a bright red headscarf tied around his head, suggestive in its way of an eighteenth-century dandy highwayman – and who styled himself, I found myself informed, the notorious rambler 'n' gambler 'Lord Offaly Of Down'.

Many of the clothes strewn around the bare floor were new and I formed the opinion that they'd been recently stolen. No one had bothered to clear up the evidence of the previous night's indulgence – mostly the consumption of alcohol and dope-smoking. The hash that I discovered, wrapped in silver foil, lay in full view and there were a number of incriminating roach ends littering the ashtrays. The ashtrays themselves had been removed from local pubs by the tenants.

There was a smell of burnt incense and joss-sticks and the room's only furniture consisted of grubby mattresses laid out side by side on the floor. There were no sheets. Inside two sleeping bags were Troy McClory (20), originally from Edinburgh, and – curled up beside him – Una Fogarty (23), from somewhere in the southern Irish Republic. She had red curly hair and a significant complement of freckles on her notably pale face.

A few tattered pop posters adorned the walls, but the main decoration was a preponderance of swirling graphic art monstrosities and assorted graffiti, including the legend:

N
U
D
E

D
I
S
I
N
T
E
G
R
A
T
I
N
G

P
A
R
A
C
H
U
T
I
S
T

W
O
M
A
N.

which travelled from ceiling to floor in crudely painted blue-and-red lettering.

Also in evidence on the ceiling and walls were drawings in an attenuated psychedelic style, variously depicting butterflies and mushrooms, overlooked by an enormous pupil, almost laughably crude in its simplicity, and haphazardly sprayed with the vivid red injunction: *EYE AM WATCHING YOU!*

I interviewed the suspect – the aforementioned Des McKeever, the self-styled *Lord Offaly Of Down* – aged 20, from Northern Ireland, and decided to make the arrest at 6.03 p.m.

When interviewed – time of interview 12.03 a.m. – the subject acknowledged that while he might support the aims of the Provisional Irish Republican Army (PIRA), he did not condone their methods.

It might be reasonably deduced that his erratic behaviour on this occasion and given the fact of his very recent dismissal from teacher training college in Strawberry Hill for possession of narcotics, that the suspect was still in something of a delusional state. Having, on a number of occasions during our conversation, claimed that the previous interviewers, PC Thornton and Det. Superintendent Maxwell, had threatened to throw him off a roof.

This concludes my statement for the moment.

Nude Disntegrating Parachutist
Woman
ha ha ha
did you ever hear the like
what a name for a song
whenever you take the time
to think about it
I wonder does Una
remember us playing that
number
which was a tune
by a now long-forgotten
rock group from
Wales
by the name of
Budgie
if I recall
yes
Budgie
Budgie

Budgie
which revolved on the turntable
as The Ponytailed Wizard
Troy McClory
outlined his latest plans.
Yes, told them all about
his proposal for a happening
to go along with the play
he intended to direct
named *The Bald Prima Donna.*
Yup, explained Troy, I am going to
blow their freaking minds
take this bourgeois town apart
& o how full of it Troy The Wizard was
with his plans, or so he said, already
far advanced, and maybe
none other than Syd Barrett set to
play the lead
Or so the Scottish wonderboy
continued to insist, waving his
arms as he described what it was going to be
like
out in The Putney Arts Centre
where he'd just been appointed
temporary artistic director
with the first act of his production
intended as a
seventeen-minute wordless epic
with a band miming
to an accompanying bacchanal of writhing
bodies – as Shuggie
& Lord Offaly provide crashing guitars and
growling, graunchy vocals
with the chicks
in the aisles serving water and marshmallows.

Ah yes, The Frolics Of The Seventies
Those old Putney old-time
caperings
with no end of light projections
& amoeba-like blobs on the walls
amorphous swirls and liquid shadows,
non-figurative drips and rolling
alpha waves

gravity-defying waterfalls.
No wonder it would turn a girl's mind
and make them want to be
naked painted dancers in far-out movies
not as yet made.

Boys o boys
yes, The Frolics
aye, The Capers
& the polysensory possibilities
of performance

& a long way surely
from the old bags of a show
that you might be seeing
God help them, in Erin
all about cruel Albin
& 'the bad times that are
coming surely!'

But you'd never have thought the like
No, not in Putney Arts
Centre
God help them
where Troy The Wizard
was now head buck-cat
assisted by his loyal lieutenants
including
Shuggie 'The Boy' Otis
Big Peter & Lord Offaly
not to mention all the chicks, including Una,
who were busy sewing the costumes,
with all sorts of wanderers
aye, every class of man-jack and
drifter arriving in with a playscript
under his arm
hoping to get a production –
their motto being:
'just put it on!'
with stragglers ambling
in and announcing over a coffee
how Knut Hamsun, maybe

had changed their life
forever,
finding themselves welcomed
with open arms
by the 'heads',
those advance scouts of
limitless possibility.

Because, as Frank 'The Blind Owl' Olson
had announced to
the *Putney News*,
his troubled eyes
blinking through thick spectacles,
there were big things coming
– things that no one, certainly not the straights,
would, could, ever have dreamed of
because the fringe was not just a space
for plays
but for travelling deep inside wherever your
heart & soul wanted to go
yeah man, this is our laboratory, our playground,
The Blind Owl had explained
& yeah, since you ask, it's experimental by
definition, a place where every voice can be
heard – because everyone is welcome to put
forward their idea…
Is cuma ce aisteach, he said,
no matter how strange
& it sure was that
is beag e an t-amhras faoi
yes, very little doubt about it
when Shuggie Otis came in one day &
Frank began telling him about the
latest, most recent visitor
a tall, gaunt fellow in a long black coat &
with a slouch hat tilted across to one
side, pulled down across his eyes,
& who wouldn't give his name
only to say is mise fear bocht
as oileán Éireann
yes, only to divulge that he was but a poor man
from the island of Ireland
a poor old fellow, a wanderer of the roads
with nothing of value to his name

only maybe a wee parcel of a yarn
aye, he said, my own personal wee
biteen of an adventure
which you'll maybe, one day, with a bit of luck
aye, if fortune smiles
you'll be making into a revue or a play
a small penny gaff
that might entertain na daoine
the peepil, aye
go ahead, said Frank
as the wanderer began to shake
& agitate this way and that way
as he spoke
& it fair put the fear of God in
The Blind Owl, he was oft to say later,
whatever way the visitor had elected
to relate it
The Witch Hare, it was called –
aye, & maybe one day, you'll have it
up there *suas ar an stáitse*, suggested
the tall, hatted stranger
played out like the *drámaíocht*
the very same as it was in real life
anyhow, noble sir, let you
be having patience
now that I tell it
I was out, do you see, tracking hares this night
aye, do you see
& what did I see underneath that big blue
globular
glowing
steel moon
only this great big fine puss of a thing
& it hopping about hither, thither
& yonder
& her whacking her ears about
now up, now down,
aye and winking those two great big
eyes of hers as she was doing it
So here goes, I said
although I hadn't much grain of
me blessed powder left in me gun
– and bang at her, then!
Well such a scritch and a scrake as

that *giorria* lẹt out of her soon as it hit her
'twould fricken a rigament, so it would,
frighten an entire battalion,
with the *fuil* & it pouring out of her
aye, the blood running in streams
from the wound where I'd got her
as I followed her all the way up
the boreen as far as
Kitty Fogarty's door
& as soon as I landed at the threshold didn't
I hear this awful keening & mourning
within
aye and a desperate and pitiful groanin' too

as I opened the door and there she was herself
one of the Fogartys
that you'd know because of the twist
that familiar, hunted, dark turn of the súil
aye, of the eye
as she looked at me
& this black cat by her heel
with the fur on its back
rising up as she stretched for to spit
at me
but I just went on never heedin' one morsel
as I says to her Kitty what is it
might I ask
that ails you
Nothing, says she
it's nothing
Then what, I says, is that there on the flure,
aye, on the flure, over there yonder
beside you in the chair
Oh, says she, I was cuttin' a billet of wood,
aye cuttin' a billet of wood, do you see, with the
reaping hook
and I've wounded myself a biteen in the leg
as you can see
& them's drops of my own precious blood.

The strange thing is
said Frank The Blind Owl
that when I looked up
he was gone

&, after that, he never came back
no, never was seen about
the place again,
ever.

What did he look like, Shuggie Otis
enquired
only to look up and see Frank glaring at
him, trembling: I TOLD YOU HE HAD
HIS HAT PULLED DOWN!
Are you fucking deaf?

Before returning to what he was doing –
in this case painting some flats.
But Shuggie didn't mind – being pretty
out of it himself, in actual fact
as he leafed through the gig guide pages
of the magazine *Sounds*.
But of course, he didn't mind
& never said anything about it again
it was that kind of place.

The production Blind Owl had been doing
the painting for
was a one-act based on an idea by
the older brother of Dessie McKeever
who had heard it from some other prisoner
with whom he'd been interned at the very
beginning of the conflict in Ulster
with them actually putting it on themselves
in the cage
all about Jesus and how he decides to come
back to earth
for to make us fuckers wise up! says Dessie,
'Last Train To Poyntzpass'
was what it had been called initially,
with Christ reading his paper as the
train comes shunting slowly into the station
with him not even looking up as this
fellow with his collar turned up

comfortable in what might be described as
the Tony Hancock look
complete with trilby
cocked over one eye
and three-quarter length
sheepskin
gets on board the train
and sits down beside him, pressing
the finger of a black leather glove
to his lips
hush now
he winks
soft-jowled
just like Hancock
& with the very same twinkle
glittering in his eye

hush now
do you hear me
&
don't say a word
he repeats
tapping the side of
his nose with the finger –
not that Jesus, still reading his paper,
passes any remarks
until Tony, or whatever his name was,
he sighs as he reaches in under
the lapel of the
sheepskin
yes, pulls it back
and grins as he shoots the passenger
who is sitting directly opposite
yes, bang bang bang

with warm blood splashing
out all over the compartment
& what does he do then
only perform a little dance:
Mr Exu & Me
The bowld Fogarty
forever together
making sweet poetry!

before pulling the trigger
& shooting him once more
one two three four times
in the face
as the train gathers speed
smiling, kind of wanly,
at the insouciant Son Of God
as he tips him a wink
you make sure now to keep your mouth
shut
I hope, now, that you hear?
As The Christ looks up
& realises that the man is gone.

The proposed production
was never, in fact,
actually mounted
which I think was a pity
although some of Tanith's sketches
all those various bits & pieces
including orange comets
showers of hail & fire, unclean birds
a raised trumpet sounding
& another creased-up one
depicting the shadowy Hancock
figure
& the particular railway carriage
in question
being plunged into darkness
so vivid you could almost hear
the awful screams
The Third Ear Band was initially
approached to do the music
at least that's what Troy had
told them all,
but that never came to anything either.
The actor cast in the lead role of
The King Of Friday – the
name selected by Una for The Christ figure
suggested
by a prayer card inherited from our mother
with his motorcycle jacket
& black leather trousers
he could easily have doubled

for Jim Morrison
of The Doors
or *The Dures*, as Dessie McKeever
innocently used to call them
much to everyone's amusement
before deciding to board the Archway
bus.

Where, sitting at the back
he didn't so much as
make a sound
heading along the
Holloway Road
already, in his mind,
having more or less bid goodbye
forever, waving farewell
to what, in a fit of what must have been
madness
he had once dared to hope
might be a burgeoning art career
Troy had even once spoken highly of him
had actually described him as
'the Irish Warhol'
that Saturday when the two of them
had been stoned
with Troy locking the door
& sticking up a notice
Achtung! Verboten! Geniuses
at work!
spreading a great sheet of canvas
out across the floorboards
of the attic
hey man now we're gonna go to it
the Scotsman had said it
and he ought to know
thought Dessie as he sat there
alone on the bus
yeah, The Wizard McClory
he was the one
who really knew his stuff
whenever it came
to artwork & the like
all those painters
Jackson Pollock

you name it
& Troy and himself
there they were
stripped to the waist
with their eyes bright and wild
tossing their colours
this way and that
with Dessie lapsing
into a trance
from somewhere deep within him
megaphone-declaring: *Presenting*
for your pleasure – the good people
at the Fair Of Currabawn!

Where were they coming from
those strange feelings
sensations
evoking, at the edge of his vision,
a small, cowled figure
holding a drawstring pouch
positioned precariously on his knee
with his face invisible
as he fingered out golden guineas
yes, laid them out, those glittering
coins one by one
upon his knee
in the eerie moonlit quiet
of what appeared to be a disused
forge
as cries and whoops in his mind
split the night
and he found its equivalent in
a crimson blaze of colour
in that painting he now thought
of as The Fairy Cavalcade
– At The Crossroads,
where two-foot-high beings
emerged from hills and mounds
riding horses no bigger than cats
and all these words
like he didn't know where
on earth they were coming from
in the middle of all these
brushstrokes

like a waterfall tumbling
out of Dessie's mouth
o isn't it a queer and terrible
night
I am going to tell you all
with the blood in my veins
seeming to be on fire
the night that my travelling coach
broke down
& didn't I see them out in the fields
on the backs of their coal-black
snorting steeds
and they skirting the edge
of the deep green glen
where the mountain stream
dashed over the rocks
may God forgive me this
night if so much as a word
I have spoke is not the truth
yes, may The Godhead lay
his unmerciful hand upon me
if I, for so much as a second, elect
to play you false
gasped the Lord Of Offaly
in what might have been a fever
swiping his dripping brush
this way and that
finishing off his picture
of the 'wee little man'
in his swallowtail coat
scuffed & buckled brogues
looking up, with a glint
in his eye
while behind him
in the distance
one of his colleagues
steered a sheep by the ears
while two others clapped and
cheered
playing football with a hen
whilst five or six others
jig-a-jigged
delirious
performing the mickey-jump-jubbly

ceilidh in the bushes
buppita-screek
buppita-screek
jiggity
jiggity
jiggity
squeal
expiring
eee!
o
God
o
God
help me
a
a
a
a
a
h!
atomised among the trees
as Troy McClory fell backwards
bawling out
for all he was worth
'O Jesus, man! That is so far out!
Man, too much, reaaaaally far out
I'm telling you, man' –
every bit as far out as his own
extraordinary effort
which, only towards dawn was he
coming close to completing
before spreading out the sheet
and hoisting it upon the wall
an explosion of colour
'experimental art' which meant
nothing to anyone else
not even the chicks
who knew shit from shit
but which, every time they saw it,
bestowed upon its executors
a warm, fulfilled glow of pride
especially when they saw Mr Exu in it
pony-tailed, grinning, in his immaculate white
suit and spotless white shoes

and whispering to them 'yes,
certamente, this is way far out'
with his tail & anglewise prick
exalted high above the world.

I'm Mr Exu, they heard him softly whisper,
smiling towards them, each in turn,
known well to the Fogartys
late of Currabawn.
Yes, constant custodian of peace
here at Abaddon's
midnight junction
quiet in the night
at the crossroads of your soul
Troy McClory
but especially you
Lord Offaly Of Down
poor
misbegotten
old
Dessie
Mc
Keever
upon whom
I have
now laid
my
mark.

Yes, young Dessie McKeever
also known
as
Lord Offaly
Of
Down
who was still humming
his favourite tune by Mott the Hoople
named 'At The Crossroads'
when he heard the driver
of the nightbus calling
Archway now
last
stop
if

you
please.
& so
it
was
so it
came to be
for poor old Dessie
the first of
many
Lord Offaly
Of
Down
down
down
from the Archway Bridge
Lord Offaly Of Down
forever
now
g
    o
        o
           d
              b
                  y
                     e.

Why do birds sing
those little choristers, can you tell me
why is it that they habitually perform,
Troy The Wizard used to wonder
during his more abstracted
Wordsworthian moments
can anyone tell me
why that might be
never considering for a moment
at least when it came to the
the *londubh*
the *blackbird*

that what that particular little birdie
what it might be trying to do
was warn him of what was in store
for him in the future
a great many long years hence
far from now
after he'd long since ceased to be
The Wizard Of Mahavishnu
with his talent & promise
as the greatest, most promising
artist of his generation
having all but turned to ash
yes, like some great city
crumbled to ruins
when he found himself
in the early nineties
working as a labourer
the sort of position you
might expect to be occupied
well – by who?
Some half-formed apeman
from Ireland
in a donkey jacket & galluses
of course
& not some once-handsome
once-upon-a-time
Rock God who bore more than
a passing resemblance
to Ian Hunter,
legendary vocalist with the
rock band
Mott the Hoople

& who, even yet,
as he sat at the counter
of The Crown in Cricklewood
with twenty-odd years now having elapsed
he still, somehow, he just could not
manage to bring himself to
believe
to accept
just what a shambles his
life had become.

The pub was like a great big
vintage ocean cruise-liner
& as he squatted there morosely
reflecting further on the wreckage of
his days
somehow, he simply failed to
accept it
in any shape form or fashion
to persuade himself to shoulder
even the smallest portion of
the blame
for what had now happened
he was shivering all over
& tossing down drinks
1
2
3
4
5
he got rid of
all in the space of fifteen minutes
trying to erase the memory
of the morning.
When, sitting in the cab of the mechanical
excavator
he'd found himself unexpectedly alerted
by what he had taken to be the faint sound
of a sob
as a huge wave of imní
came surging down on top
of him.
& it was just then that he saw it
caught a glimpse of
the thing
whatever you might like to call it
however you would describe it
only fleetingly, however
almost as if it had been barely in existence at
all.
It couldn't be, he told himself.
Because all of that had been
in his imagination
mostly because of all the drugs
that they'd been taking

all those years ago
in Brondesbury Gardens.

Please, he repeated
reaching deep into his pocket
of his overalls for the purpose of
retrieving his handkerchief.
& which, in the circumstances
proved both hasty and unwise
Will you for the love of Christ watch the fuck
where it is that you're going! shouted
the foreman
but it was already too late
as the lumbering, monstrous vehicle
turned right over on its side.

It had been a close call
with Troy McClory
almost succeeding in killing two people
before plunging
the machine into the clay pit
where it had rolled
over on its side, trapping him inside the cab.

Like everyone said
it had been a close-run thing
having banged his head a couple of times
against the wheel arch & seriously damaged
both his legs.

Lying there, helplessly
pawing at the glass
doing his best to cry out
as, quite unbidden
familiar figures
albeit now tiny
came running frantically
across some waste ground

flailing their arms
just as they'd done
in that Brondesbury courtyard
in the aftermath of the suicide of
poor Tanith Kaplinski.

Alone at the counter
of The Crown
that day in the year of 1994
Troy McClory wept.
Before ordering more alcohol
& retiring to the seclusion of
a darkened booth
where he continued, all day,
to remain alone
squatting there with his shoulders hunched
not unlike a gruagach himself
pouring one double whiskey after
another into himself.
Or uisquebaugh as, in his neck of the woods,
they prefer to call it.

Yes, it sure was sad,
for one of Edinburgh's brightest and best
or so they kept on insisting
back in '74
aye, one ae its finest ever students
to have ended up in such a bad way
as this
living the life of a woebegone navvy
of the type that he had once so
routinely scorned
like some poor 'auld' Irish
uneducated journeyman
if only, as his mother used to
mournfully lament
yes, such a pity he had taken so many drugs.
But then, Troy, as his mother knew
more than anyone
in any case
he had always been just
that little bit *over-imaginative*.
I mean, imagine thinking you could make

yourself invisible, she had remarked, somewhat
blithely, to her neighbour one day.
That was what he told me one day
& him only eight.

Yes, which the growing boy Troy
had announced one morning
in the long ago
in the McClory Edinburgh kitchen
at the tender age of eight and
one-half years.
Schooldays which now returned with a
vengeance
as he remained there alone in the shadow-booth
of The Crown Public House
recasting themselves in all their vivid
glory.

Ah yes, those wonderful suburban Edinburgh
times
especially on Saturdays
when he'd be off once more
on his regular paper round.
Which always ended, without fail
with him enjoying the most magnificent chat
with his good old friend Professor
McVittie
who, of course, wasn't really a
proper professor at all
but wore a white coat so as to make you think
that was the case.

Mr McVittie owned the newsagent's at the
corner of
the street on which they lived in Morningside.
He was long since deceased.
But was still very much alive in the mind
of Troy McClory
yes & always would be
thought Troy
as he sat there, smoking & chucking
down drink
moderately relieved now the whiskey
was at last doing its work.

He almost felt like laughing, in fact
as he swirled the amber liquid round & round
round & round
at the bottom of the glass.

How could he ever have believed in
gruagachs, he wondered
with it being like something, maybe
that you'd find in a magazine
called *Creepy*
that he used to read
or maybe in one of the scarier *Rupert Bears*
– of the type he used to enjoy in Prof.
McVittie's wonderful newsagent's
where, in the distance
you could hear a little child
singing
ever so plaintively
'All Things Bright and Beautiful'
just a little bit beyond the horizon
where all the trees
would suddenly, unexpectedly, come alive
& with claw-like roots against a moonlit sky
try breaching your bedroom
window to get in close to you.
In a world of hedgerows-come-alive,
& beyond those, the infinite void.

Because there's a heavy whiff around Albion,
the professor used to say, which reminds
one of honeysuckle growing above the
porch of one's front door
but also a sense of the destabilising
dark sublime
you remember that, my lad,
he sometimes used to say
with Troy, being young
not knowing quite what he meant
our lives at their most beautiful
they border an infinite void
he would say
as he turned each page filled with every
conceivable manner of
out-of-the-world creatures

in the land called Nutwood
including turtle postmasters and wild, shrieking
clockwork birds.

That was where such creatures as he
belonged, he thought
meaning the *gruagach*
so what was he going and thinking about them
now for, Troy wondered.
Especially having long since cracked
his substance abuse.
He didn't rightly know.
All he knew was the dread had somehow
slowly begun returning.
& fiercely so
the *imní*, as we know it.
What, for Schopenhauer, as he knew,
represented the sight of a power beyond
all comparison superior to that of
the individual
& threatening him with annihilation
whose immensity in space and time
reduces the individual to naught.

He could just about hold the glass
steady in his hand
before looking down and seeing it
again as a claw-like root,
stealthily creeping around a rock.

Such a desperate affliction, *them old
trimmlins*, Nano used to say.
Yes, a fret to the living world for sartin sure, my
lad.

Coroner's Report On Subject Troy McClory:

Number Of Units Consumed: 23
Time Of Disappearance: 00.55 a.m – 01.25 a.m.
Exact Time Of Arrival Home To St Jude's Hostel, Quex Road, Kilburn: Unknown.

With the only evidence that he'd ever been there in that room at all
being what, initially, looked like a sixpenny coin.
        But, in fact, was a small silver medallion which had been given to him
by my sister one night when he was having his way with her and when he had admired
its design, tinkling away there under her vest – to which she had it pinned.
        Being a good little country girl, of course, and never going
anywhere without her sacred Lourdes 'Miraculous' Medal.
        Our Lady conceived without sin pray for us who have recourse to thee,
read the inscription around the perimeter –
                those same lines
                he had used
                all those distant days ago
                incorporated them
                into a song which he
                had liked to sing
                serenading my sister
                about ghosts and saints
                as he gently and softly crooned into
                her willing, receptive ear.

                Poor old Troy,
                it sure was sad to see him go.
                Even if my sister
                yes, even if Una
                she'll often insist that I've got
                it wrong
                yes, the whole damned thing
                that's what she says
                that Troy was innocent
                & that most of the things he had
                said or done were blameless
                if a little immature
                & irresponsible
                with it all being down to my possessiveness
                & bitter jealousy
                but then she would say

that
she would have to, really
having been in love with the idiot
so there you are.

That's the way it goes,
I suppose.

Although I'm sure that he did
get himself quite a surprise
the same fellow
when he woke up and realised
in the night that he was, in fact, dying.

No, not so much brazen cheek from him
then I'll warrant
not so much T. S. Eliot
or e. e. cummings and his friend
so how do you like your blue-eyed
boy now, Mr Death?

O I like him very much
I like him very fucking well
Mr Semi-Rapist
pogue Iscariot
Mr Judas-Kiss McClory
as you, within seconds,
are about to find out.

I suppose, in a way, though,
it's a pity that he didn't live
even just to see
how well, against the odds,
the whole thing worked
out
for me and Una, at any rate,
God love her
& the terrific life that we've – *somehow!*
don't ask me! – managed to
make here together, in Cliftonville.
& for her, especially, & her ongoing

adventures in the world of living *theatah*
daahling!

I mean, talk about 'Fudge'
because I'm sorry
you can't
absolutely zero chance
with her
looking more like a straw
than a human being now
skating and running
here and there around the place
with her bag filled with papers
containing all kinds of notes and directions
for the cast.
With her latest preoccupation being
the upcoming interview
with the TV show host Conan O' Brien.
Who, I don't know if you know, would
be about as close as you might be able to get
to a real and genuinely convincing life-size
gruagach
with those freckles and red hair
that great big tidal wave of a quiff you see
him sporting.
She calls herself a *Conanite* now, and swears
all 'the gang' will soon be appearing on the
Saturday-night show.
'Because,' she says, 'isn't he Irish yes from
the old country, the exact very same as us, my
brother. So hurrah, mo dheartháir iontach, *Team
Coco – an dtuigeann tú?*'

Then sticks up a photo right beside his –
of Ivanka Trump standing there next to 'The Donald'
in that great big dumb Crombie coat of his
pouting & scowling like a porkie
on the porch of The White House
as the team from Fox Rolling News run around him
with a plethora of cameras and cables.

I think it must have been the day of his inauguration.
I've never seen anything like that Fox fucking News

because it never really stops does it
night noon and morning
breaking news
breaking news
with the actual truth being
that you'd be likely to get more truth
& fair reporting from Attenborough's
snouty wee lizard, I swear to God.
With very little on it these
times, at least so far as I can see
only fellows with scarves around their
faces & these big eyes
ploughing trucks right into people
yes, letting this great big roar
out of them
as they gun the vehicle &
ram right into innocent
folks standing in queues
yes, that's all you ever see
on the flat-screen tubes that
they have dotted all around
the hotel
some of them covering half
of the wall
& a long way
that's for sure
from the little white-plastic
nineteen-inch black-and-white Pye portable
which poor old Tanith Kaplinski always used to
watch in the front room of Brondesbury
whenever she came home
in the good old days of the
Winter of Our Discontent
or, should I say, in this case,
Summer.

When she'd be returning from
her nightly practice at the dance studio
thinking that she was Margot Fonteyn.
O, nothing but the best for Miss Kaplinski,
certainly not.
Who was now, by all accounts – *mirabile dictu!* – in line
for the lead role in a forthcoming Benjamin Britten
opera in the world-famous Sadler's Wells Theatre

that would soon show the lot of them
just like she'd promised she always would
show them, that is
after being flung out, unceremoniously, from
the family home in Stanmore – with her mother
contemptuously tossing all her bits &
pieces out after her, on the doorstep,
her gaunt and uncompromising, stern-faced mother.
The 'old bitch', as she called her.
Charming.
Never, of course, having known her father.

Now, as I sit here looking back on those days
relaxing on the window seat
in the lobby of The Cliftonville Hotel
what do I find Miss Kaplinski
doing
only having herself a great deal of fun
pretending she's changing her name
clad in nothing but a single wee scrap
of cloth
pirouetting in front of the full-length mirror.
I'm Margot, she said to herself, Margot Fonteyn.
I'll be dancing tonight in Sadler's Wells.
Would you like to come along?
I'll be performing in Offenbach's *Tales Of Hoffmann*,
in which I play the mechanical doll.
So come along, will you –
please say yes.
'Les Oiseaux Dans La Charmille' – come &
be enthralled by my interpretation of
the doll-woman-machine.
The automaton.

Apart from Joanne Kaplan,
Tanith really did seem just about
the coolest chick back then
with only the littlest scrap of cloth –
yes, the teenshiest *biteen*
covering her shame as she glided effortlessly,
humming along with the Offenbach overture.
& then, with a hot drink, sitting down,
flicking through the cream vellum
of her manuscript,

humming away *la la la la* –
at which point she heard it
– soft, scarcely audible indeed,
that whispering, intermittent
rustling sound
the same kind of one that
you might hear grasshoppers make.
& after which she experienced
this other odd and equally unnerving
feeling
that someone close by
was watching her intently.

But not only just observing her
– all of Brondesbury Gardens.
With the sensation, in fact, becoming
so bad that she thought that she was
going to fall victim to a cardiac arrest
which was why she leaned against
the kitchen counter.
What am I? she heard herself saying
where what who
with her lips drying up as she endeavoured to
repeat the words
trying again to say
there's no one else in the room
yes, no one else in this room
only me.
before deciding that this had happened as
a result of recent events
a consequence of the constabulary's recent visit
to the flat.

All the same, it was the strangest feeling
as if she had found herself cruelly alone
dropped & abandoned in the
middle of a huge futuristic shopping centre
somewhere in New York, perhaps.
But London, no –
because they didn't have that style
of building there.
At least not to the same extent,
she thought,
where men in suits stalked the corridors

not so much as uttering a word.
Where you heard fans swirl
air-con breezes somewhere afar
a vacuum cleaner droning.
exactly as it was doing now.
she had now become the tiniest of figures
she thought
trapped inside an immense conspiracy.
Directly above, long rows of icy-blue strip lighting
seemed to stretch to a vanishing point.
Who is Harry Kellerman and why is he saying those
terrible things about me?
What did that mean?
What meaning could it possibly have, that question?
She felt like a hand had closed around her heart
& kept on opening, then closing
in & out
becoming aware of another
equally urgent & similar question
this time in an even softer whisper:
Can
Hieronymous Merkin
Ever Forget Mercy Humppe
And Find True Happiness?
Over & over it repeated itself in her mind,
only this
time taking her back to the conversation
with Troy McClory

because it was him who had said it
yes, he who had posed the question
only three nights previously
when they'd all been in the front room
playing stoned Scrabble

so, after that, she didn't feel quite so bad
dabbing at the beads of perspiration which
were multiplying on her brow
first hot
then cold
all those small & glistening pearls
lining up.
She smiled & tried to convince herself
she was relieved

even smiling as she said
yes, that is the question
can Hieronymous Merkin…?
but she never managed to finish the sentence
because when she thought that
Tanith Kaplinski found herself laughing
because what a thing to be thinking now
she wondered
why, all of a sudden, had that come into her mind?
I mean, why on earth was she bothering about that
now?
When she should have been studying the libretto
of Benjamin Britten
why was she not doing that
she asked herself
being much too experienced to take the role
in the opera for granted
even though it was the casting of a lifetime
and the director had more or less privately
confirmed it
I'll do it later! she repeated to herself,
I'll do it in the morning
in the morning yes
yes, that's when I'll do it
study it in the morning
when all the rest of them have left the house
as she picked up one thing
& then left it down
asking herself: *now why did I do that?*
As her heart kept pounding – & then what happened?
With her elbow, she knocked down a cup.
The noise that it made – it really was deafening.
'Hello?' she said. 'Hello?'
Would you look at her, the wee girleen, unabashed
in her nipper tuck
would you look at the girleen there and
her, unabashed,
sitting there in her nipper tuck
aye, & divil a bother on her
sitting there, naked, nudie,
in her nipper tuck
God between us, do you hear me,
& all harm
not a bother on her there, ceilidh dancing in

[156]

her nipper tuck
brazen, God bless her, in her snow-white
nudie.

Before turning around and, to her surprise – discovering
nothing.
Nothing but the black-and-white TV, flickering away
in the corner.
But not with Rolling News
o no
Or David Attenborough's *Planet Earth* either.
As a matter of fact, I forget what was actually on.
'Don't worry, I won't hurt you,' she heard the
indistinct figure in the corner reassuring
her. 'But, nevertheless, I'm afraid the time has come.'
And, as soon as she heard that, Tanith Kaplinski burst
into tears.
Because somehow, instinctively, she knew
in that moment
that she was never going to see her old friends
again
whether in The Mahavishnu Temple
at college
or the dance studio in Maida Vale.
Please! Tanith pleaded, please I'll do anything.
Thinking about 'All the beautiful birds in the
garden', composed by Offenbach
which she had been assiduously rehearsing all that day.
All the beautiful birds in the garden
those little birdies,
sighed the shape as it gazed right at her
her fearful eyes falling
on the crouched shape of a
very old woman
a lady in a shawl
a crocheted black shawl
sitting in the corner by the small TV.
Saying nothing.

Nothing, that is, apart from:
Are you not well, daughter? But
don't be afraid – because Auntie
Nano is here.

With divil the bit she hasn't seen
down through the years. So, hush now,
alanna, and rest yourself aisy.
At least that was what Tanith Kaplinski thought
she had heard
as the telly went *fizz!* and *spurt!* and then *sss!*

Outside, at some considerable distance, a group of little
children could be heard ring-a-rosy-ing and
laughing.
'It's sad,' said Tanith, swallowing deeply, 'it's just so so
hard.'
Looking askance at the shawled old lady
steadily rocking back and forth in the armchair
with a hypnotic, easy rhythm
before removing her squat clay pipe,
with eyes squinting.
'You poor little *craythur*,' Tanith heard her
murmur, smiling ever so faintly,
'try not to be afraid, will you, daughter?'

But poor Tanith – how could she not?
Did you ever see a star like Margot Fonteyn doing
a pee?
With the drops going *tick tick tick*
all the way down her leg?

Well, Tanith Kaplinski did that night.
With it, in fact, turning out to be
none other than herself, of course.
As she stood there, ossified
staring in disbelief
at the small widening yellow pool
'Please, will you not hurt me?'
Tanith Kaplinski abjectly appealed.
'Because I've been so looking forward
to my show next week.'
'I know that, daughter,' the old woman said,
'I realise that, craythur.
Tá a fhios agam
But I'm afraid
I'm sorry to say
it's inevitable, can't you see
what it is that has to happen

just as it is with Lord Dessie
of Archway Bridge.
& there's nothing in heaven or earth
that can stop it now.'

Yes, that was what the old woman told her
those were the words that her visitor
that night spoke.
The old lady who had appeared
out of nowhere
– only now, you see, there wasn't anyone
there
Neither rocking chair nor Auntie Nano, either.

Just the smallest of birds sitting
there perched on top of the dresser
coolly appraising the 'trimmlin' Tanith Kaplinski
with all the bitter tragedy of the world
sharply reflected in the living pearl
of
its
unflinching
eye.

Ah yes, the old times surely,
there's no doubt about it.
You'll never guess what Una has gone
& done now –
pinned up on the noticeboard
an old comic picture of the Red Baron
flying ace of World War I.
Yes, has thumbtacked him up there
right next to 'Coco',
her famous TV host and lover, she says.
Ha ha ha she laughs,
Baron Von Richthofen
thinks he can strafe all my precious memories
him and his guns and doodlebugs
& get rid of everything that matters
just like that

with the truth actually being
like so many people
that he's full of gas and pop
the very exact same as that
other *ommadawn*, Trevor Howard
who never, in his life,
went on any
                              lousy
            made-up
commando

        missions
                              at all

        she insists
        waving her arms

        &, before I know it,
        is away off over the other side of the foyer
        chatting by the new time
        to Butley & Co.
        Pulling out bits and pieces
        from her handbag.
        Ladies & gentlemen
        I can hear her shouting
        doing jazz hands as Connie
        The Brazilian Princess,
        smiling,
        goes gliding by.

        'All aboard to begin our rehearsals!' Una shouts
        after her,
        but Her Majesty has already
        turned the corner.
        Una always gets her group together
        every Thursday afternoon.
        That's, of course, provided she happens to
        remember
        & The Baron hasn't
        come around jeering
        in his triplane

strafing her reason and
ripping up the dirt of her mind.

In which case she'll be standing
sucking her thumb, staring at iguanas
or some new astonishing undersea
creation, laughing at the very idea
of plays or stupid *Capers*,
being much too preoccupied
trying to keep up with
Baron Von Richthofen
the incomparable dandy
in his goggles and flying jacket
cruelly looping in and out of her memory
as he *rat-a-ta-tats* and splinters
her soul
even further
&, in the process,
often does the same to mine.
Well, obviously, he would
how could he not
what with my sister Una
and myself being so close
as we always have,
to an almost ridiculous degree
at times.

Do you know what,
I've never seen so many seabirds in my life
as are to be found in Cliftonville Gardens.
With this gull in particular coming right up
to the front door every day
& poking his beak against the glass
just standing there shifting from
foot to foot
as if on the point of asking:
well, where is it then?
where exactly is my lunch?

So many fowl
all these little twitterers,
where on earth could they all be
coming from?
I mean, they can't *all* be natives of Margate.

In recent times I've taken to noting
the various different species.
They say that the blackbird and the song thrush
they're the superior singers of early Springtime.
& maybe 'cos of that
it's when I hear my sister singing
like she often does
humming abstractedly
trilling these little notes of regret
that I often think
the pair of us
we're not unlike a pair of
sweet little birdies ourselves.
'No wonder you're jealous of
Troy!' she used to say.
Look – she's reading one of
Troy's favourites so she is
even after all this time
she's still got a soft spot
for *Peanuts* & all that.
Charlie Brown, you've got a failure face.
You know that?
Why, it's got failure written all over it.

Troy always used to like reading that to Una.
& then doing this funny twirly
dance just like Snoopy.

I can't tell you how much she loved that
& used to sometimes say that she thought
it was that which had first
made her fall in love with him,
his love for *Peanuts* and his childish sense of
humour.

'Do you know something, Charlie Brown?
If only you weren't so wishy-washy, you could be a
prince who flies to the moon!'
She said that out of the blue
only just the other day
& then when I laughed and said:
ah yes, that old Charlie Brown!
what does she go and do
turns around and, eating the last of her

guggy egg
says: *Who?*

As I took her hand and clasped it to my cheek
we were always doing that
but not in any kind of unsavoury way
it's just that she's my sister
that's all
& us, we Fogartys
it's our duty to stick together
me and her against the world
like an dornán slat
the bundle of sticks
that together will remain forever
unbreakable
because once they begin to separate
they can be torn apart & will splinter
like matchwood
& flitter away
broken up
destroyed.

It's just a pity we didn't manage
it in the end
setting up a home of our own
under the eaves
constructed our very own
closed-cup mud nest
At Home With The Fogartys
which had always been what I'd
hoped and longed for
&, I know
so did she,
before certain tensions got the better of us
and we watched it burn
our sweet home of dreams
right there
in front of our very eyes.
Teach álainn
Dan agus Una Fogarty
Dan & Una's
lovely, dreamy mountain home

now, sadly, nothing but a memory
but all the same,
like I promised,
I'll always be here by her side
to watch over her
& guide her
yes, right until the sixpences are
placed upon my eyes
of that I can assure you
may God forgive me
should I play you false
this night.

Because every simple human being
has their hopes and aspirations – is that
not the case?
Yes, that's the way
it just is, and always has been.

How marvellous, though, it would have been.
If, in some small way, it had all worked out
& the children she'd longed for
& happened upon
– quite by accident, of course
o, go deimhin, go deimhin! –
that special day
out of nowhere
in Queen's Park

if they'd only been able to remain
a little longer in our 'Secret Nest'
maybe even stay there for good
with the pair of us
me and Una
as their parents
yes, their caring & loving
tuismitheoirí
o what kisses & presents
we'd have lavished on our own little birdies
our two wee
babogues,
Bobbie agus Ann.

Ann & Bobbie
&
Bobbie & Ann
The two lovely *childre* we found that day
our own little personal charges
who we thought might give our lives
meaning
after The Temple it had fallen
into ruins
with nothing remaining
for to give our lives meaning
we were sure they would save us
as we, in our turn,
might be able to do the same
for them
taking them away from their heroin-addict
mother
to our secret attic
our warm nest of sanctuary
so sweet
but, sadly however,
it didn't work out
mostly because of my sister's instability
& the complete & utter unpredictability
of her moods.
Some people at the time did, in fact,
mention the gruagach
Na páistí goidte, such commentators
suggested – the stolen children.
Because that's what such entities
were reputed, in the old times,
to do.

But everyone agreed that that was ridiculous.
&, as a matter of fact,
they were right.
Because Una didn't, in fact, steal them
that glittering Sunday afternoon in
Queen's Park
a week after The Temple had finally folded
no, simply borrowed them for a while.
Something which the two *páistí* themselves
were more than glad of, let me tell you
– living, as they did, in an absolute

[165]

midden in a sinkhole estate at the
back end of Killiburn
surrounded by hyperfuckingdermics and
empty pizza cartons.
With Bobbie even saying
thank you for being so kind to us
Una
& telling us all about
The Swans Of Lough Derravaragh
where once there had lived
such beautiful swans
who had once been frightened
little children like us
finding themselves then
secure in our secret attic
enchanted & protected
given no end of sweeties and
all kinds of treats
showed
so much affection and
kindness
that Bobbie said he could
barely speak
we love you, Auntie Una!
cried Ann
as salt silver rivers came coursing
down my sister's hollowed-out cheeks.

I ndeireadh na dála
at the end of the day
we only had them a mere
three pitiful hours
some eternal dream home, for sure!

Almost as brief & pathetic
as Troy McClory's
alternative societies &
Hy-Brasil of a society cleansed
& entirely reformed!

No, *mar adeirim*,
as I say,
little Bobbie & Ann weren't kidnapped
but just for the briefest of periods

provided with a glimpse
of a heaven that might have been.

& I will say this
temporary though it was
yes, short-lived though
our improvised home in *Knocknanane*
(Home Of The Birds,
Nest Of The Fogartys)
however fleeting
it might have been
there at the top of the totally
vacated premises
in Brondesbury Gardens
in its kindness & tenderness &
magnificent sheer *ordinariness*
it was infinitely superior
to anything achieved by
Troy McClory and his
starry-eyed
inner-travelling
psychic-cosmonaut
cronies
him &
King Crimson &
In
The
Wake
Of
Fucking

O, *alanna*

whenever I think of that
so-called fucking Wizard
sitting there
in his fringed buckskin jacket
tugging on that little scrawny
scraggy beard
squinting his eyes as he pushes back
his long lank blondie hair
inhaling a long deep draught
of some more dope

before preparing to deliver yet
another blah blah lecture
about Ralph Bakshi
or Robert Crumb & the
Fabulous Furry Freak Brothers
or his most recent obsession
Fritz The Cat
the sexy moggie
in the stripey sweater
who liked to hang around
pool rooms
whenever
he wasn't 'balling chicks'
& which, by Troy's own admission,
the prodigal art student, gifted
musician & amateur scientist
not to mention God's gift to
women
thought was 'absolutely
fucking
hilarious'.

Yes, almost as amusing
as the one and only Toots
McGladdery,
claiming to be a distant relative
of Una's
arriving to stay in the flat one night
& departing as mysteriously as he'd
appeared
leaving no trace
just a milky smear
on the Polaroid
taken by Blind Owl
o but what a character
it has to be said
with everyone loving him
what with the way he made
McClory jealous
being a fabulous talker
& well-fit to charm the
pants off everyone
what with his tales of having been
places

that even they, as yet, could only
but dream of
living in the heart of the Amazonian
rainforest
and yet still well able to chat away
like he'd never left his little hometown
of Threemilecross
the smallest little poky wee quarter
that was ever heard of in the world
he kept on saying
but with a host of stories & yarns
that would keep you going half the night
such as the one that he told
about John *Sagart A'Bhata*
the parish priest of Gullion
who ended up with a wooden leg
& why, muses their visitor,
well on account of him repeatedly
bad-mouthing the fairies
especially Con Of The Mountain
known far and wide
as *The Living Man* from
the world of *The Pookies*
put on this earth
for that express purpose
because without an intermediary
between this world and the next
The Pookies are unable to act
so jealous was McClory
as McGladdery the visitor went on with his
ridiculous story
that he couldn't help himself but
scoff: *Pshaw!*
only to hear the bold McGladdery
diminishing him even that little bit further
by wagging his finger and warning the
Scotsman
in the middle of mimicking his accent
you be careful now, d'ye heer me, Jimmy,
or I'll come over and clatter ye
wae a great big bunch ae bagpipes!
& you ought to have heard the
laughter then
with even Una falling about the place

as Toots McGladdery, undaunted,
continued
well, not long after that, then
he said
didn't the Sagart A'Bhata,
feared parish priest of Gullion,
didn't he
take a breaking out on his knee,
& was left with no choice
but to go and see
Con Of The Mountain
who gave him short shrift,
I'm sorry I have to say
what happened to ye, father,
is that you've been shot through
with a bow and arrow
through the window
of your upstairs bedroom
and when you go back
if you take a look, you'll see
the little hole
where The Queen Of The Fairies
herself it was shot you
on account of your bad faith
and sad, bitter lack
of generosity in the past
but what, says the priest,
what about me leg
o that, says Con, you're
as well to ask the doctors to take
that off straight away
for as long as these mountains
rise till the sky
regrettably, your reverence, your
leg, it will
never heal
& which, God watch over you
all here tonight,
blessed hearers,
it never did.
Which is why until the day that the
poor man was crated
aye, fitted up for the suit of
boards,

he was evermore known as
Hobbledy Auld Father John
aha ha ha ha
ha
ha
ha!
whooped Toots McGladdery
whacking with his hat
until two of the biggest,
fattest tears
that maybe in your whole living
life
you have ever seen
came rolling, with impunity, down
his cheeks.
O man alive! hollered Toots
McGladdery,
glory to God,
whoopity fuck,
the things that happen
in this arse-about-face
blessed world,
I do declare!

As Una, perhaps surprisingly, kept gazing
into his eyes
as if, God bless her, she'd found herself
mesmerised
the way you might be in the old times
they used to say
Toots McGladdery continued, smiling,
cracking his knuckles as he tossed back
his head
shaking his ponytail as he looked right
over at McClory
who, by now, was literally beside himself
with envy and resentment
for no one ought to be talking to his chick,
no sir, not like that
filling her full of old *raiméis*
about how the 'Ulster leprechauns',
especially those – like himself, ha ha! –

from Slieve Gullion
in South Armagh – had always
been regarded as the finest storytellers
& poets in the fairy world
a skill which had enabled him to move with
grace, from Rio to Bogotá and to every
far-flung nook of the known world
aye, and unknown too, Toots gamely
continued
brushing ash off his trim lapel
with it proving no bother to me at all
to stand in the crook of a tree in Manaus
or Belém
& declaim every verse – all 14,402 of them,
of the poem that was handed down to me
& my wandering kin
and is fit to be recited by no mortal tongue
would you like that, maybe, I could say it for
you now?
NO! bawled McClory
for we've had quite enough
of you and your bullshit blarney!

With them all looking over
at the face of the livid Scotsman
trepidatious at the possible
onset of seriously bad 'bad vibes',
as Toots McGladdery continued
rocking from side
to side
laughing and still laughing
until the poor fellow
seemed near fit to burst
pouring scorn on the 'McClorys'
& every 'Scotty' as wouldn't
'fucking bother'
opening his purse to 'spend
fucking Christmas'
– with a faint smile, I swear to God
becoming evident on my sister's lips
as the visitor McGladdery hopped
around on one leg
& announced that, unfortunately,
he had to be going

aye, back to South America,
&, with those words, he was gone
like he'd never been there
not even bothering to stay for
breakfast
with a certain Scotsman glaring
furiously over at my sister
as much as to say: you really
oughtn't to have done that you know
given the glad eye to Mr Toots McGladdery!
because that is not a good thing to do
& so later on, Miss Fudge Old
Freckle-Face Fogarty
very shortly now
I'll be showing you some more peace
& love
Yes, I'll soon wipe the smile off your face
something of which he was
more than capable
if the truth be told,
you ignorant country-bred
disloyal Irish slattern!

With the bruise still throbbing
on the right-hand side of her face
where he'd hit her until
at last, he'd got fed up doing it
yes, off went Troy to get himself
a pick-up
maybe a snort of coke
if he was lucky
as he left her there, waiting,
lying sprawled on the bed,
waiting for what
she did not know
not, at least, until it finally arrived
for all the world
like a painting slowly inking itself
in
& there, on the hill overlooking Calvary,
what did she see standing outlined against
a burnished copper sky
only the bold 'Toots McGladdery'
with his white shoes & waistcoat

laughing his head off
as he pointed towards the crossbeam
above him
where lay slumped
the bloodless, savagely perforated
form of our unique, selfless Saviour,
he who is known as
the singular Christus.
Poor Una! screeched
McGladdery
in a voice no longer his own
but that of the ages
'For it was she!' he wailed,
as the big cat slavered on its reins,
'Her and her forebears
who forged the iron
yes, fashioned the nails
that ran through The Redeemer's
mercilessly gored hands!
Sim nosso caminho foi amaldiçoado
com muitos perigos inseparáveis!
HELP ME! she cried,
as she lay there on the bed,
please can anyone come to my assistance
I'm Una Fogarty
please give me your hand
anyone please
it doesn't matter
who it is.
Prepared, even, to forgive
what Troy had done
but it didn't matter
for he didn't hear her
anymore
as he lay, out cold,
in another room
snoring
ripped to the gills
with coke
& amphetamines
yes, snoring
&
snoring
&

grunting
&
snoring,
before
turning on
his
side
to give some other dream-chick
the benefit of his great
big Scottish penis
o yes
but of course.

Look at him again now
climbing back up once more
on the table
getting ready for another
big showing-off
with his poetry book of
T. S. Eliot open wide
delivering another big speech
about Death
I had not thought
death
had undone so many
well that just shows you
what you know
you great big
wittering Scottish óinseach
shut up

O here I am
the painter
the famous painter
& musician
Troy McClory
all the way
from Morningside
Troy 'The Hammer Man'
that is to say
who likes to ball some chicks
when he can

especially those who are
head over heels
such as, for example,
our innocent Una
who never had such
attention paid to her in
her life
partly because she looked
like Ten Ton Tessie
but also because
she had been brought up
in an orphanage, a drab and dull
but reasonably humane place
just outside Wolverhampton
do you love me she said
yes I do you're my special
Lady Ocean
&
that is the way that it's always
going to be
for you are my lady
& I am your man
& together we shall walk
in the wake of the magnificent
Poseidon.

here, let me put this
inside you, he would say
yes, ha ha ha,
let me do it again
clutching at his bud
& jumping up & down to
the sound of *Atomic Rooster*
with their swirling, vertiginous
Hammond waves of heavy organ rock
ladies & gentlemen
what you have before you
this night is the spectacle of
the Great Spontaneous Apple Creation
during the course of which
three thousand people
will be seen this night
to consume
one strawberry

ha ha ha laughed Troy again
as he fell on top of my sister
& kissed her *brollach*
yes, every part of her sweet white
breast he was seen to consume
as he rolled yet another
plump, generous number
& recited some sections from
The Liverpool Scene
yes, Adrian Henri – another poet that he
liked to boast he was fond of
& had actually *met*
although
that, of course
was another lie
yes, yet another little birdie
as Margaret Rutherford likes
to describe such attempts
at hoodwinks
I am a good friend of Adrian
Henri
Know him well, actually
ha ha ha ha ha
but of course you do Troy

But, as it turned out,
very soon there was to be a lot
less chat of that particular character
not long after Frankie 'The Blind Owl'
Olson
succeeded in getting himself
along with poor old Lord Offaly Of Down
arrested on suspicion of conspiracy to cause
explosions.
With The Temple being placed
under around-the-clock surveillance.
With it proving, in the end, a great deal
more than poor old Lord Offaly-McKeever
could seem to cope with
with the truth being
that, behind all his bluster,
he hadn't been all that assured of himself
during his relatively brief period in the city.
& which was why he headed up

on the suicide bus to
Archway
yes, to the suicide bridge
as it was known
&, as a matter of fact,

still is.
Where Dessie found it
really really cold,
for some
reason
almost unbearable
ice-cold
dreadful
in spite of the fact
that it was only late Summer.

Young Desmond McKeever, aged
20, formerly from Kilkeel in the
County of Down
stood handsomely attired in his navy frock coat
and Three Musketeers hat, which he'd bought
in a second-hand store in Brewer St
with his long straight hair parted in the middle
covering a pale oval face
flowing down past his shoulders
as he finished the last of his cigarette
before tossing it into the slipstream of the
roaring traffic below.
Then he thought he heard some birds
speaking
yes, little birds
éiníní, as Nano called them
wee éiníní
imagine, I ask you
hearing birds
but then, of course
you have to remember
that poor old Lord Desmond Offaly
Of Down
he had been really stoned at the time
yes, out of his box
as they said to him
spread your wings

& he heard those sweet little birdies
rousing up a melodic chorus
as he joined them, swimming
carelessly out into the blue:
I am the Lord Of Offaly
Silken Thomas is my name
as those few months in London
disported themselves before his eyes
trying not to think about
Tanith Kaplinski's funeral
yes, the 'wee' problem
of poor 'wee' Tanith
who he did his best to keep
out of his mind
trying to concentrate
as best he possibly could
on the memory of Joanne
baking bread in the kitchen
ponytailed Troy at his table making
neat little sketches of Charlie Brown,
Peanuts & Snoopy
& Big Peter chatting about his
plans to drive all the way
on his own back to Afghanistan.

What a dream it had been, for sure.
Except now it was over:
bye bye birdie.
This is what the *éiníní*
of Archway had to say
as Dessie McKeever sailed
away
'far out', in front of the moon.

All the way from Kilkeel,
Co. Down,
in the Heart Of Erin
never to be,
evermore.

Ah, boys oh boys,
some of the things that come
into your mind,
I swear to God
you'd often wonder
at times, did you imagine it
such as Malachy Breslin
& the secret room that he
built in the attic
& that no one knew about
only me in
Brondesbury Gardens.
& which was handy on account
of keeping a keen and watchful eye
on all the shenanigans
because, God be good to them,
they were desperate rogues entirely
that made up McClory's *clann*,
aye his precious, enlightened 'family'.

Which is how
I came to be a discreet
but, nonetheless, ever-vigilant
lodger
with a ringside seat at the construction of
a whole new society
not to mention no end of
X-rated movies
starring my sister & her lover
Jack Nicholson
that is to say
Troy McClory
of course.

With Des McKeever's
vacant room
being advertised then
in *Time Out*, no less
as yet another prospective tenant
arrived
elegant above all
with her expensive bags and baggage
& this lady's name was
Iris Montgomery

& a very genteel type she was indeed.
This would have been in the very
last days of October
not long before the whole sad project
was seen to collapse
& such a racket, I swear to God

as this creature created
& her not more than a slip of a thing
what Nano would have described as
a little *biteen* of a *kippeen*
meaning hardly there
at all, so she wasn't.
Except that everywhere she went
she seemed to be addressing adoring
crowds
for that, at least, was what she appeared to think.
O yes, I'm engaged in a very important
project at the moment,
she confided over breakfast one morning,
compiling a volume provisionally entitled
'The History Of London'.

Well, Lord above
you really do have to say it
is there anything that can compete
with the young and their boundless ambition
get out of my way or I'll take out
your kidneys and eat them in front of you
the very same as a turkey's gizzard
for I'm so special,
talented and unique
that everyone has to know
the story of my life.

But then, in another way,
I suppose you have to hand it to them
because if you're not confident then
when you're in your late teens
and early twenties
then when are you ever likely
to be
considering what's in store for most

of us
even if the greater proportion
of her particular story,
like the majority of her pronouncements,
it amounted to not a great deal more
than complete and utter fantasy
as did the opera that she claimed
to be preparing
based on the work of
Dory Previn, the composer's wife.
It was nearly impossible not to
meet her on the stairs
always in a hurry
clambering down with an armful
of books
on her way to convene
with some fellow 'soul-travellers' &
'metaphysical explorers', at The Golden
Dawn restaurant
or, perhaps, The British Library –
for she really did see herself as quite
the intellectual scholar.

Yes, Miss Iris Montgomery-Carew sure
did cut quite a dash
& stopped, at least for a while,
the poor old bruised and now somewhat uncertain
Mahavishnu Temple in its tracks.
Even if a few,
primarily as a consequence of jealousy,
vehemently criticised her attempts at poetry
describing them as 'wilfully
unintelligible' –
a view which I have to say that I found
most surprising
considering some of the *raiméis*
that they'd listened to in the past
and praised to the skies,
most notably from Blondie McBondie
the handsome Scot
standing like some latter-day Rock Messiah
blathering Bob Dylan and T. S. Eliot
on the fucking table with the eyes gone
skewballs back in his head

I mean, what on earth were we supposed to think
– the second fucking coming or what?

But class will out, I suppose you have to say,
and it has to be admitted that, in the end,
almost in spite of themselves,
many of them grew to admire her.
Because, whatever else about her, Iris
definitely did possess an estimable aristocratic grace.
She genuinely did, wandering around the flat
in a deep-blue satin kimono
declaiming her own great chunks of verse
which, on occasion, with her taking it all so seriously,
it appeared as if she might be
on the verge of incurring
a seizure of some kind.
Sometimes, indeed, you'd actually witness her break
down and cry
starting to mutter things about her father
& which was interesting
at least initially.
But, after a while, I have to admit
that I found myself becoming impatient
especially after paragraphs of this great big
so-called forthcoming London history of hers
which she routinely referred to as her 'tour de force'
& kept going on about
night after fucking night, you know?
With most of it, sad to say, amounting to
little more than sentimental adolescent
schoolgirl gibberish
more *raiméis*, in otherwords
buckets of balderdash.

History Of London?
I thought as I watched her,
A Neurotic Human Matchstick Tells Its
Tiresomely Predictable Story perhaps!
Ah yes, poor old Iris Kippeen-Montgomery.
And it was after that, to be honest
that I found I didn't really, any longer, care
as I went off and got gloriously drunk with the old
crowd back in The Bedford Arms.

[183]

Before finally returning to my
place of concealment
and, I suppose, somewhat buoyed by
a skinful of ye olde *uisquebaugh*
pressing my already flushed cheek
against the skirting and, without
so much as a care in the world, began emptying my
lungs and
giving it everything I'd got.
Rise her, Dan!
as they used to say in The Bedford
lift the rafters, me auld segocia!

& so I did,
gave it my all
right there in the middle of the night
it must have been well past 3 a.m.,
gazed upon approvingly
by a plump-bellied harvest moon.
Rise her, Dan, attaboy Fogarty!
Will you come to the bower
o'er the free boundless ocean! H'ho ye girl ye! Give
us a gander at them two luscious globes of flesh!

& finding myself deriving such a *cic*
from my escapades
not to mention the astonished Iris's reaction
to my humorous request
– even more gratifying than the one I'd
received from poor old Tanith, God rest
her soul.
I could see no reason not to go *thar barr* –
that is to say, going over the top.
As I caught a *hault* of a crock of withered flowers
& sent it flying across the room.
'Bejapers aye!' I remember cackling,
simultaneously striking the boords
a good smart kick with my foot,
'And sure why the devil wouldn't we
have ourselves a grand old *ceilidh*!
You're a topping girl, Ma'am, so you are so
you are! fair play to you, Miss Montgomery! Oh
now!'

But that was just the start of it, really
& what with me being aware, as I say,
that
not only was our most recent tenant a poet
of considerable promise, but the actual
author of the
forthcoming publication, sure to be a masterpiece
entitled, yes:
'The History Of London'
that I concluded there really was nothing for it
but to regale Miss Iris
with a personal and particular favourite of
my own, taught to me by my very own Auntie Nano
namely, 'The Green Eye Of The Little Yellow God'
& in which, coincidentally, there
happens to be a mention of a certain 'Old Carew' –
so how's that for serendipity?
He was known as 'Mad Carew' by the subs
at Kathmandu
He was hotter than they felt inclined to tell!

I flung back a chair and performed
a gay little dance,
bashing a few pots & pans
as I did so.
Before clearing my throat and once again
raising the rafters
with all the gusto I could humanly muster.
Good man, Dan, I shouted, man alive, Fogarty
but you are the man, *rip it up like the man*
you are!
There's a green-eyed yellow idol to the north of
Kathmandu
There's a little marble cross below the town
so there is
so there is
och troth indeed and sowl there is!

Well, such a laugh, I can't tell you
whenever I saw Miss Montgomery's
shocked reaction to that.
I must have danced ten or maybe even *twenty* jigs
battering and kicking the skirting as
I did so.

But then, of course, there'd be silence after that
– often, perhaps, for days.
Weeks, even.
With the result that
it was hard to even get a word out of her now.
A development which surprised a lot of her
colleagues – none more so than those with whom she
laboured, her fellow tutors in the Killiburn
Polytechnic, where she lectured part-time.

With the actual truth being – quite apart from
complaining of 'hearing loud noises' – like her
poetic heroine, Sylvia Plath,
Iris Montgomery-Carew
had once more
become privy
only this time with a vengeance
to certain familiar distressing memories of her father
which, all her life, from time to time,
had continued to plague her
with her never knowing when
it was exactly they were going to strike
– and when she discovered him, her actual
parent, standing in his dicky bow
behind the curtains
staring intently over at her
– well, I mean, you can imagine!

But, unlike Tanith Kaplinski,
Iris Montgomery-Carew
neglected to tell anyone about these, or similar occurrences,
including the rustling noise she could have sworn
she had heard
& which had reminded her of nothing
so much as the sound that grasshoppers
made.
Yes, decided not to open her mouth about any of it
– which was, maybe, wise.
Because, I mean, who's going to believe the like of
that
secret rooms and the presences of ghosts, Irish
wet-on-the-brain drunks
and concluding, childishly,
that what you were dealing with

what it was, all along, was
an evil-intentioned *gruagach*.
Whatever that is.
I mean, honest to God

when you think about it
who in their right mind
is going, for a second, to believe a
fairy story the like of that
even if towards the end of my life
or one of them
when my liver packed in
after a lifetime of supping in
them auld Killiburn hostelries
Malachy Breslin *did*
build me an actual secret room
to provide me with shelter
and, by a mysterious coincidence,
located it in the very same
place as where my very own
maw-hir
my own poor
afflicted mother
God rest her
once upon a time
in the fifties
took her own life
one sad day before dawn
in that very same attic
by stringing a
holy medal and a
scapular around her neck.

Honestly!
Such a parcel of speculative,
wayward raiméis
or *seafóid* –
fanciful garbage, as
Nano in her heyday,
would, no doubt, have insisted.
Secret rooms and little wee men
the size of goblins, *pshaw!*

Not unlike, I suppose,
a lot of the discursive old rambling
nonsense
that I used to like to put,
particularly on Sundays,
when it was raining,
into the pages of my
trusty *dialann*
yes, my personal diary
recounting my own particular view
& intimate history
of London City
as if the likes of me could
be entitled to have a history
& me but the shakings
of the Fogarty bag
the dribbly issue
of a long line of peasants
with divil the bit of
a peerage or a title
to be anywhere seen
or indeed anything
at all
as might commend our
worth to anyone
but, nonetheless,
I did my best
yes, to tell the story of
sweet Una and me
and all the old Fogartys
that were cast out to be exiles
like so many poor old Gaels
before them
landing their
sad little biteen of a
brown paper parcel
on the shores
of the Thames
with all its
ships
&
towers
&
of course

temples
once upon a time there was a city
which grew up out of nothing
a heaven on earth
for all the people to enjoy
including both my sister
& I
yes, that would be Una
not long released from the
orphanage in Wolverhampton
getting bits and pieces of
old work wherever she
was fit to find it
already seeming pale
& aged beyond her years
a great big lump
of expendable domestic *leavings,*
the shakings of the bag
clattering around with her mop
and bucket
wielding those implements
night and day
beginning at the tender
age of eighteen years
labouring in office
after
office
after
overlit
office
everywhere she goes
being watched and surrounded
by the eyes of the London
departed
furtive loafers
& policemen
in walrus moustaches
staring along with the rest of the dead
but not unkindly
in the streets of a city lit amber
by gas
where shadows fall on yellow stock brick.
Hark! Look at those Salvation
Army brassmen

with their ladies alongside
in coal-scuttle beribboned
poke bonnets.
Goodness gracious
but that's just the start of
it
for now what we have
is Una 'Lady'
Fogarty's
alternative
History Of London.
Where she would even set down
the story of 'The Mysteries'
of which not a word
had e'er been spoken in her
family
&
never would
owing to the sensitivity of
its subject
Yes, the mysteries
the girls who surreptitiously
used the very same beats
as the more established prostitutes
& who, once they had 'hooked'
their man
left him to pay
their cab fare to where
their homes were situated
often as not being ordinary
housewives
who only worked when they
had to
had to
had to
wrote Lady Fogarty
in the grip of *the trimmlins*
& who were known
as the 'mysteries'
simply because
so little was known about them
with 'Dotsy' Fogarty, our very own mother
entering the ranks
in the aftermath of a court case

not long after giving our Una
up for adoption
in 1954
where a sympathetic judge
had found her *not guilty*
of pulling the plug on
not only one
but eight little infants
in the hospital
in Paddington
where she'd worked
temporarily
as a nurse's assistant
and whose lives, thankfully,
had been saved
in
the
nick
of time
yes, thought Lady Una
I'll write all that
because it is the truth
in my own private, personal
history of this city
where I wandered after
leaving the orphanage up north
in this fabulous new land
of music hall & song
& smoky saloons
& cellar bars like Nano's
who of course was not my aunt
at all
I only made that up
a little birdie
for the purpose of keeping
myself entertained
&, as well as that,
ensuring that the story keeps
moving.
Indeed, I only wish she was
our relation
or anything to do with us at all
lovely Aunt Nano
holding court like she did

in that grand old Gaelic
flaithiúil way
down in the most blissful
anarchic dungeon among everyone
priest & pauper
because it was London no one
prevented them from making
their own rules
stage-door johnnies
bookies
&
eccentrics
here in this land of
boarding houses and
dragon landladies
& the owners of
small hotels which
she came to know well
in Bethnal Green
&
St Pancras
where you felt as if
you were up in a balloon
looking down over the chimney pots
floating aloft with the starlings
wheeling in the smoky
London sunset.
Drifting among the spires
& domes of the cathedrals
past scores of pubs
& synagogues
& her favourite the old
Metropolitan Music Hall
yes, *The Met*
with its music-hall architecture
a light touch of Arabesque
with a hint of Edwardian
art nouveau
so beautiful now that
the Spring is approaching
& the trees are speckled
with green, with the very first
heads of the tulips peeping out
Meanwhile the railway

shrieks & clatters
as the workers
clocking out
make their way to
The Star Of The East
a great Gothic pub
filled with mirrors
& low-hanging lamps
with its name sandblasted
engraved in gold
then there's the Thames
the chief commercial highway
of this place
& the foundation of its
importance
twice a day the river
brings in fresh air from Southend
whence goes back
the stale air
pulled by the ebb tides
but o how she becomes excited
yes, how giddy & filled with
a trimmlins most exotic &
luxurious
does our diarist Lady Una Fogarty
find herself
when at last she inscribes
two special words
that is to say
The Roundhouse
which is a huge circular building
in Chalk Farm, hard by Camden Lock
that can be seen from the trains
going north
& dates from
1847, with its distinctive
feature being its vast conical
roof of slate supported on
twenty-four cast-iron columns.
Where you could easily place
engine drivers in stove-pipe hats
side-whiskered men in corduroy
just like Troy the night he had brought
her there to hear some 'sounds'

yes, to see 'The Crims', as he called
King Crimson
& they were all blissed-out
with Jo & Tanith in their
coloured floppy hats
doing what everyone in The Roundhouse
was doing
choreographing themselves
to the light show's patterns
forming chemically enhanced
dance shapes that merged
with the pulsating blobs & drips
of the light-show oils.
I'm a pop art aesthete
Troy McClory used to say
an inner-travelling cosmonaut
which poor Fudge, at first, didn't
have a hope of understanding.
But, thanks in the main to her
new *beau* Troy,
she was learning.

Yes, she was learning
my sister, to this very day,
will suddenly disgorge the
most strident of observations
often out loud
& usually completely
out of nowhere
back here in our own private
home from home
that is to say
the Cliftonville Bay Hotel
occasionally in the lobby
or maybe standing over by the library
near the potted palm
where Murphy the dog is always
loping around
wandering
looking like he's about
to lift his leg
& just when I'm about to say

Una dear, don't worry yourself!
she'll just shout
or start laughing
&
rasp to nobody
in particular
well
well
well
would you lookit
who it is
Mr Dan ever-present
know-it-all Fogarty
Mr Dan who thinks
he knows it all
Master Daniel Fogarty who
thinks he knows everything
there is to know
Yes, Mr Big-Time
Know-It-All
who has taken it upon himself
this long time past
to colonise the
inside of my fucking
poor head
& is under the impression
that he owns that too
& has authority over it and all
its jurisdiction
yes, every road and inconsequential byway
every shadowed building lurking at the back of
my mind
none of which matters a great deal
anyhow
thanks to Baron
     Von
       fucking
          Richthofen
so-called air-ace
in his bright red Fokker plane
not to mention Trevor Howard
& his night-time Stukas
strafing every bit of
my brain without respite

leave me alone!
hell roast them all.

I can almost nearly tell
the very moment that I see her
just what it is she's likely to say
I'm so used to hearing it
night noon & morning
Yes, damn you to hell
you cur-dog. Dan Fogarty
my so-called brother
only out for yourself
to see what you can get
just like always!

Yes, that's what she'll say
even though I'm the only one
here or anywhere else
who might be looking out for her.
With the reason being
that I'm the only one who knows
the truth
about everything she went through
not only during the course of her life
not only in Wolverhampton
but also in
Brondesbury Gardens
especially towards the end
when I tried to talk her out
of going anywhere near her two
so-called birdies
those deprived wee *childre*
Bobbie & Ann
that afternoon in
Queen's Park.

Even though she still insists,
yes, right up to this very day,
on saying
that it was actually *me* who had
given her the idea
and put her up to it

ever so slyly sliding the suggestion
into her mind
like in the song Johnny
Dankworth used to play in Nano's
'Experiments With Mice'
except that, in this case,
it was Una who'd been selected
to assume the role of the mouse
yes, you put me up to it
it was you who made me into
Una The Mouse
yes, Una An Luch
that's what you made me
saw to it that it was
inevitable
in the way that only the *gruagach*
can do.
Having no choice
because it's in their nature
& why, she says
screwing her fists into her eyes
I sometimes hate you so much
you're not my brother
or any form of kin at all,
Times I could happily kill you
Dan 'Smiling' Fogarty
even if you are my brother
whether half-born,
     full-born

         or

              any

                  other

                      fucking-thing

                        else.

Not that it matters what she says
because in my experience
irrespective of all available evidence
people, in the end, will believe what they want.
Although, to be honest
perhaps as a result of her being a poet

and of a highly strung artistic nature generally
in this regard
I did feel particularly sorry
for sorry Iris Montgomery-Carew.
Lord, when I think of it!
She used to quote these great enormous chunks of
poetry first thing in the morning
with it soon becoming generally accepted
that poor old Iris
she had already been long since
'away with the fairies'
before ever deciding
to come anywhere near The Temple.

Una used to think *The Waste Land* was a
book on drainage.

As Miss Montgomery would declaim
another big hefty slab of it
lying there in her deep-blue satin kimono
admiring this little ornament
a cockleshell orange-bordered ashtray which
reminded her of a day that she'd spent
on a picnic in Surrey with her daddy.

Probably the item she treasured most of all in her life.

And which she woke up one morning to find on top of her
bedside locker – *gone!* as Nano used to say.
With not so much as a single trace of it anywhere to be seen.
Something which couldn't possibly have happened, she
      knew.
But of course not.

Except, of course, that it had.
Her most treasured possession.
Vanished without trace.
And, as if that wasn't bad enough,
when she goes to her notebook
yes, that little spiral-bound jotter
in which she'd entered all of her
chapter headings
what you might call a ready-reckoner
that she was never without

always used for reference
now, she says, where was I, as she tosses
back her head of lovely fine freshly washed
hair
telling herself, convincingly, that
there wasn't so much as a 'bother' on
her
wondering which chapter will she
tackle next
with her eyes going blurry as she licks
her thumb, so smooth and elegant,
never for so much as one second
considering
that what she might find there
would not be her headings so
carefully and thoughtfully and
meticulously inscribed
with each one having its
own particular, discrete significance
every single one of which she was proud
having put so much care and consideration
into its creation
only now to find it
nowhere in sight
that chapter heading
or anything else, indeed,
that she had written.
& in its place, just:
I DON'T
I DON'T
I DON'T
I DON'T
I DON'T
I DON'T
I DON'T WANT TO
I DON'T WANT TO
I DON'T WANT TO
I DON'T WANT TO
I DON'T WANT TO BE BORN
I DON'T WANT TO BE BORN
I DON'T WANT TO BE BORN
I DON'T WANT TO BE BORN
I DON'T WANT TO BE BORN
I DON'T WANT TO BE BORN

I DON'T WANT TO BE BORN
I DON'T WANT TO BE BORN
I DON'T WANT TO BE BORN
I DON'T WANT TO BE BORN
I DON'T WANT TO BE BORN
I DON'T WANT TO BE BORN
I DON'T WANT TO BE BORN,
going on for twenty or thirty pages
in the same thick relentlessly gouging
graphite.
Like An Lonradh, I suppose,
an scannán Kubrick,
the film by Stanley –
except that *The Shining*
hadn't yet been made.
So maybe it could have been that second-rate
Exorcist that had been doing the rounds
at the time,
alternately titled The Devil Within Her
or I Don't Want To Be Born
starring the equally iconic
(or so 'Lady' Montgomery, no doubt, would have
thought)
Joan Collins
but Iris only very rarely attended
the cinema
and would scarcely have bothered with
something so essentially ephemeral.

To someone like her – really quite
hopelessly worthless, to be honest.

Hey there, motherfucker!
Ah
there
you are
says Todd to me
this morning coming across the lobby,
I was looking for you
if there was going to be a rumble
between Oppenheimer and T. S. Eliot
who would your money go on, friend?

I had more sense than to try to argue with someone
like Todd
who, as experience had indicated, would
stroke his chin and nod away earnestly
& then look up and ask you did you
happen to like pancakes.
Because I myself
am more than partial to a short stack
he says
before going on to list
the various different types
blueberry etc.
for at least fifteen minutes
or more.

So I do my best to keep him humoured
until he eventually gets the message
& anyway has just at that moment
spotted Butley and goes over to talk to him
and Murphy

as off goes Una with her notes and
pieces of paper
shuffling along & repeating to herself
in two different voices
death death death and T. S. Eliot
& now I am become Death, destroyer of all worlds.

To be perfectly honest, I think she'd just about had it,
our lass,
getting into anymore debates
& wranglings with me
for, God knows
we've had our share
& most of the time
it isn't even funny anymore
not the way it used to be
at any rate
it could be, maybe, that we've both become tired
as a result of all these advancing years
& just don't have that former spark
when her eyes would twinkle
& she'd look at me

& wag the finger
I hope that you're not at it again
are you Dan Fogarty
telling me more of those *piseoga* of yours
are you Dan,
trying to trick me
with more of those wee birdies, eh?
Which is her name, of course, a wee birdie
for any form of frivolous
fancy, little lie or general
embellishment of the truth.
And which Rutherford
also uses
whenever she happens to
take the notion.
It's a good one, though,
isn't it?
Just like the *childre* of
old might say
ha ha,
Wee Birdies!

But here, I wanted to tell you about
probably
the worst, certainly the saddest
casualty of all
back in the days of The Temple,
Brondesbury Gardens
& by whom I mean Sexy Lexy Gordon
the caretaker
or 'Moody Alex' as the girls used to call him
& then other times,
sniggering behind their
hands
& for obvious reasons, as will become
clear: *Roger*

grim officious custodian of 'The Mansions Of Layabout
Lowlifes', as he'd personally christened The Temple
& its endless stream of peripatetic residents.

& who might,
when one thinks about it,
considering some of the more than negative
appraisals
he was in the habit of receiving from
many of the female occupants of Brondesbury,
might arguably have been in contention for the accolade of
supreme lowlife layabout himself
& this in spite of his impressive army service
record.
Which he never ceased reminding them of
& wondering, of course, why he
had ever bothered
yes, fighting for the likes of that
'bloody lot!'

How many eyes would you say the night possesses?
One thousand, might you say?
Double that, perhaps?
Well you'd be wrong.
Because in the apartments of
Brondesbury Gardens, at least in 1974
it simply had *one*
& it resided, nervily
deep in the gleaming
perspiring brow
of one
'Moody' Alex
Gordon, alias
Sexy Lexy,

Who had always,
always
always
wanted to be in the war
right from the very first day he had pronounced
himself King Of The Blitz
after, in his dreams, in his V-neck
red sweater and brown khaki shorts
having perceived himself
descending the few remaining functional
concrete steps of a comprehensively bombed-out

West End store
before the mound of rubble that they led
to gave way suddenly and he found himself
spiralling downward helplessly
plummeting into the middle of
what was to become his
own private & as yet undiscovered world
there to remain for as long as he
personally cared to decide,
being as he was the self-styled
Lord of all he surveyed in this
basement section of the building
a private kingdom here in this
basement part of the department store
where all the fantastic sports goods were stored.

'Yes, I'm the *King Of The Blitz*!'
cried Alex Gordon,
aged 10
furiously pounding his chest
like the proudest little gorilla
sole commander of this urban jungle.
Yes, this is jollywell good! he declared
before lifting a great big dumb-bell up as high
as it would go against his chest
& then running across to select a
pale white willow cricket bat,
making a wild big swing with it.
Before something alerted him and he suddenly noticed
something like
what appeared to be the softest pink bulb
exactly like the top part of a tulip
swaying back and forth behind a big crate of basketballs
like a mesmeric pendulum
attempting to capture his attention.
It really was most shockingly pink in colour
vivid
livid
soft
&
pliable
just
waving there
from side to side

& poor Alex Gordon
he really didn't know what to do
as he stood there plying his willow but remaining
dead dead
quite stock still.
As outside the whine of the V-1s proceeded.
While, beneath their piercing, relentless whistles
The Boy Prince Of The Blitz
he became aware of the gentlest whisper
as it came sailing across the
black-and-white chequerboard floor.
Please don't be angry, he heard its soft, disarming appeal,
please will you not be angry, little babogue. It's just that
Mummy was afraid to tell you. About the little brother
that you didn't know you had. This is all that's left, I'm
afraid.
Ha ha.
Yes, the only thing remaining from the abortion is *this*!
Meaning the little round bulb at the head of the wavering
limb.
What troubled Alex most, whenever he experienced that
dream
was the fact that he had never even known his
little brother's name,
presuming it was a boy
something which he would never know now
ever since his mother had died in an explosion
& his father was afflicted with a severe case of the jitters
or *trimmlins* as they'd be known elsewhere
it really did have the most far-reaching effects
on poor young Alex Gordon.
Yes, affecting most profoundly
that poor young sensitive
essentially good-at-heart soul
the self-appointed bomb-site magistrate
yes, would repeatedly & recurrently,
in varying degrees,
appear at the back of his mind
just waving
all through those subsequent years.

I mean – talk about The History Of London!
O, if only those old walls of Brondesbury
Gardens could have talked

what little birdies might they have
had to tell
regarding Alex and all of those many moods
yes, that old Sexy Lexy, caretaker cum
part-time gardener
whose predilection for currying favour
'wiv the birds' was legendary,
even down to accepting 'certain little courtesies'
in lieu of rent.
I mean, wot a corker.
Was it any wonder that Tanith Kaplinski
had threatened to
report him, at least twice, to the police
& even, on another occasion,
telephone his wife.

But back to Madame Matchstick –
that is to say, Lady Iris Montgomery-Carew
or what remained of her.
With what finished poor old
Iris off
more than anything else really
being the sheer intensity
of the most recent visitation.
Or what she preferred to categorise
in her own mind as
a 'callous, indifferent manifestation of evil'.

By which she meant
a certain entity
sitting there waiting
with seemingly infinite patience
when Iris eventually got home from
college
with the figure in the corner
only sitting up
whenever she heard the young student
enter,
closing the landing door softly behind her.
Half-human, half-animal was the description
Iris had insisted on
whenever she got around
to explaining it all later.

With Luke Powys, a more recent
resident,
a potter with whom she'd had a brief
relationship
having remarked
at the time
that there was no one better than Iris
when it came to painting a vivid if distressing
picture
what with her being a writer & a poet
& everything
with everyone nodding
& agreeing yes
it was really far out.
With her, at this time, growing
paler
& more drawn-looking than ever
turning a record sleeve
absently in her hands
Death Walks Behind You
was the name of the title on
the cover
directly above the horrific piece of art.
That's what you saw, maybe, Iris?
Luke Powys had suggested
tapping away with his nail himself
tracing the contours
of the fearsome medieval
image
Nebuchadnezzar, he explained,
an epochal representation
for all the world
like something only recently emerged
from a primeval swamp
yes, that's maybe what you saw
he said again
after we got stoned and listened
to this album in its entirety
that night
or *thought*, maybe,
that was what you saw
yeah, figured you did –
because that fucking hash,
believe me, it is

really fucking strong
so strong
man
yeah
really fucking out there
you know?

But Iris didn't accept this
& wouldn't
no matter how many
of the rest of them
agreed
& kept on getting more frustrated
not to mention
thinner & thinner
when it became abundantly
& perfectly clear
that no one in the flat
was ever going to believe her
maybe because they were
afraid to even begin to
acknowledge it
but they didn't anyway
& she just continued to become
more & more
like
a
matchstick.

Until one day they came home
to find the elegant Iris Montgomery-
Carew
well, to find her absent, in fact –
yes, gone.
Never to be seen again, said the note
she had left behind
having gone to stay with
some relative
abroad.

And leaving no trace of her
former existence behind her

but that didn't matter
because even in those
grim impecunious days,
accommodation in London was
still quite hard to come by
so in went the notice in the
local newsagents & before they knew it
there was a queue stretching almost
as far as Biddy Mulligan's Select
Public House
all along the Killiburn High Road
with every type of client coming
clattering and banging up the stairs
as the sitting tenants proceeded obliviously
with their 'sounds'
playing & listening to music
most of the day & long into the night.

Along with Luke, the gifted potter from Wales
who, as I say,
had only recently joined the fold
now they had Maddie Lynam &
Frank 'The Blind Owl' Olson
who had made it back safe
from his travels
in South America
sharing the big room with Shuggie Otis &
Johnny Winter
& a whole host of others
who came and went
as they pleased,
Not forgetting the larger-than-life
self-appointed King Of County Cavan
that is to say
Macaulay 'Breffni' O'Rourke
six-foot three if he was an inch
coming and going with his knapsack
in his threadbare silver tweed maxi-coat
crinkling up his nose like Catweazle
laughing and joking, mostly to himself,
with his bearded mouth breaking into
a half-smile at the corners,
reciting bits of old poetry and rhymes
and quoting extensive excerpts from

the *oeuvre* of Kahlil
Gibran.
along with Frank 'The Blind Owl'
Olson
becoming so popular
through his proficiency
for quoting mythology
and performing arcane folk tunes
on the mandolin
that at times the pair of them
they came extremely close to
eclipsing the heretofore unchallenged
hegemony
of
'the colossus' Troy McClory
the great *Grand Wizard*
ha ha
ho ho

with the exception, of course,
of my adoring sister
yes, the one and only hopelessly besotted
Una
now, apparently, going by the
name of *Amphitrite*.
Yes – that, apparently,
was her latest appellation
courtesy of The Wizard
as he wound his long 'artist's' fingers
around hers
assuring her convincingly
& at length
yet again
of just how much he wanted
&
loved her
as those two sad peepers
swum in her head
pitifully giving credence
to every single word –
but then, I suppose, that's the way.

I wanted to say a few things
about bird impressions
which Una is thinking of
including in *The Capers*.
Oo you've gone and bent
me shuttlecock all out of
shape, cooed Butley
whenever he was informed
of this development
& went away off with
the two shoulders shaking
rubbing his hands
like he thinks he's
Arthur Askey.

Anyway, bird impersonations,
as I was saying –
that is something
I've always been good at
down the years
& is how I got my nickname
An Londubh
or
The Blackbird.
'Ti-ti-pu, ti-ti-pu!'
I'd go
sticking my leg out
like I've grown a tail
& which used to always go down
a storm in The Bedford on
Saturday nights
sometimes they used to even hear
it in Mahavishnu
especially when Big Peter
would be back from Afghanistan.
That is really strong shit, they would say
'Because I could have sworn
I heard whistling coming from
behind the skirting – no, man,
I really did!'

With the next thing, I remember
thinking to myself,

being that they'll start
agreeing with one another
that everything Lady Montgomery
told them was right
& that she *had* seen a hare
sitting on a chair,
assuming the body of an elderly lady,
her brown eyes glassy,
motionless in a crouched position.

With the whole thing, in a way,
being a pity
what with the way it happened
whether hares or anything else
seeing as The King Of Cavan –
Macaulay 'Breffni' O'Rourke –
yes, everything The King of Cavan
had experienced in The Temple
he decided to make
it his business to write it
all down
put it all in his diary –
the same one, tragically,
that he'd ended up
flushing down the lavatory
on that very same
night that the police
had, unexpectedly, raided
the flat
when he'd got the dreads
because it was all in there
all of his private thoughts
& meanderings
with him thinking that maybe
they'd peg him for a lunatic
especially when they'd find
themselves
reading the section
which he'd been intending to
show, specifically, to Frank Olson
just for a bit of a laugh
because, looking back now,
what it described
was extremely funny

although it hadn't been
on the day that it happened
in fact, it had been anything but.
When Macaulay had been sitting
by himself in the front room
dicing up the hash into small pound
deals
before finding himself listening
all of a sudden
to this prolonged eruption
of hysterical laughter
& climbing the stairs
assuming there was no one else
in the house
only to find himself confronted by
what he could only consider a small,
& ludicrously so, version of himself
with similar crinkled-up eyes and
the exact same long red hair
looking up as it
stood there
right in the centre of the stark
unvarnished floorboards
with its hands on its hips
as it whispered, with a smile,
hello there, King Of Cavan.
Before continuing, examining
its nails:
'It seems to me that you're a man
after my own heart!'

By which he meant,
as he explained,
largely in appearance.
What with Macaulay's similarly
wild copper curls
& his habit of paying scant attention
to personal hygiene.
'Yes, not at all unlike
the gruagach,' the grotesque
little maneen sighed.
'Never bothering overmuch,' he continued,
'Wearing clothes as seem fancy
dirty and untidy in our habits

we are
all a-tangle with twigs and straw
& briars!'
Such an unmerciful shriek
as he released then,
turning a cartwheel,
before thrusting a weathered
gnarled digit
right in front of Macaulay
O'Rourke's astonished face.
The man that haunts this bower,
he explained, is a fellow by the name of
Daniel Fogarty
who came over to these shores
after being banished in disgrace
from the mountain village of Currabawn
& was drawn to this place on account of
his poor unfortunate mother
who went by the name of Doreen Fogarty,
God be good to her and keep her
and preserve forever the honour of
her good name.
Anyhow, didn't she strike herself down
in a frenzy, in this very room
in the long ago, in 1954.
Aye, poor Dots,
her own life didn't she take it
here
with a medal
God help us
& a scapular round her neck
die, she did,
& her roaring for her daughter
that poor sweet craythur
as she had no choice but to hand over
to the nuns in Wolverhampton
for adoption.
Una, God love her,
Una, aye.
With her brother
poor auld Dan
aye poor old
heartbroken Fogarty
didn't he get Malachy Breslin

a master carpenter, in his time,
to build for him a *biteen* of a hole
a kind of secret den
you might say
into which he could come and go
as he *playzed*
but even having a home
a dark little kingdom all
of his own
that didn't bring him happiness
either
or contentment, no,
or anything like it
with the result that
in the latter end, didn't he
do it too
by his own hand end it
like so many of our countrymen
for whatever reason, God bless them,
they have done in their time
yes, draw a line under the whole
accursed shebang
kaput
by drinking steadily
day by day, until death.

& with that, the little man,
he pushed Macaulay out
of the way
aye, with those two eyes bulging
turned back in his head
began repeating the word
Nebukkedna!
yes, Nebukkedna!
he kept on repeating
moving and crawling
back and forth across the
splintered boards
nebukkedna, nebukkedna,
with skin like hide
his toes turning into
what'd put you in mind
of talons

as he back-crawled, sneering
with his body super-long
& his forefinger extended
from which then issued
a lightning bolt without noise
as the world within and without
the room
it began shuddering and was lit
by a flash of electric blue
as Macaulay 'Breffni' O'Rourke
the self-appointed
writer-king of Cavan realised
in that sudden, unexpected moment
that it wasn't now
or even tomorrow
he found himself existing in
but 20,000 years or more into
the future
when a massive wave
of biblical proportions
had engulfed the city of
London
so vast and overwhelming
that even the thought of it
had the effect of making
Macaulay O'Rourke
helplessly succumb
in that moment
to what can only be described
to the father & mother
as a God-Almighty fit
yes, a quite spectacular episode of
the trimmlins
one might say
as Big Ben
The Tower of London &
The Houses of Parliament
went crashing past
on the surging tide
reduced to nothing but matchwood
in his mind
& everyone he'd ever known
his mother, his father
himself as a child

& all the boys and girls
that he'd ever known
or had yet to meet
a chick that he'd known
down in Devon, who'd died
endeavoured, agape, to be heard
above the screech of an ugly
down-sweeping albatross
reaching out their arms
calling help us please
can you help us
we're drowning
from the inside of a
helplessly buffeted
life raft
we died and all those others
took our place
who are we does anyone remember
even know that we once were here
as the portico of The Royal Mint
went sailing by
and it was then that he heard it again
the brief, cruel, rattling
injunction
of Nebuchadnezzar
who, just as quickly,
now was gone, almost as if
he had never existed
which, like the police had always
insisted when they read it,
he hadn't.
I mean, after all,
what in heaven's name else
could they say?

I was thinking about all this
the dramatic submersion of the
City of London
& so forth
and
continuing to run it all over
in my mind
as I was
sitting here by the fire
in the front hall of Cliftonville
when I heard Una shouting
calling over to Roystone Oames
and complaining that she'd told
him she needed him 'soonest' –
like be there, you hear?
onstage in 'five'.

Boy, this is gonna be one hell of a show, remarks
Todd, coming strolling by
plucking his phone-buds out of his ears
as he bays some more Creedence Clearwater
Revival
Hey! Born On The Bayou! he roars over
when he sees me
& I'm not surprised when I hear
that Una wants
him in a star part in the show
because, whatever else,
he really does have a voice
like gritty sandpaper
pure rock and roll
even better than Ian Hunter!
I laugh to myself.

Then who arrives over
only the one and only
Butley Henderson himself.
polishing his cornet
as he sits alongside me
just as Attenborough introduces
another episode of his show
this time *Planet Earth II*
& the plucky little reptile

comes skittering along
making good its escape
from those vigilant, dead-eyed
merciless scaly-backed predators
as it deftly ascends
the face of the cliff &
somehow, miraculously
makes it again to high ground
safety
Don't talk to me about iguanas, says Butley,
as the tough little green-and-copper escapee
makes yet another break for it
Hooray! cries Una, tossing
her sheaf of notes into the air, *maith an bookil!*

As over arrive Margaret Rutherford and
her trusty lieutenant
Consuela Gomes The Brazilian Princess
& you can see that they've been rooting for the little fellow
too.
'O, those beastly snakes!' Margaret complains, hitting
her clipboard a little blow with her knuckle, 'tormenting
that poor defenceless little lizard hatchling.'
'Iguana,' corrects Una, 'it's an iguana, Miss Rutherford.'
'I do beg your pardon,' Maggie Rutherford smiles
reluctantly, 'forgive my ignorance but I was under the
impression that an iguana was, in fact, a lizard'
– clearly not a little peeved.
Because she can get like that
impatient, you know?
But then, I suppose, it goes
with the territory
all the things she has to put up
with
from early morning
until late
with everyone complaining
about this and that
making up their own personal
'Cliftonville Rules'
yes, constructing them all
as they go along
doing what they please,
more or less.

So, is it any wonder
that from time to time
poor old Miss Maggie Ruthers
she'd be fractious?

Madame Snap-Jaw
is what I sometimes call
Miss Rutherford,
especially when I think of
her riding along through the fog
on her bike
like you'll often see her
doing in the movies
playing the doughty society matron
particularly on Sundays
when they're showing
all her old afternoon matinees.

As we chatted away, about this
and that, I found myself
thinking that Connie The Princess
that she was looking particularly
well
Must be over her difficulties, I decided.
Because I knew she'd had some.
All you had to do was look at her –
losing weight, temper a little
frayed –
all of the usual things, I suppose.

But I was telling you, wasn't I
about the woman in the flat –
or should I say, 'old lady'.
Or, more accurately, perhaps
the squatting *giorria* –
that is to say, *hare*.

Because that's what it was! Iris Montgomery had
kept on insisting
immensely frustrated by their
persistent, wilful scepticism
doing her best, through constant floods of tears,
to somehow make herself understood.
But, even more importantly,

to enable herself, at some level, to be *believed*.
That's what it was, don't you see? That's what I saw,
with my own two fucking eyes!

After she had gone
eventually
everyone thought that this was great
with Troy even sketching a little picture
of what she'd described
with a huge debate then ensuing
as to the finer details of difference
between a rabbit and a hare
Man, she sure been smoking some heavy weed,
observed Big Peter,
I mean, I've seen them, man
come and go in this place
but this little lady – she, for sure,
is out where the buses don't run.
Where they ain't, in fact, been for decades.
That was what Big Peter had to say
& that was
even before
the
whistling
trousers
Or 'Na Bríste Feadaíl'
as Nano, in all likelihood,
would have preferred to call them.

O, those fun times in London
& Brondesbury Gardens
when your refuse
it still was not being collected
with rats
& flies
dead fish
&
bin bags
& everyone terrified
of

bombs
going off
on
the
tube.

& having, as a result,
a lot more to contend
with
& far too much
on their minds
to be having to deal with
the likes of

whistling
t
r
o
u
s
e
r
s

with that just, in fact,
being really the start
of a whole new
really quite dreadful
phase
as they saw it.

These particular
trousers
these *briste*
what they were called
was Oxford bags
big baggy loon-style pants
in crushed purple velvet
which Troy liked to wear
maybe at special, dress-up style
gigs
cool, sit-down type

maybe Nick Drake
or a coffee-house acoustic session
but anyway, there they were
standing right in front of
him in the still & fish-grey
light of the morn
when he'd been awakened by
what he didn't know
just a creaking sound or something
not rustling, anyway,
and, to his amazement, he saw the pants
concerned
positioned
barely two feet in front of him
stiff as a board, in actual fact
as if they'd
filled with liquid concrete
two trunkless legs of stone
thought Troy
presenting a spectacle which, initially,
had been amusing
but that was before, one by one, the fly buttons
began to pop
and what emerged then only this tiny
little head
along with a voice which started
piping the strangest tune
one which made poor McClory's skin
crawl
the words of which I won't repeat here
but, thankfully, thought Troy
that ancient tune or whatever it was supposed
to be
it hadn't actually lasted very long
before this really quite hilarious
lilting took its place
gradually morphing into what
was actually the most melodic & uplifting
whistle
which Troy recognised as 'Annie Laurie'
a song favoured & very often sung by
his old friend Douglas McVittie
The Professor.

Man, that was some good shit
we were smoking yesterday
he casually remarked to Joanne at breakfast
the following morning
checking out the cheap mail-order
high-waisted purple loons out of the
corner of his eye
now a pile of crushed velvet
lying in a disconsolate bundle
on the floor
yes, it really & truly was,
he said again,
as he made a half-hearted
oval with his lips
but with no sound
whatsoever
whether that of a whistle
or otherwise
showing any signs of
emerging
like a flock of living notes
through the gaping
mocking
aperture of a wide, unbuttoned fly.

Even though some of the things
Troy said were silly
such as why not come to my show
this weekend
yes, come & see some Ionesco down in
Putney
The Bald Prima Donna
where the price of one ticket admission is
your mind
that's all, he would say,
that will suffice, he would confirm,
somewhat portentously, as he nodded.

& even Una would be just a *beagáinín*
yes, a little piece embarrassed
not much
just a little

by this fresh display of
McClory-style braggadocio.

But then, as I say,
there were these other times, too, when
you would listen very carefully
when Troy, he seemed
in fact quite vulnerable.
That is, whenever he
wasn't standing up on
tables pontificating about 'golden visions'
or 'coming Utopias'
& didn't see the need to
pretend that he
knew Syd Barrett
or had recently been to see
the writer Angela Carter
about his 'latest project'
or some other 'workshop'
he was planning for the actors' lab.

No, when he was just Troy
'the boy' Troy that our Una liked
had fallen hopelessly *i ngrá* with
in fact
as she lay with her head against his chest
& in that dreamy, troubled way that he sometimes
had
he wondered aloud
what happens *after* the afterglow
for he had always said that the
comedown is the worst
that can be hard to handle, he said
– as, right at that moment, on her
way home from another party
across town, Tanith Kaplinski
was in fact discovering
having consumed a great deal
more than usual
yes, a very great deal
at six in the morning disembarking
from the nightbus
and dropping all the contents
of her bag onto the pavement in

the middle of Kilburn Square
as she pretended not to care
in fact, laughing about it
as if it was nothing,
everything she had taken over the
course of a very long night at
the party, every amphetamine she
had willingly accepted adding a *frisson*
of nail-chewing neurosis to her ever-
present female anxieties, with the
brain-mashing onslaught of LSD
heaping further chemical layers on top.

But she didn't care – as off she went
back to Brondesbury Gardens, at the top
of her voice chanting *1000 Micrograms Of
Love* ha ha!
& not being one bit surprised when, at the
turn of the landing, on the half-flight leading
to Iris's room, the man with the staple-shaped
bushy black moustache – a handsome fellow
too! – nodded courteously and gave her a playful little
wave of acknowledgement
as she heard him say:
'Oh hi – I'm Peter!'
To her amazement, then, on turning
the key of her flat in the latch
finding him waiting
on her bed inside.
Yes, as I say, I'm Peter!
he had grinned – only now seeming completely different.
That is to say, dressed in period
Edwardian costume – most notably
a fashionable high-buttoned jacket.

Then what happened – his moustache fell off.
As the other Peter appeared in the door.
Hi, I'm Peter, she heard him say, smiling as he extended
his hand.
He was wearing a matching paisley shirt and tie.
& that was it – with everything rising up inside the shaken
Tanith Kaplinski – who, right on the spot broke down anew.
Not that anyone heard her pitiful sobs – for down in the
kitchen, after a skinful, Troy and Iris had managed to gain

their second wind and were already cooking further plans for
yet another production in the little theatre in Putney.
One that, this time, would *really* blow everyone's minds!
Meanwhile, upstairs, Tanith was in the grip of *the trimmlins*,
digging her nails down deep into her skin.
Having become convinced that, only seconds
earlier, someone had touched her intimately – Peter.
But which one – was it the second Peter, Wyngarde the actor
she recognised from the series *Jason King*?
No – because now she knew.
She realised now at last.
Even if her sense of relief, as she'd suspected, it transpired to
be momentary.
As the lilting triplets came drifting through a crack in the
wall.
& she heard the distinctive voice of Peter Sarstedt, like
crushed velvet, crooning as the signature French accordion
slowly began to fade away: Where Do You Go To My Lovely?
he told her he wanted to know.
That's the reason I'm playing my song for you, he explained,
just like I will one day when we meet again, on a hill overlooking the Holy City, beneath a red sky over Jerusalem.
Ha ha! he laughed.
As, just at that moment, the bedroom door burst open and
Troy, sporting a wide-brimmed western cowboy hat,
flamboyantly waved his joint and announced, without
preamble:
You really have got to hear this, babe. Zachariah the father of
John The Baptist had no name for his son – and was struck
dumb, yeah? But when he heard the name *John The Baptist*
his speech – astonishingly, it came back. Our show is gonna
be the story of John The Baptist – & how he became the
Prince Of The Hippies. Yeah, & how he had grasshoppers in
the desert for dinner – he was a true non-conformist, but
when he told off the Emperor, he really lost his head.
It'll be called Zachariah, kinda like Jesus Christ Superstar,
only way cooler. London's first electric western – it'll
speak the language of the seventies, Tanith – are you
listening?
But Tanith Kaplinski wasn't.
Being much too busy sucking her thumb, laying there spread
eagled on the floor – her eyes like something familiar from
the popular film *Fritz The Cat*.

Stop it, will you, for heaven's sake,
picking endlessly at those threads
of your fucking cardigan,
I'll sometimes say
rather intemperately, to
my sister
but all she'll ever offer
by way of
reply is
do you know what, mo dhearthhair
do you know what, my brother
are you listening to me, our Dan
yes, do you know what it's like
it's like you're walking
along & at last taking command
when all of a sudden
the very ground underneath
your feet
it has unexpectedly given way
and there you are
you've just
the phantom whistle
& here they are again
V
V
V
V
V
V
yes, and there you are
hurtling down a mineshaft
& then landing
splay-legged like
a doll
in the middle of
a city under fierce attack
from who else but
The Luftwaffe
of course
strafing off this bit
& that bit
but that's not enough then

                    then they're coming   coming
back for more

        rat

                              a-
        ta-ta-ta-ta-ta-ta-ta

                              ta-ta ha ha!

        with the tail-gunner
        laughing his heart out
        shouting Donner und Blitzen
        Fogarty rat-tat-tat!
        Why it's nearly as bad as the night
        back in the Temple Of Old
        Mahavishnu
        when Saigon fell
        yes, back in Mahavishnu
        that fateful night
        when we watched
        it as it happened
        in living colour on our rented TV
        with Big Peter white as a ghost
        imagining himself back in
        'Nam even though he had never
        been there
        no, Afghanistan only
        but if he hadn't ever
        been anywhere near
        the South Vietnamese
        capital
        he sure as fucking hell
        was in the middle of it now
        God knows
        with Jimi Hendrix
        the Seattle Prince
        in his red bandana
        playing at full volume

        as Big Peter
        pleaded *Please!*
        no more, no fucking more!

covering his face with his arms
because we're running out of time
crawling under the sofa
weeping and shielding his eyes
with his fingers
& The Stars That Play With Laughing Sam's
Dice roaring away like lions
with a wild shrill of shrapnel bells
chords locked in Spitfire dogfights
& racing-green Ferraris tearing around
Brands Hatch
until the Seattle Prince in his military regalia
like the dandiest highwayman
the music pouring out of his fingers
finally reined it in just a little
now
gliding
riding
sliding
before loosing off again into even
more belligerent bursts
head-warping
scintillating
as the firefight over
Saigon continued
with the stars
displaced
& everywhere
the smell of a world
that is burning
as overhead the night
birds fly
Huey
Apache
Chinook
whooshing with
infinitely murderous
potential
as the rotor blades keep spinning
flattening the foot-high grass
as Lieutenant Troy McClory
comes running with a rolled-up
canvas stretcher
and Luke and Maddie Lynam, hysterical

with junked-up laughter
jump from the cabin
and run towards the wounded
men at the edge of the trees
as the lieutenant, blood flowing,
flowing from his neck
walks slowly towards
the helicopter
as a second helicopter skims
overhead
at the very last moment
Big Peter Hanlon
pulls the pin &
hurls a grenade
as he covers his ears
with Jimi wrenching
every inch of acid out
of his axe

&
just like Una
is doing now
watches the buildings
of the world
we thought we knew
in silent slow motion
already collapsing all around
him
& us.

In The Temple Of Mahavishnu
many years ago
when Southern Asia
burned and radio chatter
filled the air
a long way
from livestreams
webcams
& avian police
&
indeed
David Attenborough
& his

iguana *beag*.
Aye, his little wee impudent
reptile
who daily puts the run
on the *nimhe*
aye, the snakes.

A queer world surely
& no mistake
as Nano would say
domhan iontach ait
gan amhras.

I mean, like I was saying
who ever heard of
britches the
likeathat?

Honestly: Whistling Trousers
incandescent quavers
waltzing out of a pair of breeks
– in your wildest imaginings
could you ever
possibly
conceive
of
such
a
thing?

Because I don't think even Nano
would have paid much heed
to a silly old *pishogue* the like of that.
Another little birdie,
as Madame Snap-Jaw
Rutherford
might say
a likely tale indeed
she could conclude
before clipping along
down the corridor
in her little white shoes
the spit of *Mr Exu's*

ha ha
no I'm joking
because hers are more
chunky
clunky, even
standard medical issue
I should imagine.

Ah yes, *bah*! I can loudly hear
Nano scoff
at the very idea
of whistling trousers
pulling that black crocheted shawl
around her shoulders
hysterical at the likelihood
of such a thing ever taking place
but which, of course,
it had.
Although, admittedly,
not long after
that poor old Scotsman
he had given himself
a mild electric shock
trying, as he often did,
to wire the stereo
up to the light socket
the crazy cat
but then, he was always up
to wheezes the like of that
fixing things
trying to blag electricity
rewiring the system
to feed from the meter
next door
with some considerable
degree of success
it must be said.

But then, as we all know,
that young Scotsman

yes, good old Troy McClory
whenever he put his mind
to it properly
why the fellow could almost fix
absolutely everything
but when it came to women,
especially those.

Yes, more than anything, he liked to fix
na cailíni.
But you couldn't
at least wouldn't
have said that back then
no, not in those days
when women were referred to
as 'chicks' or one's 'lady'.
And, publicly at least, you preferred
to be seen to consider them in a
somewhat old-fashioned, perhaps,
but nonetheless respectful manner.

As you lay on some mattress
stroking their lovely bare buttocks
in this case those of my sister
whilst enjoying a nice, protracted
stinging toke
as you both examine an album cover
in profound detail
or engage in stoned Scrabble
as the rest of the tenants
go about their various bits of business.

Yes, Troy 'The Hammer'
as everyone knew
he was capable of repairing almost anything.
If anything went wrong in the building
they usually never bothered even
contacting the caretaker
no left that cranky old bastard
Moody Alex alone
& went straight away
without any further hesitation
right up to the top floor
where the brightest student

in all of Scotland
was in the process of
nibbling Una's toes and
chewing away at the backside
of
my
sister
yes, mo dheirfiúr deas dílis.

He was particularly good at mending fuses
but whenever it came to musical equipment
Troy really and truly was the last word.
But then, of course, it came as no surprise to anyone
whether in the rooms of 45 Brondesbury
or anywhere else
that this ought to have been the case
with him having spent such a
long time with his old friend Professor
Douglas McVittie
who had, more or less, been a physics
genius
& had taught him more or less
everything a young chap
could know about electronics.

& which is why, I suppose
that it came as such a shock to him
what happened that night.
that particular bank holiday weekend
when all the other tenants
had vacated the premises
& returned home to their various outposts
including Land's End, Exeter,
& even as far afield as
the Orkney Islands.

Which meant that there wasn't so
much as a single sound throughout the building.

Apart from the saxophone at the circus
in Queen's Park
which happened to be playing
'Welcome Home' by Peters & Lee

yes, come and cross our threshold
because this is your home
forever now
& in here you'll find
everything ever in your life
that you dreamed of.

Una loved that tune
he knew because she had acquainted
her new lover
of the fact many times
while they were lying there together
& although he'd felt like
bursting out laughing
because it was such a stupid piece
of old sentimental *raiméis*
he didn't
out of pity

as he stroked her hair
and listened to her as she confided:
It reminds me, I don't know quite why
of the heartbreaking, lonely pain of my life, Troy.

What she'd been referring to
of course
was the day
she'd been placed in the orphanage
in Wolverhampton
but Troy Mr Fixit
he wasn't really listening
being much too busy
leafing through
the pages of a children's comic
& laughing his head off
at all the adverts in the back

Before rolling over
& saying to her
stark naked
I wonder could you get me this for a present?
For my birthday, you reckon?

It stung me
having to listen to that
yes, you figure you might possibly
be in a position to fork out a

couple of your hard-earned pennies
for the purpose of procuring
one of these for old Hammer Man
Troy McClory?

It was a baseball glove he was talking about
as he went on to describe in great detail
the stitching
& the soft pliable quality
of the polished calf leather
& telling her just how much he had
wanted to have one of them as a boy.

When I used to go down to Mr McVittie's shop,
he explained
with whom I used to enjoy such fabulous discussions.
O, about all sorts of wonderful things! Troy went
        on
& you could tell by her expression
that poor old Una, our silly billy Nunie
that she really was entirely & quite
hopelessly entranced.
As her lover proceeded,
yes, that old Mr McVittie
and myself – we were quite a team! he
told her.
Yes, you had to hand it to
that old Douglas
there was just nothing he didn't know!

He rolled another joint & swept back
his great big lion's mane of hair
with his eyes moistening up as he sighed
at the reminiscence
as Una McNunie
silly billy that she was
she continued to marvel
at the startling exactitude of
his recall.

I have to tell you this, that old Douglas
used to always say to me, elaborated Troy,
that your destiny
young McClory, is to become a
world-famous scientist.
And which I have to say, Una my love
I actually did consider quite seriously for some
time – before being admitted to The Slade, to study art.
I'm glad you did, replied my sister
for I love your paintings
I love them so much
really and truly can't bring myself to tell you
because words fail me.
One of his paintings was entitled: *Mahavishnu.*
'I got the inspiration from John McLaughlin and his band,' he
informed her, 'after I went to see them one night – a couple
of weeks before you and I met. You familiar with The
Rainbow, babe?'
And Una 'Nunie' Fogarty nodded again, even more eagerly
this time.
Confirming that she did – know it, I mean.
The Rainbow.
And all the other places that he mentioned – including The
Roundhouse and Dingwall's, not forgetting the legendary
Marquee, where of course he was familiar with the owner.
He had just been to The Roundhouse to see Arthur Brown –
The Crazy World Of.

Mind-blowing, he said.
But then, of course, 'Art', as he called him, always was.
Una's eyes rolled back in her head.
Tell me more about Mr McVittie, she requested.
And on he went.
We even used to talk about such concepts as invisibility, he said –
laughing as he did so.
We were going to make a cloak of our own – and wander around
Edinburgh, spying on all our neighbours.
An invisibility cloak, laughed my sister, why that's something else.
She was even beginning to talk like him now.
As she lay right back in his arms and told him again how much she
loved him and was glad that he wasn't invisible.
'I know you are, Lady Ocean,' he murmured, 'I can see
by the look in your eyes that that's the case.'

And I think, looking back, that for me, perhaps, that was what
represented the very last straw.
Yes, the final one, I'm afraid, I'm sorry to have to say.

As Troy McClory fell back and drifted into an initially
pleasant slumber
where he found himself confronted by the sight of
the avuncular Mr Douglas McVittie
alias 'The Prof'
working away into the night
in his garden shed
humming away to the tune of 'Annie Laurie'
which was the one that 'Hammer' McClory remembered most
vividly of all.
Then what does he see
only himself as a boy
at the bottom of Professor McVittie's garden
toiling away at a canvas
effected in the familiar and now popular
style of Roger Dean
with a great big green pterodactyl
emerging from the top left-hand corner
with a wingspan so vast that it almost blocked out the sun.
but then, sad to say
found himself looking down
having been disturbed yet again
by who else only that great big dew-eyed
lump who went by the name of Una Fudgy
Wudgy Fudgy
gazing up abjectly
& and asking him all sorts of irritating questions.
What brushes are you using, what species of bird is that.
But that, if he had only bothered to give it some consideration, was
because there simply didn't seem to be anything left inside of my
poor little innocent sister's mind that she hadn't already gone and
shared with 'Mr Fixit'.
And whose face she was still dwelling on as she made her way
northward that very same morning towards Middlesbrough,
where she would remain for a few days
with the contract cleaning firm she worked for.
For his part, Troy hadn't bothered going into college – preferring to
lie there as a means of getting rid of his hangover and his somewhat
understandably fuzzed and fucked-up head.
He groaned and turned over, smiling as he thought of her

remarks – all those daft, incessant questions – so innocuous.
Instinctively, he found himself reaching under the pillow for his
smokes – before, suddenly, becoming privy to what, initially at
least, was a muffled and somewhat indistinct sound, albeit close by.
Before it gradually began to increase in volume – until, hilariously,
he realised what its actual source was – a bird, for heaven's sake,
trapped underneath his discarded britches.
His precious blue Oxford bags – so admired by poor old Fudge.
And which he now shook out, before releasing the swallow – for
that's what it was
from its fluttering captivity
out into the bright blue yonder,
through the open window of the bedroom.

As he sat on the edge of the bed, lighting up a joint
wondering, somewhat aimlessly, might it make a good subject for a
song.
My little swallow
swallow can you fly
to freedom can you make your way…

Having decided it was a little
too much like 'Blackbird'
by the Beatles
& Paul McCartney
being somewhat startled & taken aback
when he heard the sound of a *knocking* of some kind
which appeared to be coming from
behind the wardrobe door.
'Who's that?' he called out, puzzled because
he wasn't yet stoned. 'Is that you, Una?'

How could it be, he snorted, shaking his head
because she would be halfway to Middlesbrough by
now.
Is that you, he repeated.
Una…?
It was still quite dark so he tried the light switch, but it
wouldn't work.
I must fix that, said Mr Fixit.
Yes, I must remember to fix that, he repeated.
As he flung the door of the wardrobe open

only to find – he couldn't believe it!
the tattered old remnant of:
an American baseball glove!

Where on earth could that have possibly
come from? he wondered
because he hadn't remembered ever seeing it before.
Man, but it was funny – I really do have to admit
& say that.
As I stood there, looking over his shoulder
& felt like tapping him on the cheek once or
twice.
But nothing was funnier than him
acting as if he wasn't perturbed
there were even tears in his eyes
for heaven's sake
och, Troy, ye cod ye, he exclaimed aloud
ye'll hae to ease up a wee bit on the *ganj*

as he reached down, lifting it up &
stroking its chapped and weathered leather,
acknowledging how much he liked
its shape, the suppleness
& the soft yielding texture of the worn brown fabric.
It was almost, in fact, as if he was back there
leafing through all the mags
in Mr McVittie's imaginative wonderland
his tobacco-smelling fragrant emporium.
Mr McVittie's Morningside shop.
Where he used to love reading the *Valiant* comic
especially The Steel Claw
which was where, he assumed,
his particular little 'head-picture'
had come out of right this minute
so colourful and real, inside his mind.
O man, he repeated, this really is far out.
It's way too much, he said, as he continued
to stroke the bashed calf-leather object in his hands.
Only to discover, upon momentarily looking
down that, in fact, it was no longer there!
With both hands open – but
bewilderingly, now containing nothing.
And that was when I made a little form
of identification

electing to warn him, as best I, civilly, could
that if he ever so much as laid a hand
on my sister again
or even went near her
that I'd…
well, I wasn't in a position,
not as yet, to
tell him what.

But it was more than enough to make him blanch
and to do so severely, as a matter of fact
a whiter shade of pale
as he might indeed have put it himself
'I'm sorry,' I whispered, stepping forward into the
light, 'I don't expect you to understand.'
The Little Old Man Of The Barn, we're called
sometimes.
'I never do anticipate any form of understanding,
Troy,' I explained.
Impressively, he wasn't seen to flinch.
No, he didn't flinch.
But that may have been because he was stone-cold
numb.
Ró-mhairbhiteach, as Nano would have put it.
To such an extent that even the slightest of
movements would, likely as not, have been
quite impossible.
Because there are just some things that even
wonderboys cannot fix.

Then, when he looked again, I was gone
& what did he see
lying there between his feet?

Yes, the baseball glove
the very exact same as he remembered
it, as a boy.

Back at the ranch here in Cliftonville
the very latest is
that Una my beloved
she has recently been considering
the inclusion of an excerpt
in her show
from a popular farce
current during the period
with which we are concerned
& entitled
if you happen to remember
around the 'Troy' time
No Sex Please, We're British
& I'd suggested to her maybe
we, she, should consider Sexy Lexy
Gordon
for some role
seeing as he would be absolutely
perfect for the play
if we could find him
if he happens to be still alive
only what does she go and say to me then
looking right at me in naked contempt
& utter disgust
I thought I told you
I thought I told you
you effing fool
I've already allocated
that part to Mike Yarwood
& before I can say anything
by way of response
I look up & realise
that my sister
she's already left
& is sitting over on
the window seat
beside the library
reading the exact same page of script
over & over & over again
as she dabs her eyes
crying out her poor little heart
it would help of course
if you knew what it was she
was weeping about

but most of the time
like a lot of folks
hereabouts in Cliftonville
in actual fact
she doesn't.

Anyhow, no matter what she says
I do think I'm right
about Alex being her man
although I can see straight away
why she might not be interested
because that old Moody Lexy Gordon
he really could be an irascible and
contrary individual.
Although, from his point of view,
considering what he had to put up with
from 'that crew' over in Brondesbury
particularly the women
was it any wonder
any bloody wonder he would say

even down to phone calls in the middle of the night.
which was true.
regarding recent 'disturbances' of course

what else
most notably, in his case
from Joanne Kaplan
who, as he knew, like
The Duchess Tanith,
as he had christened her,
was no stranger to late-night parties
and as well as that was a hair-trigger
emotionally
with her open sandals and great big sweeping
floor-length dresses
give you the pip so she would
– always blathering out of her,
Alex thought, brag brag brag.
Nearly as bad as his commanding officer
in The Sigs,
during the time

he had spent in Aden
which was as close as the
King Of The Blitz
could get to a proper war
& whom he had taken his share
of shit from
& so hardly was going to allow himself
to be intimidated
by yet another overeducated middle-class
diva
some hippy dolly the likes of Miss Joanne
bleeding Kaplan
or any other would-be revolutionary dreamer
who happened to 'crash' in The Mahavishnu
bloody Temple.
He hadn't been overly impressed by the manner
in which she'd decorated her apartment
either,
transforming, in the circumstances,
a perfectly well-appointed
room into something resembling an Indian
ashram.
Which he didn't object to, really – remaining
mindful that times, as they always had been, were
changing, and that he would have to move along
with them.
But then why all the fuss when he had asked
her for not one single thing other than the
tiniest of little pecks on the cheek?

& o then, all of sudden
all this talk of sharing
& 'hanging loose'
had suddenly & mysteriously
seemed to evaporate.
& Duchess Kaplinski – for all her dancing
around the flat in the nude,
she had turned to be the very exact blooming
same.
Especially that night before 'it' had
happened – when, directly after yet another
blistering argument with his wife Vonnie,
he had found himself summoned once more
from his bed in Northolt

across the city to No. 45 Brondesbury
for the exact same reason as per
usual
& by the same urgent & agitated voice.
Whose owner had met him, ashen-faced,
in the hallway – standing there blurting out all
kinds of hopelessly unintelligible
rubbish.

Before racing on ahead of him and flinging the
door of her apartment open, breaking down in
tears as she once more appealed for help
with an even greater
vehemence.
However, just as before,
he could make little sense of what she
was saying,
or trying to.
What kind of sounds, he pressed her
exasperatedly
Furniture moving, she confided hoarsely
& what sounded like a table being knocked
over.
Or perhaps an armoire.
A-*what*? he said, but she had already moved
on – shifting from this spot to the next as she
shredded a Kleenex tissue in her hands.
O God, she stammered, o my fucking God,
covering her chest in the middle of it all
having caught him in the act
of enjoying the briefest, fleeting glance.
Christ Jesus, groaned Miss Kaplan.
Madam, thought the caretaker,
a prude for all her talk.
Just the very same as her
friend, Tanith Kaplinski
for hadn't Alex Gordon
seen her himself
o yes, many times, through
the tiny fissure he'd discovered
quite by chance in the wall –
a cherry-sized aperture
one which had lit Miss Tanith

Kaplinski beautifully, whenever she'd
perform her private, solitary dance.
Attired in that swooshingly voluminous
orange-and-red dressing gown of hers
acting as if she was some
kind of extraordinary magic human bird.
Les Oiseaux Dans La Charmille, the
performance was called.
Cor, those bristols, Alex used to think
as he twitched in his hiding place
behind the wall
but none of that was in any way relevant now
as he sighed and
followed her friend, Joanne.
Wondering how on earth he could ever have
properly fancied her
or even bothered to ask her for a peck.
Much less give her one.
I heard the sound of laughter, Joanne said.
Yes, the sound of laughter – I heard it, after the
noise.
I see, said Alex.
Assuring her that he'd look into it.
Something else – like the sound of a drum, she
stammered.
The sound of a drum? the caretaker said.
Like a beating drum sounding – that's what I
heard.
A tom-tom.
A tom-tom, uh-huh, he repeated
writing it down.
Before repeating once more:
I'll definitely look into it.

And, at the time, had definitely meant it.
But whether he had or not, what with the marital
troubles he and his spouse of twenty-five years,
Vonnie, had been experiencing, he didn't get around to
doing anything in the end.

Not that it really mattered, considering that only a brief two days later,
he was on the receiving end of another nocturnal telephone call – but
with a convincing note of urgency about it this time, from one of the
layabouts, a longhaired Scottish artist who rarely saw water
wouldn't have known it
if you'd upended the twat in a barrel of it.
You've got to come over, Troy McClory urged.
So Alex Gordon called a taxi and succeeded in arriving in
less than three-quarters of an hour.
Paying the cabbie, he looked at his watch and saw that it was
approaching six thirty-two a.m.
On the cobblestones of the courtyard, he could make out the
shape of a body covered over by a sheet.
It was Tanith.
A knot of spectators stood huddled above her – gazing
upwards to the open upstairs window, where a light gauze
curtain was billowing outwards.
And it was then, for the first time, really, that Alex Gordon
realised how damp his forehead actually was.
Before finally, with the deepest reluctance, raising his head to
once more appraise the wide-open window
only now noticing the outline of her form, imprinted on the
shattered glass portico through which she'd fallen – in what
was soon to be established as a suicide.

Not that,
& I am very keen to
point this out
this is in any way
to suggest,
his appetites & weaknesses
notwithstanding,
that
moody Alex Gordon
was in any way
to blame for what happened

at least
not
entirely

even if there
can be no denying

that when Tanith &
Joanne
got together to practise
their movements
(often as not in the nude)
rehearsals which were
dominated by spare piano arrangements
– with Tanith's pianoforte excellence
being admirably complemented by
her friend's warm & languid voice
Les Oiseaux Dans La Charmaille –
Mr Alex Gordon was always to be found
loitering nearby
watching
breathing
sometimes behind the
skirting
observing through his
spyhole
in livid tumescence
so, obviously, being
ladies
& possessed
of certain instincts
regarding such things
his behaviour was not
without some degree
of significance

Even if nothing
had ever been proved
ah yes
it's sad thinking back on it
her poor young body
lying there in the rain
of early morning
& her with all her life
yet before her.
It's sad
the way
things have to work
out
& if only there were some way
to turn the clock back

then, believe you me,
I would gladly do it
may my heart cease to beat
if for one second
I play you false,
God knows.

Because, even after all
of these years that we've spent
together here in
Cliftonville
with my poor sister, God love her, in and out
of who knows how many institutions
being to this very day
still visited
by dread remembrances of one sort or
another
as were the tenants of The Temple
back then in No. 45
Joanne Kaplan in particular
especially one lunchtime
not long after her best friend's
suicide
when she had arrived home
early from college
& found herself confronted
by a scene of what can only
be described as one of
unutterable chaos

with great streaks
of jam smeared all along
the flock wallpaper
& random clothes flung
around and books with their pages
torn out
hurled indiscriminately
about the floor
not to mention
her mattress completely torn asunder
& her treasured,

most favourite china cabinet
thoughtlessly overturned.
Such sobs she released as she
sat there in that chair – and, convinced
that she'd just heard
a falsetto peal of mocking
laughter
looked across the room
for her moist eyes to descry –
absolutely nothing.

Faic, as Nano would say.

At least until I found myself
unable any longer to resist
the nagging temptation…
Why do little birds whistle?
That's a question that
you'll often hear posed.
Maybe, just simply,
because at the end of the day
they have to.

In any case, there she remained,
barely able to move a muscle
as I released a sharp little
arpeggio of notes
but which possessed a strange
sound.
One evocative of that which the spinner
makes when turning her wheel
now near – now distant
the song of the dream-bird
whose velvety flight haunts the clearings at an
indeterminate hour.

Yes, a wee birdie piping
on a window ledge, warmly
liberating itself
of a vital plenitude that it simply can
no longer contain.
Ti-ti-pu, *ti-ti-pu*: can you hear
me, Joanne Kaplan
come

over
here
come
close
to the wall.
There's a good girl
easy now
easy
aisy
aisy
aisy
now,
lass
hush there, alanna
there's a good girl
it's all OK
it's you and me
oh Lord blessus
would you look at you now
& you all abashed
as a girleen in your nipper tuck
sure, I'm only making
game of you so I am
with the pair of us soon to be yarnin'
& enjoying maybe even
a biteen of a snuggle
maybe even a little pogue!
yes, a sweet little kiss
& them all there wringing
their hands and keening
where have they
gone
where could they be gone
ah lookit here girl
don't you be going
all colleen-style flush
come over here, gentle
so I can give you a hug
yes, there we are
there we are now
it's
just you
&
me

&
with the two of us
smiling
as you
come to me
and I hold you close
aye, taking you in my arms
& I wonder
how do you like her now
your lovely, blue-eyed
girl
Mr Death?

Luke Powys it was
who found her later
that very same afternoon,
making no sense
& frothing at the mouth.
He heard things too –
things he never spoke of –
alarums & such like,
unique scatologies,
warring souls,
that, in their pain,
have turned on themselves.

As I'd so often seen happen
& remember with startling
clarity
like that night, God be good to it,
when I'd arrived back
on the late-night bus
to The Spike, a men's dossing-house,
& which, at that time, was situated
in Camden
aye, arriving back to find the place in chaos,
with this pair of lousy beggars
Con Colleran and Mickey 'The Gawp'
Divney
being right in the middle of a rumble
with The Colchester Robbers, as this
other brace of brigands were famously known
at the time.

& with Colleran, in particular,
making it abundantly clear
that he was in no 'fucking hurry at all to
back away from a ruck'.

And that, before he ever did,
or had any 'fucking intention at all'
of 'going anywhere fucking near his *leaba*'
he would be more than willing to smash the
head aye and the back and bones and any other
part as might be necessary, of any fuck-robber
that had ever come out of Galway
or anywhere else, if it came to that.
With a right old barney starting up after that
until in the end they succeeded in
mollifying him
& a bit of an auld *ceilidh*
began to raise the rafters
which was often the case in The Spike after
a scrap.

So off I skipped and got the old
bodhrán
& away we all went
as I struck my iron-tipped brogues on the flags:

There was an auld man down by Killiburn Brae
Riteful, titeful, titty folday
There was an auld man down by Killiburn Brae
had a curse of a wife with him most of his days!
        With me folderol do, titty fol dol
        Foldol dol dolda doler olday!

Rumpity-pumpity
Schwish, ba-boom!

Sawing and stomping until we were rudely
interrupted.
& looked up to see
the fearsome *phizzogue* of The Priest O'Donnell

with the two eyes standing out blazing
in his head

as he faced us
standing, with *the trimmlins*,
there in his long grey nightshirt

& o how did he weep
& bawl as he raised his fist
& him with the pages of
Christ opened up there before him
o´
you cunts
bad cess
to all of them
as ever dreamed
about you or raised you

Why, the birds, do they bother to sing
to alert us maybe,
& sound all alarums
with regard to the
preponderance of shameless blasphemers
the likes of this
the cur-dogs that, daily, elect to stride
among us in this world
just as they did on a hill beyond Jerusalem
beneath the rusted copper skies above Calvary
bringing *náire* like the Romans
casting lots for the garments of The Saviour
as among the trees a riot commenced
in its heart the cries of wanton birds –
lamenting the sorry pass of our country
and its kin, the low depths to
which it has descended.
So would it be any wonder that
any day now, just as it did on
that final, fateful morning,
that they'd show their face upon
the mountain once again
those unclean *éiníní* who
scout & warn of
impending famine and martyrdom
that red dragon, that lone pale horse
those guardian cherubs but who
now have the blood of the lamb
on their lips. Now atremble,

as the panther spreading out its wings
like those of the eagle
he emits his mighty, earth-shattering
roar and declares both to you
and all of your misbegotten issue
yes, let ye hear the sound of the trumpet
before this dawn which
is fast now approaching, you find
yourselves plunged into darkness
before the moon, and hopelessly
stand upon this hill as you
behold your crops and they failing
before your eyes
as fire flows and consumes
the very surface of the water
as this last mighty angel, he
sprouts horns and then vouchsafes
Behold The Sorrowful, Atrophying
Kidneys Of Christ And All That
Remains Of Erin-In-Her-Waste
behold him too, punctured and ruptured
as he slumps
like a pierced, traduced *baste* slung there
upon his crosstree because of you
to name your shame, *sin é an fáth*!
That is the reason that they pine in the heavens
those winged angels
because of you and all your sins!

We thought, in the extremity of his passion,
that at that very moment, he was surely
about to drop.
But, somehow, he rallied.

So, goodnight to you all – and, by the bowels of he who
made you
may each and every one of you standing before me
here
this night perish on your pillows as you cry in
misery for the oils of a priest
as he lifts his skirts
& tears across the fields
except that, you see:

he
    will
        not

           come.

Speaking of death, our very own mother
in her turn
did exactly that
in 1954, as I was telling you,
and I really would like
to be
able to say
that
poor old Doreen
– 'Dots' Fogarty
as she was affectionately known –
aged 40
that she was
what you would
describe as
solid and matronly
not unlike our custodian
Margaret Rutherford
but she wasn't, in fact
no, that wouldn't be true
at all
at all.
No sir.

Although if she had lived, I still retain
hopes
that that is possibly how she might have ended up
instead of becoming a fragile little thing
slinking around the place

as though afraid she had done something terrible.
Because that's the way she was
literally terrified of her own narrow shadow
and to suggest anything else
anything would be just to make up
yet another of Nano's silly 'old pishogues',
more little birdies
digressive hoodwinkings
none of which, as I'm sure you've guessed,
are true.

But, regarding poor Dots
our very own dear old departed mother
is it any bit of wonder
that the poor unfortunate lady
God be good to her
that she could have been
any way other
than the way she was
and her having had to endure trials in her life
as no mortal on this earth should have to
put up with.

& which I probably wouldn't
have referred to at all
or bothered my head
bringing up in any way
only Una said this morning
that she'd been tossing
& turning all night
in her sleep
with this dream she'd had
all about Dots
and the days when she'd
lived as a young woman
in London
& that in this dream
our old friend
Bonnie from Currabawn
she'd been playing a lament
on the violin
that'd be Bonnie,
Red Jack Sugrue's daughter

who was a wizard on the instrument
& used to charm the auld birds
with it, from the trees
as well as making every man-jack
as ever sank a pint in The Bedford Arms
swear they'd get themselves wed to her in the morning
you see if I don't
with the only difference being
that Red Jack's daughter
she loved women, do you see
& didn't have all that much
time for men
not in that way, anyhow.
O, the curls on that lovely girleen
they used to say
aye, men and women alike they
used to remark on it
as she swept her bow
why, this way, & then that
that it'd make you think of a flock of
birds itself.

With her maybe getting everyone
well way overexcited
because that, as I recall,
was the very same night
that Maddie Lynam,
God rest her soul
(long since deceased, in a car crash
in Italy, outside Naples)
who had also stayed at 45
on any number of occasions
& never complained of anything untoward
now awoke in the night
being short-taken
&
going off to have a piddle
when what did she see
half in shadow
or so she said
when she was going
to the bathroom
only the suspended figure of our
very own mother

still attired in her assistant nurse's
uniform
yes, none other than poor Dots Fogarty
herself
who had spent some time
in that very same
room
hanging there, unmoving
from a bare wooden rafter
with a few drops of *fuil*
yes, the darkest of blood
falling ever so slowly

ploc!
they went
& then
ploc
again
ploc!
ploc!
ploc!

& such a scream as poor Maddie
Lynam let out of her
when one of the droplets
say, about the size of an old Irish
sixpence
didn't it land smack
dab in the middle of
her forehead
yes, right in the
centre
that it was like nothing on earth
that ever you have heard
is all could say
– as regards poor Maddie's scream, I mean.
Wake the dead.

And how did all this
come about
do you ask
for to make me little

more than an obstetrical *hembridge*
going ploc ploc ploc

what exactly happened
far away in
the long ago
to make all this sadness
& madness come to pass
because make no mistake
ba bhrónach é, cinnte
it certainly was sad.

Anyhow, to make a long story
short
God bless ye all, if you're listening,
you patient old craythurs
what happened
do you see,
wasn't it that Doreen 'Dots'
late in 1953
she encountered this *latchyco*
(that is to say, an irresponsible,
if charming, rascal)
after drinking most of the day and
a goodly part of the night in

Nano's
yes, she met this fellow
who went by the name of
Slack Port-au-Prince
Or Slack John Timmoney
as they called him in The Bedford
a sailor, rarely home,
a high seas wanderer o
a rare fellow too
cagey, talking out of
both sides of his face
a rum *currahanach* indeed
which means restless soul
& one to be wary of
but poor Dots was tipsy
& what would she care about
that or anything more than
the liking that she'd taken

to his jet-black curls
and cheeky smile
& agreed, in the heat of the moment,
to perform the mickey-jump-jubbly
with him in an alley just off
the Commercial Road
yes, got stuck in enjoying a spot
of that good old:
ruaille
buaille
No Sex Please, We're British?
Not 'arf!

& which she definitely
most certainly
had enjoyed at the time
but then, as so often happens
& will continue to do so
sight nor sign of him was
ever seen again in spite
of all his talk about setting
up home
& there being no place
like your own fireside
with Dots, for a while, being
employed in St Mary's Hospital
in Paddington as an assistant nurse.
But no,
not anymore
no longer after that
when she discovered there
was a little *babogue* growing inside of her
and, because of that,
in fury at what had been done to her
she started to take against all
that went by the name of
living babbies
& which was the reason that she
pulled out all the plugs
& all the infants nearly
got kilted
well, eight of them anyway
except that they were somehow

saved in time
by another vigilant
member of staff
who somehow knew
that skinny Dots Fogarty
no, she
wasn't the girl
she had been
at all
& certainly would never be
now
after that
most especially when they said
she would
have to go to court
so Doreen Dotsy she hadn't really much to lose
at least that was how
she herself saw it
after buying a little trousers
& jacket for her babbie
yes, a wee pair of *bríste*
& the loveliest little pair of brogues
she would sit there at night
just staring at them
in the attic
laid out like the babogue
was alive
&, just by coincidence,
in the very same room
yes, the very same place
where all of the *ruaille buaille*
got started
in The Temple
at No. 45 Brondesbury Gardens
much much much much later on
in the late summer of 1974
to be exact.

But, long before that,
as Dots knelt by her bedside
coming close to
midnight
on that occasion in the year 1954
folding her fingers

around the one single thing
of value that she possessed
a small holy medallion
a miraculous medal
which she had bought
& brought back from
a trip to Lourdes
& always
without fail
wore on a string of blue wool
underneath her white cotton vest
like a good girl should
as her mother had instructed her
O Maria Concepta sine peccato qui
ad te confugimus
O Mary conceived without sin
pray for us who have recourse
to thee
entwined with the scapular of her
beloved St Anthony.
Of which it was said
that none who died wearing it
should suffer eternal fire
with it being nothing less than a
salvation & a safeguard in perils,
a covenant of peace
a pledge of his special protection
ha ha ha
until the end of time
her precious St Anthony.

He whose name,
in actual fact,
was the very last one
that she spoke on this earth
yes, the very last words
before, astride two chairs,
emitting a somewhat regretful cry
or a peal, more like,
she flung herself forward
blindly into the dawn.

& what was left of her child
her little *babogue*

namely *mise,*
myself in otherwords,
I regret to have to concede
came slowly
dripping out of her body
her womb, yes,
going
ploc
ploc
ploc
& then
ploc
again
as she kept on swaying
tick tock tick tock
to
&
fro
going *ploc*
ploc
ploc
the whole night
long.

It is said the first leprechauns
were the greatest of harpists
& that it was they
who taught the early
bards of Ireland
their skills & music
but nowadays, like myself,
they are more at home
with the fiddle or the Irish pipes
also, of course, they are known
as great drummers
percussionists, aye

the very same as I am
myself
late at night
behind the skirting
after I've had
a skinful of porter.

Rumpheda-baum!
that'd be the sound
that the bodhrán makes
the handmade goatskin drum
which beats time to slip-jigs,
reels & hornpipes
& which, according to Nano
at any rate
was the very same noise
that was heard by The Monsignor
Padna
who was the man most responsible
for chasing the poor, hopelessly
innocent Fogartys long ago
forever from the village
of sweet Currabawn
the lousy bastard
& such a racket as he'd heard
that morning
in the quiet of his confessional
rumpheda-baum
& it starting up
getting worse & worse
thumping and thudding
till he nearly lost
his mind
vacating the soft velvet
darkness of his booth
& flinging the
door of his confession box
open
roaring, in the grip of terror
& all-consuming trepidation
come out you wicked devil
for I'm the man'll have you.
Don't think I'm not!
Only to discover there was no one

there
for to make goatskin *baums* or
any other type of repetitive noise
either
so it was no wonder that the priesteen
he'd be a little bit embarrassed
& he going the roads to the presbytery
that same night
filling himself a *gloine of fuisce*
yes, a mighty big glass of strongest
uisquebaugh
which saw him safely off into
the land of waiting slumber
at least for a while
until what did he do in
the middle of his *brionglóid*
yes, right in the middle of his
scarlet vivid, bright-blue
dream
didn't he start
stuttering over the Latin
incantations
& knocking over candles
before hauling the starched
linen altar cloth towards him
tossing over everything
till, glory be to God,
didn't he look down at his *stomick*
which was beginning to give him pain
& see that he was growing this belly
it was moving
and then he started
to scream
as inside this *bolg* it made this
muffled beating
yes, this thumping sound
which followed him all the
way down along the centre aisle
going
rumpheda-baum
landing him smack dab dead
in the middle of the churchyard
lawn
with his ageing pins

spread out like dividers
help me! he pleaded, but
instead of doing that
everyone was running away
screaming
& it wasn't any wonder
when you think about it
when they saw what it was
that was lying there on the grass
& just what had
tumbled out of his
abdomen onto the green
nothing only
a new-born leveret and
it there writhing in its
slobbering liquescence
before, all of a sudden,
shooting bolt upright
with its two ears up
as stiff
as pokers
with one eye swivelling
up the Currabawn road
& the other still and glassy
inclining towards Moondice
yes, a great big pussens of
a thing
so it was
& it scraking like a bird
Cuntspawkus, it screeched,

Cuntspawkus, skree!
like a bronze statue raised
in the middle of his wound
right in the middle of the
bewildered padre's *bolg*
that is to say
his now unswollen stomach.

Rumpheda-baum!
Rumpheda-baum!
Pa-rumpheda-bumpheda
Rumpheda-baum!

Yes, the very same sound as had been
reported by Joanne Kaplan
on the very same night
Tanith Kaplinski had died
issuing, she swore, from the
other side of the wall
behind the skirting
pounding & pounding & pounding
as it groaned:

Inside of the wall,
inside of the wall!
pounding the boords
& then back to the wall!

Followed by the X-ray echo of the
searing, soaring jig
once so vigorously performed
in The Bedford
by the legendary daughter,
Bonnie Sugrue,
of Red Jack.
Ta-rumpedy bumpedy
Bonnie & her bow!
Aye, Bonnie & her bow!
Ta-rumpedy-bumpedy
Bonnie & her bow!

Ta rumpedy bumpedy
Red Bonnie's bow
Rumpedy pumpedy
Red Bonnie's bow!

Och, howareye *childre*! was
Red Bonnie's catchphrase.
You would hear her a mile away
coming bounding up the stairs.
But Bonnie Sugrue, unlike
her father,
she was far
from forward

or abrasive
being the highest
& sweetest nut in the wood
as her own father called her

So
was it really any wonder
yes, was it likely to
come as any surprise
that the Welsh potter
Luke Powys
that he, the poor fellow,
that, in spite of himself,
he would fall completely
head-over-heels in love
with the same colleen
Bonnie *álainn*
the lovely Bonnie
Luke who was himself a very
good musician
yes, as fine a percussionist as
had ever made his way up to London
from the valleys
& who would delight in conversing
till the small hours with her
aye, & in Welsh to boot
which she spoke proficiently
along with Gaelic

as they squatted there, cross-legged
on yet another of the grubby mattresses
beating away at his hand-drum
lathered and showered in sweat
as his wild matted hair flew all around him
and he walloped the goatskin
again
&
again
trying his best not to let her catch
not to let her catch
not to let her catch him
God love him
staring hopelessly into her eyes.

Because that old Luke Of The Valleys
as I say
he was madly in love with Red Jack's daughter

& would, without thinking
have happily married her in the morning
heck, who knew
maybe even have a bunch of kids with the lady.

It was often said that
they invented Celtic Rock
her & him.
Incidentally, it was my sister
who had specially woven the
traditional Irish cloth belt, called a
crios,
which Luke
had recently taken to
displaying,
somewhat ostentatiously
acting out the role
of the Celtic psychic
cosmonaut from the hills.
Encouraged in such tendencies
by the full-bearded
Eastern wanderer with the
glossy black corkscrew curls,
Big Peter from Dundalk,
chaser of poppies among the
Afghan hills
at all hours arriving
on the doorstep of 45
just like now
bleary-eyed with his haversack
raggedly attired in his
long scarf and balding ermine
coat
wheezing '*hi!*' to whoever
it was
might have admitted him

before starting into the tales
of his exotic peregrinations
flipping a joint
in one hand with impressive
expertise, running his tongue along
the gumline
with his jeans tucked into his
new hand-tooled leather boots
which he'd been given, he said,
on the way to Karachi
starting to laugh as he exhaled
twin plumes of smoke
'I'm Pazuzu
the auld man from Karachi!'
he chuckled
sighing as he shook his head
and went on passing the
jay around
you wanna have met this guy
– his own mother I kid you not,
dropped a trip into her Horlicks, he did.
And, man, the next thing you know
she's heading off
to Mass
& what does she hear
leaping six feet in the air
so she is
for what is she hearing
only this blackbird perched in the fork of
a tree
shouting out after her
'Hey, you, lady – get back here at once!'
whistling its heart out
this little birdie.

The very same as Big Peter
was doing now
smoking away until
they were all so exhausted
that not so much as one of
them even woke up
to see Troy McClory
investigating the commotion
what had sounded like a wardrobe

filled with bricks
coming
bumpeda
bumpeda
down
the stairs
yes
one
two
three
four
steps
after the other

but in spite of all his
searching
succeeding in finding
nothing there.
With the rest of them,
at breakfast
in the
beer garden in Willesden,
of course,
every Sunday
where they'd gone
to meet Stu The Dealer
already
beginning to start up again
with Big Peter drumming
his fingers on the table
to the rhythm of
'What Are You Doing Sunday?'
baby baby baby, he whooped
as Tanith, even louder, waved her
great big floppy hat above her head
as, with gay abandon, she declared:
Because we are getting out of our
heads!

Leading to what was the funniest
hallucination, if that's what you
want to call it
when Frank 'Blind Owl'

just as soon they got back
he went out to the kitchen to get some
sugar
there encountered the tiger-striped
tabby from No. 53
just resting his head
on his paws
next to the fridge
with those great big eyes
and that wicked, impish grin
mewing to Frank
who stood there, open-mouthed
swaying in the doorway
'Tell me this, my friend Frank Olson,
how would this appeal to you –
your arsecrack in place of
a caubeen on your head?
Because that's what is coming
that is what's gonna happen
if you think for
a second
about fucking with
Fritz The Cat!
Know what I'm saying, Blind
Owl, baby?
Because I sure do hope so!'

Which explained
why Troy
having arrived into
the kitchen
for the purposes of investigation
came upon his flatmate
arguing with 'The Main Man Fritz'
in the most reasonable and rational
of tones
wagging his finger
telling him that he was
a 'very freakin' naughty pusscat, man!'
before collapsing into
hysterical laughter
lying, foetally crouched,
underneath the kitchen table,
in a high-pitched shriek

repeating 'your arsehole for a hat!'
A mantra which saw Troy also,
not surprisingly,
dissolving right there beside him
beating his fists on the old
torn carpet
as o man o man, they kept on
saying
before everyone arrived to find
out what was happening
& the whole place became
House Of Unbridled
& Uproarious, Happy Laughter!

Many years later
long after any of this
Red Bonnie played support for
the London Irish band *The Pogues*
in The Mean Fiddler venue in Harlesden.
I saw them there myself in actual fact,
in the early days, when they'd gone
by the name *Poguemahone*, ha ha,
if you can believe that!

With Bonnie, God love her, giving as good as
she got
virtuosically delivering
among others –
'The Rakes Of Mallow',
'The Smile Of The Moon'.
Or my own personal favourite,
'The Sorrows Of Currabawn'.

with the latter
of course
never actually being performed
in reality
but whose sentiments & rhythm
have always been ever-present
in my blood
they really have

because, ah boys,
whenever you think of them
all those sorrows and longings of Currabawn
aye and Killiburn too
in its own way even worse
what with the way it abandoned us in the end
with the way it left
me and my poor unfortunate
sibling, lovely Una.

With something which ought
to have been so happy,
uncomplicated and simple
ending up bitter & filled
with disagreements
recriminations which have pursued
us
right down, even,
to this very day.

O! They say that
the women
are worse
than
the men!

Well, as far as my sister
Una
goes they are
& let there be no
hint of equivocation
about that
for she drove
me fair to distraction
around that time
especially when The Temple
finally fell to ruins
with those changes of mood
those endless
mood swings
& changes of mind
sometimes even
screaming at me

out of nowhere
& insisting it was me
who was to blame
for all that happened.

Do chuir tusa lámh orm!
was the first thing she said
when I told her that
on the peril of her life
she had no choice
& would have to
leave back the children
the *páistí* that she'd taken
literally stolen
kidnapped, yes
seduced with promises
away from Queen's Park
to our home that day.

Yes! You struck me, Dan Fogarty!
is all I can remember her saying
over
&
over
& of course
you're going to deny it
for all you've ever been
all you are is a liar
that is all you've ever been
& it was you
yes, you and no one else
who put the thought
of the *childre*
into my mind
in the first place
for us to get ourselves a pair of *páistí*
& once and for all have ourselves
a proper *clann*
one we can enjoy
at home with the Fogartys
a proper nest
a right loving family
that's what you said

& why you made me go and
do it
follow little Bobbie & Ann
every Sunday in Queen's Park
when smack-addict Judy their mother
used to go off to Carlton Vale
for an hour or so
yes, that's what you said
take the children and give them
some presents
& then bring them back so as
you and me could look after them
and now here you are
blaming it all on top of me
I hate you, my brother
I despise you, Dan Fogarty!

Yes, was all she had to say
&, as well as that, this:
I loathe and despise you,
my so-called fucking brother!
Ah dún do bhéal, I said, and hit her a *sciob*.

But here, what's this I was saying
I was telling you, wasn't I
about Red Bonnie Sugrue,
yes,
& Luke Powys
& the little romance
that had been growing up
between them
at least as far as that eager
old Luke
was concerned
but what the valley-man didn't know
of course
was that for quite some time,
Red Jack's daughter had been *coorting*
this other woman
by the name of Maggie Breen
a musician, the very same as herself
& who sometimes joined them
for sessions in *The Bedford*

or late at night in the back bar of
The Fiddler.

What ultimately ever became of
the banjo-girl Maggie Breen
to be perfectly honest
I never did find out.
Although, I do know this
that whatever it was that she and
Bonnie might have had
somehow it hadn't worked out in the end.
Aye, had finished badly
by all accounts
the very exact same
as Una and myself
but, sure, that's the way
that's the way
for sure
        ha

            ha.

But what a beautiful picker
Maggie was
she'd guested with her one night before
Shane McGowan & The Pogues
'The Lark In The Clear Air'
was one of the ones they'd played together.
Lord bless us & save us
there they are again
them sweet little old birdies
you look around & there they
are everywhere
monitoring everything
going on down below
you just can't be up to them
so you can't.

So she never married, Red Jack's daughter.
& as for Luke Powys
he ended up working in Barclays Bank.
In Glasgow of all places, never again
mentioning his time in Brondesbury Gardens.
Especially that night when he'd swallowed

a handful of bennies
& spent six hours doing his best to
count out all the eyes yes trying to count
all the eyes in the flat
all the eyes that he thought were there
in the flat
looking at him
I'd forgotten about that
neglected to remember the 1000 eyes.
Which was how many he said he could find.
1000
1000
1000
bawling his own eyes
out as he counted.

1000
I often wonder was that the same number
the same number totted up
by our mother Doreen Fogarty
yes, poor old Dots
as she twined the brown scapular
that revered, weathered 'yoke of obedience'
around her little bony fingers
and then went sailing
away off out into the blue
Yes, 1000 eyes
perhaps
or maybe
more
yes, maybe even
more
before
taking that final
plunge and

leaping
right off
into
that
cold, fogswirling
dawn
with

St Anthony
&
Mary
strung
around her
neck

Yes, 500-plus eyes
600
700
up to even
1000 eyes –
or who knows,
who can say
maybe
even
more.

As a matter of fact
I think I'd plump for that
Yes, err on the side of more
because what with the *náire*
the shame of it
of which there was plenty
yes, thinking of it somehow
getting back to the place where she'd
been born, the quiet little village
that is known as Currabawn
she would inevitably have experienced
psychological problems
imní
depression
&
all the rest of it
because after
enjoying
the ruaille buaille
with Slack Timmoney
who of course
had upped and gone
yes, completely disappeared
whether to Port-au-Prince
Rio de Janeiro
or wherever

she did not know
making it really
impossible for her
to do anything other
than what she did
arrange to have a *ginmhilleadh*
which'd be an abortion, aye
of the backstreet variety
yes, that is what
she went
&
did

only,
the Lord above
save us
didn't it all,
as so often happened
back in those medically
rudimentary days
yes, didn't the whole blessed
thing
go hopelessly wrong
with it mainly being the
responsibility of that
sleepy old ex-midwife
going by the name of Madge Mannion
who had been supposed to perform
it in her back kitchen
but hadn't been paying attention to
what she was doing-
with Dots, God love her
knowing if she didn't stop her
she was going to
end up next thing to mutilated
as off she tore up the street in
her overcoat
& nothing else
with the *lickle babogue*
still alive & kicking inside her.
So, between the hopping and the
trotting
& drinking far too much

wasn't the next thing she was doing
arriving late at night in
St Mary's Hospital
down Paddington way
doing her damnedest
to try & pull out all the
little baby hospital plugs
to bring them peace
as she kept on saying later
but, as you can imagine,
as far as everyone else was concerned
police included
that was definitely no way
to behave
with it only being by the grace
of God that another young nurse
came upon her in the nick of time
saving the babbies
but, all the same,
I'm afraid Dots Fogarty
she was now in very serious trouble
indeed
coming back half drunk
to Brondesbury Gardens
that cold night in 1954
carrying a little empty baby-suit
in a bag and all the time
laughing her head off
waltzing around in our
little attic room
along with it
& not a sinner to be seen inside of
it.
No, divil a baby or toddler
or nothing
Before being arrested
but thankfully not charged
instead treated by a doctor
after which she embarked on
an entirely new occupation
becoming what they called
a sin-girl
of mystery
with what eventually emerged

in her little attic room
not at all what you might call
a babogue
or a *leanbh* at all
nothing like a human infant
in fact
something, maybe,
not of this earth,
going
ploc
ploc
ploc
for all the world
the blood of ages.

Poor auld Dots.
No wonder she'd imagine
that the eyes of 1000 little birdies
– and more! –
monitoring her every move.

Yes, the eyes of little birdies
súile na n-éan
which, to this day,
even yet
remain relevant
to this story
because Tanith, you see
yes, *The Duchess* Tanith Kaplinski,
as she'd been christened by Alex Gordon,
in whatever spare time she
may have had at her disposal
she often made a habit of
visiting the West End
and this exotic club in particular
called *The Mandrake.*
Where, after having consumed a few lagers

she would eventually relent
(after all, they knew she was a dancer)
& perform a routine, a special little one of her own,
which never failed to bring the house down
her own very unique interpretation of
the James Bond theme
'You Only Live Twice'
rendered in as impossibly an erotic manner
as she could manage
with her hourglass silhouette wantonly
rhythmically swaying
as though Miss Kaplinski
she hadn't so much as a care in the world.
And most certainly, in recent times
hadn't been hearing any 'odd noises'.
O no, not at all.
As a performer she became quite entranced
whenever she found herself
'in the moment'
which is where she was now
in a cherry-red sports car
cruising a cliff road in the French Riviera
as the orchestral theme attained its
familiar crescendo.

She had brought the house down
with the owner pleading with her
to come back
will you, Nancy Sinatra?
Nancy, she had laughed
& had never felt better
making her way home in the
taxi, over the moon
what on earth have I been worried about?
she kept on asking herself
throughout the course of the journey
did you not see the reception
that I received?
Ha ha ha I'm a star
she kept on laughing

before finally arriving at No. 45
& whistling the very same bravura tune as
she flung her bag away from her
plugging in the kettle on the draining board
feeling so silly for ever having
been so ridiculously & unnecessarily
apprehensive
ha ha, she laughed again
& that was when she heard
the single dead, muffled beat of
the drum
just one single, abbreviated *thupp*.

But that, however, was just the beginning
as, one by one, the originally dull
scarcely audible sounds
ever so steadily began merging & ...
coagulating was the word she kept thinking of.
Until, directly, diagonally opposite
her across the room
she could plainly make out
what appeared to be an eye.

Not 1000, or anything close to such a number.
No, just one
eye, that is
just one single solitary
súil.
Gleaming there, lasciviously.
As over she went, to her dismay finding nothing.
Not, at least, until she turned around.
And saw me sitting there.
Observing her with my *little birdie*
eyes.

Súile na n-éan.

Knowing, of course, that no one would believe her.
Not even Troy McClory
who was usually sympathetic
but, like the rest of them, in recent times
had begun to manifest
identifiable signs of impatience
& exasperation.

But, if nothing else,
at least he had done this much
– recommended her to an alternative
therapist in nearby St John's Wood.
Who'd suggested she avail of the benefits
of St John's Wort, a herb she herself
swore by.

And which, for a while,
it has to be said
had actually worked like a dream for her
at least until another type of dream
or *brionglóid* took over.

When poor Tanith Kaplinski,
ironically in the aftermath of yet
another triumph onstage
in The Mandrake,
miming this to Nancy's
equally popular tune
her very own version
of the popular tune
'Secret Agent Man'
handsomely attired in a gold-spangled
mini-dress
combined with glossy white go-go boots
finding herself now really
quite euphoric
flinging open the door of her apartment
& falling down, laughing, onto the sofa.
& presently drifting off into a
deep and most contented slumber
only to wake up, she estimated afterwards,
less than an hour later
with her attention being drawn
to the elaborate white plasterwork bordering the light bulb.
& realising that the small round spot she'd just
identified
dark crimson in colour
& approximately the size of a small coin
it had now begun spreading ever so slowly
positioning itself
directly above her
she found herself dumbfounded

& as well as that discovered she
couldn't move
as the first droplet hit her
ploc, was the sound it made
&
ploc
ploc
then
ploc
after that.
As she heard me whisper,
or was it the swallow
who'd appeared at the window:
'Isn't it an awful pity,'
I sighed in her ear,
'that all of us on earth,
we only live *the wanst*?'

&
God knows it's true
but sure
what can you do
because that's the way
we are only around in this world
the *wan* time
oh God aye
aye aye
surely
& with the divil a one of us
knowing what to with it
no, half the time not knowing
where to go or what to do
only to be muddling along
as best we can
for, i ndeireadh na dála
at the end of the day
as Nano used to say
there's divil a much else as
any of us is fit to do
are youse listening to me, *craythurs*?
Auntie Nano'd commence anew

pulling away on her *píopa*
in the corner
yes, puff puff puff
on her auld clay pipe
because damn the much of any of
it do we know or understand
whether it's now
or
back
in
the
times
of
Mike
Yarwood
that it is

aye
in the long-gone times
of Mott the Hoople
&
T
U
B
U
L
A
R

B
E
L
L
S

when not only did the demon Pazuzu
come all the way from Assyria
to terrify the citizens of London
and poor old Killiburn, in The Grange Cinema
in *The Exorcist*
but, perhaps emboldened by his notoriety,
appeared to be becoming a considerable
deal more assured

with everyone in The Temple a lot more
edgy, even worse than they had been
at the start of the summer
even after the eventful intervention of
Donald 'The Fumigator' Butterworth
as they stared at each other & wished
there was someone they could justifiably
accuse
or blame
or even point the finger of suspicion at
because everyone seemed to be
looking at them
yes, everyone looking at everyone else
with pressures mounting both at work
& college
& the summer which had started
so replete and trembling with love
& hope in equal measure
now seeming to fade before their very eyes
as Troy dropped the joint for the third or fourth
time running
as he turned around & remarked to
no one in particular
yes, spoke the words of the plaintive
Sandy Denny song and the sadness
of Time and where it might go
just like the birds in the Autumn.
Who knows?
As indeed, was what happened
as the very first leaves
began to fall
with Big Peter being the first
to announce his decision to 'fly the coop'
with Maddie & Jenny Venus & Shuggie
'The Boy' Otis
with Johnny 'Fuzz Box' Winter following him
not very long after.

Until soon there was just Frank Olson
& Troy and Una left remaining
as Una, God help her innocence
lay beside him, stroking
his forehead
whispering as she did so: *acushla dílis.*

Which, she informed him, was one of
the names she was considering for
their child – *Acushla*,
if they were ever fortunate enough to have one.

Which they wouldn't, of course,
I'm happy to be able to say,
not a full one, anyhow.

As my sister,
however reluctantly,
eventually, in the end, came to realise
with it dawning on the poor little lady
that Troy and all the others
why, all along, they'd been laughing at the
very idea
of someone as clunky & clattery
not to mention, looks-wise, plain as day,
of her having a baby with the Scottish Prince
– of Fudge Fogarty giving birth to his child?
I mean, honestly, really and truly, to
goodness,
what on earth was wrong with the girl?
Hadn't he allowed her to do the *ruaille*
buaille with him?
& so surely that was enough
instead of now looking to be having
her own *childre* as well!
Why, really, Fudge!
you would often hear the others
gossiping
in the kitchen
Tanith especially
but Joanne Kaplan also
the very same as they'd done
on the night they
had helped her to dress for
Atomic Rooster
the gig they were all attending
at The Roundhouse.
Yes, fussing around with
no end of pins and bobbins
chatting away about all the

little babogues
they might have one day themselves
before laughing their heads off
just as soon as they got her out of the room
saying that maybe she might call her little
babogue Baba Cass
– after, of course, Mama Cass,
the fattest singer in the
Western world
chanteuse of The Mamas & The Papas
during those times
already in the process
of fading
far from view.

Yes, like that once-cosy living room
which had so reflected the artistic taste
of Tanith The Duchess
with its great big Chesterfield sofas
upholstered in William Morris fabric
hand-sewn fringed covers, shawls and throws,
Morris wallpaper, art nouveau posters
with vivid colours, wild swirling fonts &
wild imagery,
ceramic pots and beaded lamps
now hopelessly neglected

but with Una still being so hopelessly
in love
that she didn't even notice
as she took Troy's hand and they
went off to catch the tube
to see Atomic Rooster
with Vincent Crane and his Hammond
organ swirls
which Troy kept chatting about all
the way to Camden
most likely, I thought, to distract
attention from his 'lady'
sitting there grinning, shaped
like a sack of potatoes
as she hugged him and hugged him
all the way to the doors of The Roundhouse
with his face still burning in case

anyone might see her
& notice the way she walked
like some old country farmer's daughter
whinnying hopelessly
at every single stupid joke that he made
clattering along beside him
looking up adoringly
stumbling like a donkey
with its hooves stuck inside a bucket.

& if Una says
that all the time I imagined it
yes, that right from the start
I conjured and fashioned and rendered it all up
any old way I wanted it to happen
for the simple reason that
all along
I had been
jealous of the Scotsman
well, if that's what she thinks
then, very well, that's fine
yes, that is absolutely fair enough
because I know she liked him
& as well as that
she isn't all that well up top
but, you see, *I* know the truth
& that truth is this –
that if she wanted children
& I know she did
& just how badly
it wasn't him she was ever going
to get them from
but someone else who truly
and genuinely did care about her
& who is that?
Why, ME – who else?

Because it was I who got her the *childre*
so it was,
for all the thanks or *butochas*
she ever demonstrated.
Only to give me no end of grief
and aggravation.
I had observed them for months

with their so-called mother
coming up from their midden
in South Kilburn
to Queen's Park
That was where I first
clocked and identified them.
That pair of little birdies
who became
the páistí goidte,
the stolen children, little Bobbie & Ann.
Except that, you see,
it wasn't the case
no, it wasn't the case at all,
in fact,
with the actual truth being
that they were never *stolen*
or *goidte*
as was alleged
merely... *borrowed*

&, as it transpired,
for a short while only.

Because, you see,
it simply had to be done
particularly after the dream of The Temple
came asunder,
with our Una, God love her
being at her hopeless wit's end.

And there was only one thing
that I knew could possibly cure her
& that was for us
we Fogartys
to, once and for all, engineer
our own personal, private family
the same as we'd always
all our lives

yearned for
ever since leaving
being banished from Currabawn.
Yes, At Home With The Fogartys,
that was all we'd dreamed of

& now at last, we had it
the lovely wee Bobbie
in his blazer of bottle green
& flaxen-haired Ann
in her bonny wee bottle-green pleated kilt.
Secure now and safe
in the lovely
little home that we'd made
our own
our own private Phoenix
rising up from the ashes
triumphant once more
right here in the attic
our secure nest
forevermore
right up here
at the
top
of
the
world

&, I think,
to be honest,
that never in my life
had I ever set eyes on
happier or healthier *childre*
right from the moment
we walked out that gate
right onto Salusbury Road
& sang along with Una
before arriving
in to live amongst us.
A long way, surely, from the
drug-addict's den
that Godawful
rat trap that they'd been reared in.

Or, indeed, the likes of the former
Mahavishnu Temple
place of so-called new society of
dreams and possibilities
which, all it had done
was to
scramble our Una's mind
& make her thoughts
like pieces of

stoned

                    Scrabble

        bits   &

        pieces

                        which
        obstinately

                will not connect

                & which

                if it's bad now

                        here in Cliftonville

                now that

                we're getting older

                it
                seemed
                even
                worse
                then
                if
                you
                can
                believe
                it

                    & all of which was
                    so upsetting
                    & which made you
                    so unhappy
                    to witness
                    even yet
                    thinking back on
                    it makes

me
              so
                              enraged
              I can't even think straight
        can't think
                                        fucking
              straight
                    I mean
        why were
                                    they blaming
        me & Una
                  why put the blame on
                              the Fogartys
              again
                                    when all
        we were doing
                              was trying our best
                    to build a new home
                                    just the very
        same I can't think straight

                        it's like the Vs are coming
              but they're here
                              then there
        all over the place
                    going
                    V
        and then V
                    & then
        VVVVVVVVVVVVVVVVVVVVVV
                                        V
                                              V

                    until it's worse &
                    you
                    can't

ALL WE EVER WANTED WAS A HOME!
WHY CAN NO ONE UNDERSTAND THAT?

Mar
níl aon
tinteán
mar
do thinteán
féin.

because the plain facts are
that there isn't any home
as can compare with
the one you make yourself.

That's what Nano
used to say.
& she's right.

& we, the two of us,
were aware of that,
yes, knew it well.
which is the reason
why it was the only thing
we decided we wanted
for our two new *babogues*
who had come to dwell
forever in our nest.
It's just a pity
that Una wouldn't shut up
& I know she was nervous
but then, you have to remember,
so was I
because we're very alike
indeed, practically inextricable
& that's always been a defining Fogarty
trait,
hasn't it?
Imní, I mean
or what they prefer to call
now
anxiety & depression
yes, down the generations,
it's always been a blight.

However, happy here in Cliftonville,
all of that is now ancient history
and, although you
couldn't really say it's the perfect
home situation
at least we don't argue in the same
way we used to
and I certainly
don't manhandle her, physically,
the way I once might have done.
Why, indeed, would I
when, most of the time, the lady's like a lamb
compared to the difficult, argumentative
deirfiúr I used to have.

Aye, a sister who could not only be
by times bitter & confrontational
but violent herself, too, if she happened
to take the notion
accusing me regular of telling *bréaga*
& fancies
wee birdies, as Margaret calls them
arranging the facts to suit myself.
Ah, all the same, though,
she's been through an awful lot.

& she really does manage to
put a smile on my face, as we
go about our business these days in
Cliftonville Bay.
With me only thinking that
when the next thing I look up
and who do I see only herself,
Margaret Rutherford,
& her all got up in a green hat
& big boxy glasses
like Olive from the series
On The Buses
& Una alongside her in this
great big sweeping fedora
as over she comes *yak-yak-yakking* away.
Then who's alongside beside them
only Todd the ex-marine.

'Maybe we'll be booked for the entire season!' shouts
over Una
not looking of course where it is she's going
as bang headlong
she goes into one of the waitresses
sending her Zimmer frame sliding
across the lobby.
No sex please, we're British!
she squeals as she
retrieves the walker.
With Todd still braying on about
the rock band
Creedence Clearwater Revival & how
their lead singer John
Fogerty
is coming to the UK on tour.
He never addresses himself to me, of course
– it's always Una.
'Aye!' agrees my sister, 'On tour!
The very same name as myself!'
wobbling for a bit before
finally righting the frame.

With Todd, of course, having moved on to
something else entirely
don't ask me what
as Una, all of a sudden, stops
talking as well
& leaves down her notes
lying there scattered on the stairwell
before ambling across to the little
mini-library
& just sits there, motionless.
Saying nothing, just: blank.
Or so it seems.
But then, it's often that way
that's how it seems
with her telling you afterwards
just what it was
that was going through her mind.

The Homes Of Currabawn
that's what she's thinking of
enraptured by the show

that's in her own mind
proceeding
& that no one will ever be aware of
only me
with her sometimes even insisting
that it's me who's responsible
that it's me who's causing it
Because you're the invisible director! she says
it's you
who's doing it
&
not me
at all
because all I am
is a fucking vessel
for your thoughts
poor Una
sitting there as she rocks back & forth
& before you know it
has once more drifted away.
Is that you, Una,
Nunie is that you?
I'll whisper in her ear,
what are you thinking about
now,
Ickle Nunie?

& you want to hear the sobs of her
as she sits there listening to Troy
as he recites,
every bit as flamboyantly
as before
standing up there
on the kitchen table
only this time wielding a hand-drum
yes, pounding a *bodhrán*
wherever he got that
performing a rhythmic lament
for a poor old forgotten
potter from the valley

which, of course, is sad
that he has slipped from memory,
I mean
old Luke
because in a way
Luke Powys
was the most innocent party
of them all in Mahavishnu
with his only
crime
having been
to have loved
Bonnie Sugrue
yes
to fall helplessly in love
with the daughter
of Red Jack Sugrue
&
nothing bad should have
happened to him
I mean I didn't want it
but these things happen
when you're not looking
they can take place
occur on your blind side
as it were
& this is what happened
one night
in
Brondesbury Gardens
a long long time
ago
when there was a young man
from the valleys
yes, a young man by the name
of Luke,
Luke Powys
who
woke up
woke up
in the middle
of the night
& heard
whuppity whuppity

Yes, when he awoke
& like some fellows
& like some girls
He thought for a moment
that he could maybe hear a sound
what was it
he thought
that sound
he had heard
what could it be

why but it was but the rumble of a precariously
swaying pit-head
yes, that is indeed what it was
that had been the sound he had heard
pray pity him
for Luke do you see had been born in Aberfan.
Aberfan
hear its beat
I wonder was *the gruagach* there
The gruagach
do you think
in Aberfan – was he present?
on that dreadful night
when all those poor innocent *páistí* died.

Then the next night did it happen
I wonder did it happen
did it happen once again
to Luke Powys as he lay
there, in Mahavishnu,
upon his mattress
did it happen
do you think
do you think
did it maybe happen
o yes it did
only this time
even worse
when Luke awoke
yes, he awoke
lovelorn and immensely stricken
thinking of the face
of Red Jack's gorgeous daughter

but not just that
for what did he see
right beside him by the bed
only Bobby Moore
the captain of the England team
yes, the boss of the UK
World Cup squad
standing by the side of his mattress
in Polaroid glasses.
Polaroid
glasses
Polaroid glasses
&
a
red
shirt
he
was
wearing
them
a red shirt
with
lions
3
of
them
just like in 1966, wept Luke.
1966
1966
yes, the year 1966

but
why
was
he
thinking
about that time now?
Why now
of
all things
&
of all times…

Thinking about
back then when
there had been on the telly
on the moorish landscape of
that black-and-white screen
why, this most beautiful radiant horse,
the most graceful pony
coming sauntering through
the mist
or fog
which is what he was
dreaming about
tossing and turning
with no end of needlepricks
under his skin –
o how hot I am yet cold
he thought as he lay there inert
on a grubby old mattress
corpse-stiff beneath
an ageless moon
talk about moors
yes, I'll talk about moors
and a slot of white sky where
all that's audible anywhere is the wind
with not so much as a habitation in sight
in a carbonated world
with unbroken prospect
where the sound of water is
overwhelming
somewhere just beyond small
cliffs of ash-coloured shale
until down the sharp turn and sudden
descent
what did Luke hear – only the sound of
cantering hooves
followed by a brief sneeze,
then a whinny
why, he thought, it's Flicka
yes, Flicka the graceful TV pony
who had given his name to Luke's
best friend
My Friend Flicka!

That was the title of their favourite
show, and so why wouldn't
his bestest little friend in the world
Flicka Evans be proud to bear such a
name, wear
it as his own private badge of honour, indeed,
especially since he had always been so
taken, absolutely mesmerised in fact, by horses
and their unique ways.
So no wonder they would watch it
every single Wednesday afternoon
without fail
why wouldn't they
My Friend Flicka

He must have fallen asleep then,
Luke –
because all he could feel now was a
stillness the like of which you might
imagine was prevalent in the
moments just before Paradise the garden
itself came into mortal being.
& it was then Luke Powys
heard his name being called
& looked up to see his little friend emerging
through a door in what he took at first
to be a great mound of leaves but, on closer
inspection, revealed itself as earth.
I was hoping you'd come, he heard Flicka
say, you see I got this great free gift in *The
Beezer*
& it was then that he saw it, the multicoloured
spinner
Look here I'll show you what it can do,
said Flicka, as he pulled back the elastic
and *whee*, away it went – for all the world
a little balsa-wood bird coloured blue
soaring and then diving,
before wildcat-tumbling against a
sweeping backdrop of sky.

It's wonderful to see you again, said Flicka,
because I didn't really think that I would.
You see, I thought that the Mountain Of Death

had seen to that
having become dislodged and ending the
life of not only me, Flicka Evans, but
of the 115 other small children who happened to
be present at school that day.

Luke, you see, had had a bad flu that morning
and his mother had decided it would be best for
him to stay home.
But now that you're here, he heard Flicka say, you
& I can play with my spinner.
It's going to be such fun – for all eternity, and
with no silly mounds of sludge coming down
to land on top of us and end our happy laughter.

Such was the tone of complete conviction
in the voice of his friend Flicka as he spoke
the words
that Luke, as he lay there, could still hear the
whirr of the little bird spinner as his eyelids flipped
right open and he called out Flicka's name.
Only to see that already his friend had
vanished, along with the spinner,
whose after-echo now indifferently
enquired: why were you not at school
that day
on that very same day when all of
your little classmates were plunged
into the cold grey maw of infinity
how convenient did that prove to be
Luke Powys
in order for you to survive
survive
& your friend Flicka
perish instead of you
so welcome forever
to the soul's unbroken prospect
where you'll stand alone
unguarded, underneath a metallic,
ageless moon.

the very same thought
as had entered the mind
of a comparably perturbed
Joanne Kaplan
just as soon as she'd heard
the pony hooves trotting
click-clacking past her window at dawn.
At dawn?
Yes, at dawn.
Going clippity-
cloppety
past her window
at
dawn
& had parted the curtains
to see the figure of a blackbird
looking across
& then down
at an ancient famine
axle-cart
bearing the body
just one
of a grinning heathen
which then came alive
& rose up to its full height
scarcely more than that
of the *londubh*
the bird that then screeched
& was gone before the face of
the moon
or was it the sun
through her tears
Joanne Kaplan couldn't say.

Before plunging her face
in her hands
& committing herself
to a renewed torrent of sobbing.

Wide awake now
Luke Powys was standing
there shivering
trying his best
not to remember Bobby Moore

only now, even worse
or perhaps better,
very clearly descrying the figure of
the actress Patty Duke
standing tall & statuesque
by the looking-glass
backbrushing her hair
before turning around to give young
Luke a come-hither, pearly pink smile.
Just as she had done
when he had seen
her that same morning
on the cover of *Screen World*
on the morning
on the morning
the same morning
that it happened
when he hadn't bothered
going to school
when he hadn't even bothered his head
on that day that 116 children had faded away
& he was tingling, experiencing
strange, unaccountable feelings
for the womanly attractions of
Patty Duke
statuesque beauty
world-famous
Valley
Of
The
Dolls
curvaceous queen.

So, then: how do you
like them now,
Mr Death?

All those innocent
blue-eyed boys, including
Flicka

& indeed poor
grown-up Sexy Lexy,

let's not go forgetting
Corporal Alex.

Yes, lonely Alex Gordon
the caretaker-cum-gardener
of No. 45 Brondesbury
Gardens
once upon a time
yes, once upon a time
when, that is
some new naughty features
had been playing
in the Astral Cinema
Soho
on the same day
Sexy Lexy
had argued with his long-suffering
wife, Yvonne
&
taken the bus as far as
central London
& went into Soho
to see Robin Askwith
in *Confessions Of A Window Cleaner*
who, with his collar-length dirty-
blonde hair looked
not unlike a handsome, cheeky baboon
cor, look at
them bristols
that old Robin would say
you don't get many
of them
to the *pahhnd*
no you don't
do you Alex
do you Moody Alex
you don't get many
of them
to the
pound
at all
Sexy Lexy Gordon, he wouldn't have, normally, been
given to taking much drink.
Maybe a couple of bottles of pale ale – but divil the

much more now, the truth for it to be told.
Because even that amount would be enough to
disorientate him, easy.
Aye, aisy,
so it would.
He was walking now through the busy centre of
London. Through the middle of London, that's where
he was walking.
Coming out of Dean Street making his way towards
Soho Square. Experiencing once again that old pain in
his head.
The source of which had been the argument with his
wife.
He knew that Vonnie, God love her, that she suspected
He'd been having an affair
With one of them
trollops
that was renting
in Brondesbury Gardens
Even if he wasn't
because he actually wasn't
not an affair
All is not well, o not well, not well at all, his wife she
had kept on repeating.
No, all is not well – there, she'd said it
again – standing over by the sitting-room china cabinet
in her housecoat
with her back all the time turned.
Wringing her hands.
Ra-rumpity-rum
Her two hands
With her wringing
them

There used to never be any concealments, she said to him
then.
No secrets
No lies
No furtiveness
Sick smiles
so why o why
has it come
to this, Alex.

Come to what, she heard her husband say.
Alex Gordon was sixty-two.
Born in Walthamstow, he had lived there all his life
before eventually moving to Northolt
where they now resided.
And so he knew London well.

Although now, making his way through the centre of
the city, he felt like he had somehow gone and
completely lost his bearings
& not only did he not know
Walthamstow
or Northolt
but didn't know
anywhere
or anything
indeed
anywhere
anything
in
the
world.

So he was glad
when he finally
reached his destination
of the movie theatre
& that strangely comforting scent of
woody pine disinfectant
sliding anonymously, quietly
into his seat in the back row
of the cinema
where
Confessions
Of
A
Window
Cleaner
was already halfway through.
Cor would you look at the bristols on
that! gasped Sidney Noggett,
I wouldn't withdraw my
ladder, not 'arf.

Alex could have sworn
he had heard a bomb going off.
Because of course nowhere was safe.
No, not these days.
He wished he was back in the Arabian Peninsula.
With his beloved Sigs,
the Royal Corps Of Signals.
Even if he had to
take orders
from that cunt
yeah, that cunt
Sergeant-Major Scrogue
prat
he was
what was it for
eh
all of that
Scrogue!
Aden!
the Arabian bleeding Peninsula
risking your life
for the likes of them
yeah, for the likes of that lot
McClory the arrogant twat
& those dolly birds
over in Brondesbury
flashing their boobies
walking around
half-starkers
what was it for, eh?
The IRA
International Marxist Groupings
Gay Freedom
Maharishi Mahesh Yogi
Women's Liberation Workshop
World Of Islam
The Angry Brigade
'Continental' films.

Except that, of course, he didn't mind those.
O no – not at all.
Or, if he did, gave very little indication of it as he
huddled down in the back row, greedily consuming a
packet of salted crisps.

[313]

Going crackle
&
munch
&
enjoying a full plastic beaker
of tangy
Kia-
Ora
juice,
which was nice.

As he tried not to think about Yvonne and what her
parting words had been that morning
Alex I'm sorry, but we really have to talk.
A heart-to-heart, you know?
Because it really has – it's gone on too long.
Then the *Pearl & Dean* concerto
came starbursting onto the screen.
And a whole new feature began to unfold.
With hands being flexed inside of shiny black gauntlet-
style leather gloves – as a beautiful college student in a
flimsy pink negligee came running across the
glistening cobbles of a courtyard, trying to scream but
not being able.
With skin so fresh and fair it might have been that of
the biggest pink doll.
Yes, a large smooth *babogue*.
Then on the soundtrack you could hear
the hoarse wheeze of the killer drawing
his breath.
Or so the former signalman thought.
But you couldn't.
It wasn't.
Because it was he.
He, yes, he.
Corporal 'Sexy Lexy' Alex Gordon himself.
Dutiful caretaker of Brondesbury Gardens.
Yes, Brondesbury Gardens, No. 45.

And who, with those great big triangular sideburns to
which he was partial, might have been mistaken for an

extremely popular cabaret entertainer, Engelbert
Humperdinck.
Which was, perhaps, what made him think of a
light going on – only to find his wife, not an audience
looking up at him centre-stage – but standing there
quaking in the bright sudden blaze of their bedroom,
shaking a tattered and creased magazine.

'*Come Play With Me*' read the caption on the front.
What's this? she asked, who's this Mary Millington?
Come *choke* *Play With Me*, was the feeble response
offered by her shamefaced husband.
Do you realise – I *choke* mean do you realise –
that inside of this disgusting publication – inside here
there is a picture of me
how could my photograph possibly have got in it,
she demanded
even if she was only wearing a bikini
a degraded image from long ago.
From a weekend she'd spent
with him in Brighton
how could that be, she wondered
how could Yvonne 'Vonnie'
Gordon have succeeded in getting herself into
Playmates?
It wasn't me, her husband choked.
He hadn't put it there, he insisted.
He really hadn't.
He really
&
truly hadn't,
he sobbed repeatedly
the one and only star of
Confessions Of A Lonely Caretaker
Alex Gordon.
I really
&
truly didn't
so help me
he stuttered
someone, I swear,
is interfering with things
endeavouring to destroy
us

so help me God
so help me God
my good Christ
he repeated
before, at that very moment,
sitting there in the back row
of the theatre
he couldn't seem to bear it
anymore
flinging himself
blindly into the rain
towards a bar filled with
grimy Paddies in moleskin trousers
& donkey jackets –
where, feeling so trapped
&
miserable
&
downcast
he
didn't
even
seem
to
notice
that the tune that he'd been
whistling
in a vain attempt
at trying to seem
nonchalant
that it was, in fact,
an Irish jig
which was why all the patrons
appeared to be greeting
his presence with approval.

With that being, of course,
a longstanding habit of the
former Sigs corporal
the very same as Donald Trump, in fact
pursing his lips in the shape
of a gooseberry
& permitting

a little line of notes to go wavering
& wafting away off
wherever they
might take the notion
Yes, Alex 'Sexy' Gordon
the whistling birdie-man
The *londubh*
The blackbird
the fáinleog
or the swallow
absent-mindedly
sweeping up leaves
ti-ti-pu-ti-ti-pu
tootle tootly
whistling away

Except not anymore.

You see, *craythurs*,
for some time after a relative calm
had reasserted itself within the confines of
The Mahavishnu Temple
in the aftermath of the poor Duchess's demise
Sexy Lexy Gordon had persisted with his habit
of being *ag feadógach*
that is, of course,
whistling
while in the course of sweeping up more
leaves in the garden
or clattering with a sweeping brush
in and out of the banisters along the stairs.
Where, through the landing window,
you could look out directly onto the courtyard
where the unfortunate act of
self-defenestration
had occurred.
And across which, every morning without fail
at least up until now
that self-same caretaker
in his petrol-blue overalls
could be viewed pedalling
along, insouciantly, on his bicycle
with his little fold-up ladder tied to the crossbar.

And who always seemed to be in good humour
whistling & trilling along
to a song by, perhaps,
Max Bygraves or The Beatles

Max, in fact, being one of
his favourites
with that happy-go-lucky cheeky chappy
way he had
& which, up until now,
Alex Gordon would often do his
best to emulate.
There could be no mistaking that upbeat
sprightly singalong manner that he had.
At least, as I say, up until now.

As a certain Troy McClory
was to discover one particularly grim
and extremely wet Wednesday afternoon
when all his lectures were finished for the day
& he'd arrived home, breezing through the
door in his Afghan coat
with him actually whistling too
as up he came, bounding along the stairs
taking them one two three at a time
& finding himself being quite taken aback
when he made his sudden discovery on the landing.

It was as if the caretaker had been lying in wait.

Yes, that was definitely how it had appeared
with that thin, ungenerous expression
seeming not a little vindictive, as he remained
there in silence
on the landing
holding a brush.
'Come here you!' Troy heard him say,
'What have I ever done to you?'
to which the student pronounced himself
'really quite flummoxed'
as the caretaker reacted by literally shouting into
McClory's face.
'Don't you give me all that!' he snapped,
'Because I'm well aware – don't think, my friend! Don't

think for a second I'm not aware! So come with me!'
Subsequent to which, & somewhat to his
amazement, Troy McClory found himself kneeling
alongside Alex Gordon
as the wheezing ex-serviceman
ferreted away furiously
with his oil-covered hands working like pincers
poking relentlessly underneath the fleecy layers
of dust surrounding the small hole in the wall of
the apartment.
The student could just about make out the tiny object
inside.
'Wait a minute!' the caretaker demanded sourly.
Still scowling as he returned,
armed with a pencil
which he used to pry out the concealed wad of
cotton.
'Why did you do it?' the student heard him cry. 'What
have I ever done? All I ever do is try and make things
better. I do my job, that's all I do. Yes, I clean the
windows, occasionally mend pipes or fix the
heating. Now this, you hear? How did this get
here? Don't you know I've been searching for it for
weeks?'
With the object in question turning out, in fact,
to be his wedding ring.
'I thought I'd lost it somewhere in town,' he went on
to explain, 'maybe in the cinema. I was petrified when I
realised it had disappeared. But then what happens – it
turns up in here! What's going on? Is there a plot to destroy
me in this house?'
Then he confided in the student that in a moment of
madness he had done a terrible thing. 'You know the
Irish girl Una, Miss Pasty-Face with the
freckles? The awkward overweight one that comes and goes
at all hours, I think she maybe works as a chambermaid
or something?'
'A contract cleaner,' Troy corrected, 'she's with an
agency – they give her work.'
'Contract cleaner,' sighed Alex
absent-mindedly. 'Yes, well that's her – the one I know
that you sometimes laugh at, calling her
Fudge. Well, I gave her one, you see – one week she
was here on her own. Said she wasn't going to be able

to pay her rent, so I helped her out.
It was just a one-off, mate, that was all it was. In the
services, pal, we'd have thought nothing of it.'
At that point he looked like he
was about to whoop or cry or bawl.
Or do something far more irrational – like turn around and
just jump straight through the window, landing in the
courtyard.
But Alex Gordon didn't – just sat there morosely, on one end
of the bed, turning the gold wedding band between his
fingers.
'She was the loveliest, kindest, sweetest woman you ever
seen, my Yvonne,' he wailed, 'and now she looks at me like
I'm nothing but a piece of dirt. Like the lowliest creature that
ever walked the earth. How has this happened? I mean, as a
general rule, like the next man, I don't mind a bit of blue, I
mean, I'll watch whatever's on BBC2 late at night. But this?
Have you had anything to do with it – was it you that gave
Playmates my personal details?'
'No,' replied Troy, not knowing what the man was talking
about.
As the caretaker groaned and leaned directly over
straining himself, pitiably, in an effort to produce any kind of
sound – something that might, however tenuously, resemble a
casual whistle.
But nothing emerged.
Before he slunk off, broken.

So wasn't that a queer old turn-up for the
books?
I'd be inclined myself to say that it was.
But if that was the case, it was nothing
to the burden
Troy McClory found himself
bearing
the very next day when he received the
letter he'd been waiting for, in the post.
And which informed him, bluntly: I
regret to say this but you've failed
all of your exams.

Every one, in actual fact.

He had looked like death when he left
down the envelope.
Both Iris and Joanne had extended their
sympathy.
With Joanne by the window
quietly disrobing while trying not to think anymore about it –
as her turtleneck sweater fell to the floor and she emitted a
little groan, unbuckling the belt of her brown suede skirt.
How neat and well-cut was that fashionable, feather-cut
hairstyle.
She removed her octagonal glasses and smiled – gently
stroking the small of Iris Montgomery's soft white back.
Miss Carew wasn't chubby – o yes, that much we have
established.
In fact, she boasted a rather shapely figure.
Was rather attractive, indeed – even if on this occasion she
was attired in a somewhat shabby knitted pullover and jeans,
as if she had just come in from weeding the garden.
But which she most certainly wasn't doing now, indeed even
giggling a little, but when who appeaed in the doorway of the
bedroom, only His Majesty Mr Troy McClory,
gripping the base of his bud as he tumbled
in on top of them
yes, alongside the two *sicíní* in the *leaba*
doing his best to forget his failures
and ease the pain of his confused
& somewhat disordered mind
because it's not every day your whole
world comes crashing down
& you emerge as no genius
no, not one at all
in fact, an abject failure
who didn't even secure one pass
as he laughed
& laughed
pretending not to care
before plunging his livid
bata deep inside of Iris Montgomery.
Christ, girl, that was great, they
heard him moan.
That old mickey-jump-jubbly.
For there's nothing to compare with being '*ag marcaíocht*'.
And then going – *phléasc!* – exploding inside of a warm
waiting colleen.

'O, chomh hálainn ata se, macushla dílis
deas!' moaned Troy,
however he had managed that
like those
unsolicited voices
from before
and which meant:
'O how I love this motherfucking fucking!'
as he bounced up and down,
shedding literally gallons of sweat.

As, somewhere not so very far away
that great big tub of lard that they
called *Fudge*
yes, Fudge Fogarty she
chewed on the sheets
as she listened through the wall
to absolutely every single thing
that was going on –
pretty much
devastated, really.
Yes, more or less *briste*,
it would have to be said.
A destroyed mess of emotional jelly.
Like a bundle of old sticks that you'd
throw on the fire.
Before hearing Troy
strumming his trademark
Sandy Denny ballads: 'Who Knows Where The Time
Goes?'
as Una imagined them kissing him all over.
Especially his *bud*.
That, in particular,
splintered her heart.
With her tearing, in the end,
her treasured little *mawla bag* to pieces
out of frustration.

Yes – believe it or not
her precious *mawla bag*
that she treasured why nearly
as much as her Lourdes
miraculous medal
& which, if I didn't happen to tell

you about, at least kind of proper,
well then – I will now.

Because Fudge, do you see – Fudge or
no Fudge
at the end of the day Troy McClory
he wasn't the only one
who was good
at telling a story
& maybe even not the best
as he might think
for, glory be, & if it didn't come as
quite a surprise
when he discovered, yes found himself
considerably taken aback in his tracks when this
particular day it became apparent
that, given the fairest of
circumstances
one might say
an even playing field
that a certain Miss Una McCloona
like all of us Fogartys,
i ndeireadh na dála
at the end of the day
there was no one who could match her
when it came to relating a little
fireside yarn
or
tale
or
schkale
what with it being,
I suppose,
bred in her blood
and every single one of those Fogarty
bones.
Especially when she unlaced
her embroidered bag
yes, popped it right open
that little wee bag of memories.
No wonder Troy was mesmerised.
By the Fogarty magic, o yes ha ha.
As out they came waltzing
performing figure eights

of blissful recollection
all around the room
where the lovers lay together
underneath posters of the
San Francisco scene
Ralph Bakshi's Fritz The Cat
Easy Rider
&
The Crazy World Of Arthur Brown.

Arthur who sang, in his hat
made from tongues of flame
insisting he was a god
but he wasn't no was he
because that was just about as far as
you could get from the blissful state
in which Troy and Una found themselves
now
in Una Fogarty's Mawla Bag
Of Wonderland Imaginings
encircled by drifting, beating clouds
of dusty-winged *féileacáin*
a Painted Lady here
a looping Cabbage-White there
as a bright mottled Monarch
as maybe had been painted by
Roy Lichtenstein,
suggested Troy,
it performed a little curtsey
by way of saying goodbye
& then was gone
through the open window
off to Hampstead to join
all the others of its species
already, no doubt, convening above
the gleaming mirrors of the ponds
ferrying reports of Una's eulogies
& all of that Summer's memories
that she treasured now
& would, always
& forever, including:

1. The first time she and Troy McClory
    had 'made it', as he described it – with Sandy

Denny playing in the background.
Who knows where the time goes, she had sung
& then there were the Saturdays
yes, those first weekends when they'd
all gotten together in the garden, with Shuggie
& Big Peter & Lord Offaly sitting around a table
smoking hashish in Jenny Venus's home-made
water-pipe, as Shuggie read excerpts from a Richard
Brautigan book (*Trout Fishing In America*) aloud &

2. Someone strummed a sitar, and you could hear
the ripple of laughter from the kitchen where the
stereo
was turned up loud & Tanith & Jo
kept stirring away at a great big saucepan of
chilli in the kitchen
& the woodsmoke came
languidly drifting
high above the garden fence
as The Pokey Twins
Roystone Oames
&
His Majesty Butley Henderson
from next door glowered,
resentful not only of the fact
that Troy McClory, among others,
had been pilfering their electricity,
but also that the wartime world
the only one they knew
had passed them by.
&
last, but not least:

3. The primrose Troy had pressed into
her hand, specially selected from their private
place upon The Heath.
'Our Summer Of Love,' he'd said, running his
fingers through her hair.
'Our Summer Of Love,' she'd replied, kissing his
nipple.

Ah, them was the days, murmured Una,
popping her *mawla bag* shut,
as the tornado-tail of fled memories

receded
somewhere out in the spectacular blue.

But look here – *fan nóiméad* beag!
Yes, just for a second
take a moment there
lest you go & forget that, ultimately,
where me and my darling sister are
is right back here
in wonderful Cliftonville Bay
getting ready for Una to be putting on her show
yes, charming all the guests in the way that only
she and us Fogartys can
preparing every day for our fabulous
Cliftonville Bay Revue
starring all of our inimitable guests,
including:
* Todd Creedence
* Butley Henderson
* Roystone Oames
* Margaret Rutherford
&
Connie The São Paulo Princess
&
last but not least
a certain little iguana
courtesy of the BBC
& David Attenborough worldwide
productions.

Yes, just so long as you can remember
that we're here
we can forget all about stupid Troy McClory
aye, me auld flowers
we can for sure
him and all his pals
& any of that auld *raiméis* that he
tried to pass off as poetry
him & that

NUDE

DISINTEGRATING

PARACHUTIST

WOMAN

or:

BLUE

E
Y
E
D

B
O
Y
S

O
R

A
N
Y
T
H
I
N
G

E
L
S
E

Because what I want to tell you
now before we come to the end
which is our show
I want to tell you
about Una's relic

the stain

aye,
that irreplaceable little relic
which is the reason
why she took off up to
London in the first place.

But perhaps I should first explain.
You see, the brown scapular bearing the

image of St Anthony Of Padua is fashioned from 100% wool
and embroidered with the promise of Mary.
It is generally worn around the neck and may often be
accompanied by a small crucifix or miraculous meal.
But in the case of Joanne Kaplan – did I happen to mention
that the girl was Catholic?
Well, she was, believe it or not.
Even though you mightn't think it
not when you think of her auld shenanigans
in the sack
rowling and yowling
in the featherbed along with God's Gift
to Scotland and hungry women.
Anyway, Jo had decided this day to retire early – fed up
listening to the rest of them in the kitchen – just sitting there
glumly, as they had tended to do, ever since Tanith's
traumatic death,
dazedly watching *The Magic Roundabout*
on the television, indifferent to the
mounting chaos of the flat around them.
Roaches, overstuffed ashtrays
torn & wilting posters with faded hand-drawn
swirls & liquid text
pizza boxes, empty vodka bottles,
etc.
No end to it.
When she threw back the covers, Joanne found herself really
quite surprised
yes, immensely taken aback.
when she discovered between the sheets
the exact same holy relic of which
I've been speaking
lying right there in front of her.
She knew it couldn't be hers
because, in fact, at that very moment
she was sporting her own around her neck.
But, after some moments, she realised her mistake
& that it wasn't, in fact,
a relic at all
or even a piece of delicately
embroidered cotton
but a little circular
stain of blood
whose source appeared to

be a crack on the ceiling
She continued to gaze
in mute perplexity at the
bronze-coloured spot.
Try as she might, she just couldn't
understand it
&, in her confusion and
vulnerability
found herself calling out Iris's name
but that night her friend had been working late
in the British Library.
Don't ask me why, but at that
precise moment
Joanne reached up
& tore her own scapular off
swearing as she flung it,
trembling, across the room.
Later on insisting someone had
instructed her
to do it
& suggesting in the process that, considering
certain aspects of her behaviour in recent times
she merited neither the interest nor likely forgiveness
of her so-called master, Our Lord Jesus Christ.
Not with
the way
you've
been
going
on
ha
ha

She started weeping, on the edge of the bed
poised, with her elbows on her knees.
And it was then that she heard it
exactly the same as
her departed friend Tanith.
For all the world like a little clock ticking,
ploc
ploc
ploc,
with the whole thing

beginning
all over again.

However, succeeding in
calming down somewhat afterwards
and, with the assistance
of some others and a mild sedative
procured for her by Troy
she found herself, eventually,
becoming convinced,
relievedly deciding
that was the end of it.

It wasn't to be, however.

Some weeks afterwards she'd been at a party
in college, just drinks and nibbles,
subsequent to which she'd arrived back
to Brondesbury full of the joys
of Spring.
Deciding, all the same, that she'd prefer to 'crash out' –
instead of, like the others, heading out to The Bedford Arms.
Sure, they agreed, no problem at all.
As Joanne replied *ciao*, wiggling a couple of fingers and
slinging her leather bag over her shoulder, seeming a little
flushed but quite contented.
Only to find herself waking in the middle of the night, to the
sound of rustling, which appeared to be coming from the
direction of the air vent.
It reminded her a little of grasshoppers, she thought.
Before rolling over on her side – experiencing the dull
throbbing of what promised to be a very severe hangover
indeed.
Her lips were cracked and dry, fumbling as best she could for
the toggle of her bedside lamp – and which she, finally,
though not without an entirely uncharacteristic degree of loud
complaint and ceremony, proved successful in locating.
And which she resolutely tugged, bathing the room in a
haze of pearly light. Gradually approaching the realisation
that the relic which she'd been wearing around her neck, and
had been doing for as far back as she could remember, never
in fact let out of her sight – *it was nowhere to be seen!*
Exactly why she didn't know, for ordinarily Joanne Kaplan

experienced little difficulty in sourcing considerable
resilience – but now she broke down and ran out to Troy
McClory in a panic, seeking assistance.
Troy, who in turn looked up from his pillow where he'd been
lying in a stupor beside my sister, blinking contrarily as he
prevailed on Joanne to do her best to try and calm down.
I'll get you a glass of water, he suggested.
No, I will, interjected Una – I'll go and get it, you stay here
and talk to Jo.
& which he did – she was shivering like a jelly.
But, laugh though we might – it wasn't really amusing.
No sir, no how.
I'm afraid not, *craythurs*.
I'm afraid not, not at all.
Because, by now, Joanne Kaplan – she had actually vacated
the bedroom & gone off to the landing bathroom to vomit.
With my sister finding him stroking her lower back
whenever she returned with some water.
God bless us, all the same – but you have to hand it to the
boy for cheek.
I mean, when you get to thinking about it, Troy –
wasn't he an awful divil doing something like that, in the
middle of a crisis!
Lord above, now honestly – I ask you.
Anyway, he probably couldn't have stopped Jo if he'd wanted
to – for the poor girl was already well on her way.
'Don't ignore me when I'm speaking! Because I'm telling
you what I saw!' she screeched.
Even though, in fact, she hadn't *actually* spoken or
said all that much – not that they could understand, at any
rate.
Probably knowing that if she had, most likely what they'd
have said was: maybe you ought to lay off the hooch – &, for
a while at least, if this looks like keeping up, maybe the *ganj*.

And which is why she never mentioned again just what it was
that had confronted her whenever she returned to the bedroom.
Because I mean, let's face it, who on earth is going to believe
something the like of that – anymore than the existence of a
so-called secret room.
When she claims to have been 'intimately touched' by an
invisible old man, who had growled under the covers: 'That's
the loveliest little pot of gold that I've laid my fingers on this
many a long day, so it is!'

God bless us, *craythurs*, who in their right
mind would credit the *likea***that**?

So, as I say, that was more or less
the beginning of the end of the
would-be revolutionary headquarters of
The Mahavishnu Temple
in late September, early October
the year of Our Lord
1974.

With the exodus, once it got
started, soon building up
considerable momentum
& a right-looking sight they
presented too
with this seemingly endless caravan
of ne'er-do-wells and floppy-hatted

wastrels
pulling out from the kerb
in a convoy of battered old vans
& transits
half of them suggesting
more skeletons than people
as their neighbours the city
accountants
Royston & Butley had observed
as they watched them go.

Regarding those two chaps
what's perhaps most amazing,
when you think about it,
is how those two very same individuals
ended up here
yes, right here in Cliftonville alongside
me & my sister
such a coincidence
you would have to say
but then life is full of
coincidences
isn't it
if it's even a coincidence at all
& wasn't ordained from the
start
like so much of what we
do in life
or think we do
with Una even remarking
one day
that she wouldn't
be one bit surprised if she
goes back to her room
after lunch or maybe tea
& finds in there

as cool as you like
just sitting on the bed
as he strums his guitar
yes, the one and only
Troy McClory
fat chance Una I felt like
saying unless it's some kind
of Gothic-style
horror story you're
thinking about
seeing as they found him years
ago and not only in a bad old state
but, as a consequence of liver failure,
entirely deceased
in a back room in the
Quex Road hostel
so I wouldn't be holding
my breath if I was you.

Anyway, I was telling you,
wasn't I
about Butley & Roystone
our two contrary neighbours
one an accountant
the other a 'jobbing actor'
& who, irrefutably,
at that time
were the pair of nosiest
nosey-parkers in London
certainly in the district
of Killiburn
never passing up a chance
to go poking their old pokey noses
into other people's business
especially when one of their friends
in the Queen's Park Old Bill
had told them that they'd had it
'up to here' with
that 'appalling den'
that so-called 'anarchic coven'
which, over the past two years
had driven the authorities to the

edge of distraction
so when the pair of missing kids
had been reported to the station
the Old Bill had decided
to concentrate their efforts
mainly in the
Carlton Vale area and, of course,
Queen's Park
itself
where the boy
Bobbie
& his little sister
Ann
had been last seen
playing by the sandpit
having a go on the swing
there had been talk of
the two of them
chatting to some lady
a vagrant type
by all accounts
who might even have been
associated with the hippies
who had once lived next door
& which was the reason
that Butley and
his 'colleague' –
that is to say, soul-mate or
partner –
having heard the muffled
noise beyond their kitchen
wall
had decided to transform themselves
into freelance investigating officers
and take it upon themselves
just to see what they might see in
what remained of 45 Brondesbury
Gardens
now that the impertinent vagabonds,
supposedly, had at long last
left the neighbourhood in
peace.

& what a going-over
the two of them gave the place
with Roystone carrying on like he'd
somehow been transformed
into the bumbling eccentric
Inspector Cockrill
from the film
Green For Danger,
of course
making various comments
in a suave and eloquent big Scottish accent
as he went about the place
skimming surfaces
with the tips of his fingers and acting
like he was wearing a cloak
harrumphing and grumping and tugging
away at the whiskers on his chin
& it as bald as a baby's backside.

Coming out with all these quotes from the film
in which he claimed to have had a small
part.
But which, in fact,
he had never had any such thing –
with his so-called acting career
having amounted to little more
than the role of Mr Mercury
in Rocket Ship To Mars
which had been made in Elstree
in 1959
but never, in actual fact,
been released.
But that didn't stop him being cheeky, o no
going around the kitchen laughing
about the blind innocence & stupidity of
the pampered idiots who had once inhabited
the now almost completely devastated
premises
with the remains of a poster making his
laughter even more scornful
not to mention louder
Who Is Harry Kellerman & Why Is He
Saying Those Terrible Things About Me?
did

you
ever
in
your life
see the likes
of this,
snorted
Roystone
I mean
did you
Butley Henderson,
holding up a battered
old paperback
a copy of *The Exorcist*
whose cover
was displaying Linda Blair
with her face all boils
and pus-filled suppurations
rocking back and forth
as he kept on chortling
to such an extent that Butley
on the verge of actually choking
listening to him
insisting that
no
no
no
the
like of
it he had never
ever
heard!

Ah now,
there were some queer
carryings-on
back then in

Killiburn
let there be no doubt
about it.

But if you think that's funny, craythurs,
yes, if you think that's funny
and you find yourselves tickled
or even in the slightest bit amused by it
then I suggest you
pay attention to what old Roystone went &
did then
availing of the opportunity
to further demonstrate
his thespian prowess
yes, started showing off
more of his acting skills
& reading out bits from the paperback
making these sounds along with the dialogue
growling, in fact
& starting to say that his name
was Captain Howdy
yes, ha ha
Captain fucking Howdy do you hear me Butley
Captain fucking Howdy
& not anyone like Inspector Cockrill
no, not Inspector Cockrill
or Alastair Sim at all
at one point actually going down on his knees
hunkers and making this awful death-rattle noise
but which wasn't scary!
No, it wasn't, why of course it wasn't!
Because right from the beginning
it wasn't meant to be, because
what you were witnessing, if you happened
to be fortunate enough to be present
at that moment in the kitchen
of No. 45 Brondesbury Gardens,
what you might have considered yourself
to be witnessing was an impromptu
performance of the well-known radio
feature *It's That Man Again*!
Starring, as he proclaimed:
The incomparable Roystone Oames
& featuring his long-time partner

& friend Butley Henderson
along with *Ivor Novello*
Johnny 'Warbler' Norris
Benny Green
        &
The Clitheroe Kid,
with all of whom
'The Man' Roystone
claimed intimate friendship
as he crawled around
– astonishingly! –
yelping & barking
for what else could you call it
wondering what all of those
they might have to say
if they happened to see him now
playing the part of a twelve-year-old girl
but not just that
o no
for The Man Roystone Oames
was nothing if not
versatile
simultaneously filling the role
of the Catholic priest
who had exorcised her,
the one who had waved his golden crucifix
and, afflicted with a horrendous dose
of the trimmlins
had demanded that Pazuzu
get out of there!
Yes, a similar bout of the tremblings
which appeared to be affecting
Roystone Oames now
or was he putting
it on Butley wondered
he couldn't be sure
no, not 100%
certain
even as his friend caught a hold of
him around the neck
and in a voice perfectly identical
to that
in the film
demanded to know

your cunting mother
does she do it Henderson
tell me about your mother
you hear
does she
do it
do it
does she
your mother
the mickey-jump-jubbly
would she do it
in hell
tell me, Butley
tell me about
your mother
your mother
your mother

& it was funny
yes, it had been funny for a while
but why wouldn't Roystone
stop when he had asked him
especially after they had both
heard the laughter
& a noise like a wardrobe
filled with bricks
going *rumpeda*
followed by a
calamitous crash
of glass
stop it Roystone
for Christ's sake stop it!
&, thankfully,
eventually Roystone did
with the sweat
literally pouring down
his face
& those eyes
which, temporarily,
had been half-turned
back in their sockets
now normal again.

But then he said that
he couldn't remember
doing it
which made Butley Henderson
grumble that he wished they had
never come near the place
& which was the reason
they both started arguing
something which they had
never done in their lives
why did we have to go in there anyway
because I didn't want to
it was your idea
no it was yours
why did we have to go in there why
what business is it of ours
they're gone
very well I'm sorry
said Roystone Oames
really seeming quite taken aback himself
insisting it had been a joke
that had just gone that little bit far
even though he'd just said he
couldn't remember
& which maybe he couldn't.

But later on that night
he certainly did
when he awoke around three a.m.
or so
& descried Donald Butterworth
that is to say
Phil Mitchell's double
The Fumigator,
drawing on a cheroot
in his Puffa jacket, staring:
Your mother – does she?
An marcaíocht-jubbly?
An marcaíocht—?

Between midnight and especially between 2.30 and 3.30,
that's when the human body is at its lowest ebb, the part-time
exorcist whispered.
Are you listening, he said.
Roystone Oames McPokey are you listening?
Then listen good, Phil Mitchell sighed, stubbing
his cheroot out in a tray but now seeming,
unexpectedly,
as if he was about to cry.
During the war, he began, I'd stand at the bedroom window
and see these brilliant searchlights lighting up the sky at
Lincoln's Inn Fields. You could see the planes trapped in the
spotlights. It was like a Marvel comic. The dogfights were
eerie because of their soundlessness. You couldn't actually
hear the screaming engines because of the machine guns. It
was strange, like a silent film. Every once in a while, you'd
see a plane hit and start smoking. You might even see the
pilots bail out or float down in parachutes over London.
But you didn't know exactly where they'd come from or
where the planes had landed.
Please go away, pleaded Roystone Oames, I want to get out
of here.
I didn't tell the hippies the whole truth that day, said Mitchell,
for to be perfectly honest I was so terrified by what I'd found
I was literally afraid to speak.
He pressed on his eyes with the heels of his hands.
All the way from Assyrian sands – that's what they
say about *Pazuzu*, Mr Oames.
But he was chicken-feed compared to what I'd discovered.
Roystone Oames didn't move – just lay there as though
invisible blocks were being stacked, one by one, upon his
chest.
& when he looked
Phil Mitchell was gone.

O, yes, they say that the women
are worse than the men!
Riteful titeful titty folday
they say that the women
are worse than the men
& it's certainly true
you can say that again

Just ask Big Peter Hanlon
Aye, Big Peter from Dundalk
who didn't scare easy
& who had been to Afghanistan ten times
or more.
& who'd laughed aye and loud
whenever he'd first heard
Tanith's story
about what she'd been seeing in her room
of late
did you ever hear the like, boys?
Lord! he had scoffed,
o man!

I mean, did you ever—?

And then what happens
isn't he arriving home this
night
& turns the key in the lock
& springs
aye away on up the stairs
&
one two, hop, maybe three at a time
phweep! he whistled, and
then *phweep* again
having the time of his
life thanks to this
chick that he'd been seeing
man, she was—
what was that
he stopped for one second
& then stepped right inside

jiggledy jiggledy
whoop, me boys, piggledy

with the voice that he heard being
soft now
aye, soft as down
ever softer maybe
as it said to him Peter isn't that a grand song
it'd put you in mind of
The 'Killiburn Brae'
did you ever hear that
aye, that one, I wonder:
the killiburn brae
did you ever hear that
the killiburn brae
it puts me in mind
of
the killiburn brae
I'm sure you heard that!

then it said how are you Big Peter
are you well Big Peter Hanlon
& that was when Big Peter looked over
to see the face of his grandfather looking
right back at him
but with his wispy grey head
turned around
360 degrees
are you looking at me, Peter
his grandfather said
with the strange thing being
that he seemed a much older man
yes, a great deal older
than Big Peter could remember

before then his head turned around
& then around again
& then did the same
all over again
what would you do
if your head it turned piggledy
piggledy jiggledy
turned right around

what would you do if your head
turned full circle
go back to the start
& fix it again—!

yes turn the fuck around and
get this second right out of here
now
said Peter's grandfather to big Peter Hanlon
by the wasted bowels of the living Christ
will you listen to what
it is I'm saying to you!
turn around, son
& don't look back
don't, for pity's sake
even think about looking ba—!

For many years after, anyone
who had known Big Peter Hanlon
during his time in that North London
flat
they had often wondered what
it was had become of him.
And, although they never did find out
they would probably have found
it difficult to believe.
That Big Peter Hanlon had become
a Capuchin monk – stationed,
in fact, on the Isle Of Islay
not far from where Andy Hamilton,
the night porter
of The Rambler's Rest
had, in actual fact, been born.
Yes, born
that's what I said
unlike some of us less fortunate
anamacha.

Souls.

Incidentally, as regards poor Andy Hamilton,
not long after my sister Una's
visit to The Rambler's Rest
he had tendered his resignation & returned
to the Scottish isles
never telling anyone just what it was he
had found in the room some weeks later
long after she had left
a little bird, in fact
– a dead blackbird,
rotting away underneath the floorboards
& which he had been taking away to
bury in the garden at the back of the motel
only to find it taking wing when he left
it down
yes, stone-cold it had been,
dead for who knows how many days
& when he looked again
there it was
resplendent as though in nuptial plumage,
with the living pearl of the eye framed
by the arch of its brow,
full-throating high above in the fork of
a tree.

Before leaping forward
& circling madly on a level
with the roof of the street
its shrill cries piercing the silence:
God bless them all, the tipsy sailors.
the roving Slack Timmoneys, aye them
that have roamed
the seven seas, from *Port-au-Prince* to
London town – having bred as many colleens
as there are waves crashing upon the
world!
Haughtily rationing
fragments of considered mockery
but then when he looked again
well – what do you think?

Yes, but of course it was gone,
with nothing remaining of its
presence but a single call-note:

tá tú freisin
anois faoi gheasa

Now you too are
under my spell.

with the most peaceful silence ever
then seen to reign
with not so much as a whisper anywhere
in The Rambler's Rest Motel.

So no wonder he thought
he'd imagined the whole thing.

When I say that the women are worse than the men,
I generally mean excitable-wise,
with a certain tendency towards emotionalism,
maybe.
Because, petrified though he had been
during the course of his grandfather experience,
Big Peter Hanlon hadn't released so much
as what might be described as a single
word of distress.
Unlike a certain Maddie Lynam,
God bless her,
lovely *craythur* that she is,
that day when she found the
squirming cluster of woodlice
or *slaters* as we used to call them
which had appeared, out of nowhere
in a crack just directly above the skirting
soldered into a great big squirming ball.
Before dramatically breaking asunder
disintegrating, yes,
and
covering every inch of the walls,
then after that, then, can you believe it
before her stricken gaze turning into:
why, *eyes*, as a matter of fact.

And not just 1000, either.
Hundreds of 1000s.
Blinking.
& then blinking again.
Thousands – here there and everywhere.
Walls.
Ceiling.
Even massed inside
the body of the light bulb.

It's just a pity she hadn't mentioned them to Luke
but she couldn't, seeing
as he had been back in Wales at the time.
Because, in actual fact, he had experienced
the exact same thing
on another occasion.
One particular night when all was quiet
after they'd had a real good smoke-up
& enjoyed some of Troy's best *rogan josh*.
Because did I tell you that as well as everything
else
Troy McClory, man could he cook
o what a genius

& Luke could still taste the
pungent spice on his lips
as he lay there, blissed out, snugdeep
in a sleeping bag.

O, man alive, Lukey o Luke Luke...
Luke Powys, aged nineteen, all the way from a
South Wales pit-town.

With it soon transpiring, in his case
that in terms of undergoing inner turmoil
Luke Powys was far from being alone.
With recent events in 45 Brondesbury Gardens
in the process of exacting a heavy price
on the potter.
Although, as no small number of neutral observers
had already pointed out, it would have done
the Welshman no harm at all
had he elected to significantly curb
if not altogether terminate

his considerable intake of both narcotics
and alcohol altogether
instead of moderately curtailing it
a fact of which he was volubly proud.
With the truth, of course, being
 that he was still drinking heavily
&, regular as clockwork,
was still to be seen at the counter
of The Bedford Arms
consuming bottle after bottle of
Newcastle Brown Ale, along with
chasers of Crested Ten whiskey
when he wasn't engaged in continuous
stoned games of pool in the back room with strangers.
Where they had only just
started with the latest fad of
'underground discotheques',
where everyone now
so unlike before
appeared to have taken the trouble
to dress up to the nines
in kipper ties
& polyester
not to mention
eight-inch platform heels,
their myriad reflections
reflected in
speckling mirror balls
revolving above
a continuously flashing, tessellated floor.
Which wasn't what Luke & his friends were
used to at all
with their tatty ponchos and stonewashed
jeans
not to mention the music
its beat a continuous non-stop shuffle
dance dance dance
urged the deejay
like a space explorer
gum-chewing in mirror shades
in his cylindrical glass booth
high above
with a twin turntable

pushing buttons &
sliding levers
dance dance dance
to the discotheque rhythm
where the hi-hat drumming
infectiously rolled on like a loop
beneath the baroque strings
and gliding horns
& Luke all glassy-eyed now
like some stranger in
his own skin, discomfited
by all these elements
which, all of a sudden, seemed so alien –
so far from the parties they'd had in
the garden
where drifting smoke from the barbecue
rose up above the sounds of Captain Beefheart
& Jethro Tull
white-hippie days
so at odds with this,
skinny women wearing
great big hats
and shaven-headed black men
sporting pastel sharp-cut suits,
interested in nothing
only dancing
boogie-ing, yes
and the all-nite party
no books
no politics
high on drugs –
stimulants,
astonishingly,
whose names he didn't
even
know.
Which was hard to credit
but
true,
nonetheless.

Something is leaving
but you don't know what it is
do you, Mr Powys,

he heard himself say
now you who were once
on the inside laughing
at everyone there
on the outside looking
in
why, that is where you are
now yourself
how did that happen
that happened suddenly
didn't it, Mr Powys,
with those self-styled psychic warriors
all of a sudden having become
citadel-storming
establishment-burning
children of the revolution
no longer
hiding your eyes
behind dark shades
partied-out hippies
with their Socialist Worker badges
lying slumped,
supernumerary,
in their rainbow beads and
tie-dyes
a shadow gliding past
the decade of the sun.

'It's time to take the A-Train, my friend,'
Luke heard a soft, grating voice begin to play
inside his head,
'with the only problem being I don't
know where it's headed. One thing's for sure.
It ain't going home.'
Lifting yet another glass of whiskey
as the rhythm section thumped
while he did his best
to relegate such unnerving thoughts –
the idea of them not being numero uno,
of being at the very centre of everything! –
to the edge of his mind.
With them only, even more,
infecting its core

& he found himself stammering blearily, to no one:
'It's history, Powys.
Your motley crew
of ragbag nihilists – it's finished, my friend.
Your privileged time in this world is done,
or can't you see it?'

Repeatedly muttering those same sentiments
as though attempting to precisely determine
not only their particular sense and meaning
but also that of every single aspect of his surroundings
– most pressingly the ebbing, flowing, super-clean
extended electronic, highly mechanised
and deeply sensual nature of the music palpitating
from the space-shuttle booth –
hissing, heliumated – with that
distinctive, string-heavy chunk-a-chunk
ba-ba-ba-ba-ba-
ba-ba-ba-ba-ba-!
As, in their genital-hugging polyester trouser suits,
the lissome dancers in ice-cold sequins
and disco glitter
gyrated underneath the
revolving mirror balls
to the thudding
bumph bumph beat and the basso profundo
of soul-man Barry White
who insisted *baby yes*
yes baby that
love could conquer all.
Except, I'm afraid, not for you,
astral traveller inner cosmonaut,
Luke Powys –
because everyone gets their chance
& you and your friends – you've had yours.
Your time in the garden
your day in the sun
like I say – it's almost over,
taken a walk.

So, screw the poetry of e. e.
cummings,
the Bhagavad Gita,

The Angry Brigade,
Angela Davis
& the Furry Freaks.
Because, whether or not you accept it –
your dreams are,
already, passing into myth.

Capiche?

Which were the last words remembered by Luke Powys
that night
as, back in Brondesbury Gardens
now in an inebriated haze
and having failed to wring any sense
out of the broken stereo
he had stumbled, snorting defiantly,
across the floor, aiming a hopelessly inaccurate
swing with his boot at the infuriatingly recalcitrant
machine.
'What's going on? I say – what's going on out there, man? That
you, Luke?'
he had overheard Troy calling out from the bedroom
but decided with a chuckle to ignore him completely.
And, within a matter of seconds, had fallen into a
deep deep sleep.
Not suspecting for a moment what was going to happen
that he was on the point of encountering *Cailín Éan Aberfan*
The Bird-Girl Of Aberfan.
Luke hadn't actually been at school that day.
'You're not going in this morning,' his mother had said,
'because even by looking at you I can tell that
 you're in no fit state.'
As a result of which
at his mother's unswerving insistence,
Luke spent the day tucked up in his bed and being as far away from
his school as he could possibly be.
Yes, far from his desk in the front row where his teacher, a lovely
lady in her forties, was explaining to all his classmates just how
funny and flighty fairy tales can be. Especially in the way that not
only the same tales but often the very same characters as well,
except maybe in different guises, can often turn up in all cultures
around the world.

With some of them being funny and some of them being sad – and, just as often, both at the very same time.

Take the German *kobold*, she continued – and no doubt Luke would have been rapt had he been there, being very interested in such things.

Yes, take the German kobold, his teacher went on, a diminutive race who live far underground and who are extremely hostile to all of mankind.

And who are not unlike, she smiled, some of the little rascals one tends to find in this class – in that they play tricks but look after lost children and guide them home.

And the English fairies – tiny sprites who dwell in lakes and rivers and who maintain perhaps an ambivalent attitude to the human race.

But, the teacher concluded, perhaps no other people have differentiated between the various forms of supernatural entities as have the Irish.

Strictly speaking, the fairy creatures of Irish folklore belong to the otherworld. They co-exist with humankind but generally remain invisible to human eyes.

The colliery tip began slipping to the side of the mountain at approximately 9.15 a.m. on October 21, 1966 – killing, eventually, 116 children and 28 adults.

When Flicka and Luke had played World Cup, Luke had always been George Cohen and Flicka Bobby Moore the captain, sometimes wearing plastic sunglasses that he had got out of a lucky bag, kicking the ball as high as he could, shouting: 'Cross it, cross it – use the wing, Lukie! The wing, my friend – come on.'

He had even had a special World Cup jumper, a red one with three lions that his grandfather had brought him after a trip to London.

Luke never got over it – because Flicka Evans wasn't the only friend he had lost, even though he was his best one.

Though he rarely spoke of it, ever since the 21 Oct of that year, his relationship with the world had never been the same. Always that little bit dubious and fragile, he now found it conniving, selfish and untrustworthy, with part of his soul burnt away.

Only not gone down abruptly in flames, like Saigon – but ruined in a much more subtle and substantial fashion, as though erased, wiped away – by a single deft swab of a giant blue thumb of ice.

Which was why they had found him one night on the landing of Brondesbury Gardens

with a knife – a kitchen knife, waving it –
hysterically pointing it at something.
'I can hear it!' he was shouting, 'It's over there! Surely you can
hear it! It sounds like birds…!'
That's what they had called it at the funeral – the mass funeral, at
the open graves.
'These precious creatures born of our hearts,' the vicar had said,
'Gone at last, those precious little birdies – to rest with Him in His
beautiful bower. Along with God at the end of the sky.'

Who would ever have believed
yes, I mean
who would ever have believed
ever, really,
that the memory of that night waving his knife
on the landing in the squat
swearing there was something lurking in
behind the skirting
would never, not properly –
be seen to fade from Luke Powys' mind.

Because, after all, we grow up, we forget.
& let's remember
it was a long time ago
But that wasn't what happened to Luke.
O no
not at all
in fact, if anything
the memory
it grew
stronger
&
stronger
&
more vivid
with every
single
day
that passed
And was always to be apprehended
just lying there
a little beyond the perimeter of his brain.

Just as it was, many years later
when, leaving the hospital where he was now employed as an
ambulance driver & looking extremely smart in his white
paramedic's uniform – he had been coming just past
Selfridges when he heard that same familiar sound,
and found himself distracted by what at first had been
nothing but a blur
slowly transforming into the unmistakable waving image of a
little boy
standing there alone, just a little ways
up ahead of him,
on the traffic island directly opposite Oxford Circus tube.
With his eyes twinkling as he smiled:
'Lo, Luke,' the paramedic heard him say, flicking back his
darkish hair. 'Lo, Luke,' he repeated, 'Lo, Luke.'
And then was gone.

That was all he had said, his best friend Flicka from Aberfan.
And one thing was for sure – Luke Powys was lucky he
survived, what with the way his vehicle had mounted the
kerb.
As, indeed, had been the bus-stop passengers.

Well, anyway, as I say
those visions 'proper', they'd begun that
night
when someone had turned down
the cover of his sleeping
bag
as he lay there licking his lips
& dreaming about the rogan josh
that the famous Troy McClory
had made
hello, said Flicka Evans
I really have missed
you so much
Luke Powys
I really & truly
have missed you
Luke
Luke
Luke

&
I suppose, here in Cliftonville
or anywhere else
most folks would
say ah sure at the end of the day
what is it
it's just an auld story
like something the old people
maybe
used to tell us all long ago
another wee birdie
a hoodwinky fib
of the Margaret Rutherford variety
one to be taken, for sure, with
a pinch of salt
the way that Una's always
coming out with things
& then not following them up
with an explanation that
might make any sense
but then, sure, of course
aren't the country people
in Ireland renowned
across the world for that
wee fibby mc birdies
they don't even know
they're doing it.

'You couldn't believe their oath,' you'll
sometimes, often good-naturedly,
hear visitors say.
& maybe that's true
but this much I will tell you
that you cannot doubt their abilities
whenever it comes to the fields
of drama & variety
with Una's plans for her *Cliftonville
Capers* now rattling along
full-steam ahead
the greatest show ever in The Cliftonville
Bay Hotel
she promises
pinning up a whole pile more

new posters
really colourful ones
with everybody now
getting caught up in the excitement
even Margaret Rutherford
&
Connie The Princess
but here, what am I talking about
especially
Margaret Rutherford & Connie
The Princess.
With everyone, as I say
over the moon with excitement
wondering what my sister is going to do next
coming barrelling along
directing operations
with Butley Henderson,
I think,
being the most
agitated of all
with it being nearly impossible to
get him to stop interrupting proceedings
on the stage
blowing these solos
willy-nilly
on his cornet
especially since he heard Terry Wogan died.
No, you just can't stop him parping away
delivering his very own special & personal
arrangement of the radio DJ's
only hit record
the seaside summer brass special
'The Floral Dance'.

He's a changed man, Butley,
these days, all the same,
& just can't seem to get enough of
my 'old yarns', or so he tells me.
And I have to say that I do believe him
clapping me on the back
& laughing away goodo
almost wetting himself,
I swear to God
with the old-fashioned ways
of the seventies,
racism, etc.
now long gone
although, in retrospect,
I think they were a little
exaggerated
for, to tell the honest truth,
they weren't, in fact, all that
bad.
Or so I thought,
until:
'Isn't that right, Butley?' I says to him
one day
when, to my surprise, what does he do
only turn around and give us this
unbelievably filthy look.
'Who let *you* in here?' he says. 'All I can say is that things must have
slipped very badly in this country when it has come to this. I think I
have no option but to have a word with the management.'
As he goes off, muttering to himself,
waspishly polishing the big round
lenses of his spectacles.
'Ignore that motherfucker!'
Todd Creedence shouts over.
'I'm mighty familiar with fucks like that
from Saigon. Here, have a Kit Kat.'

& it's funny for sure
but way too late to stop Una from
crying
because you never know
when she'll take these things
to heart
like if someone says

for example
you're a liar
you're a liar
Fogarty
talking away there to yourself
pretending that you have
a brother
yes, pretending that you
have a brother who makes you think
& do all these bad & ignoble
selfish things
such as stealing children

that's the thing that she fears most
of all
& that Rutherford or someone will
make her check out
saying there isn't any such thing
as Dan
as Dan Fogarty
or anyone else
because it's just you, Madam
yes, it's just you, Una Fogarty
you and your battered and bruised
subconscious
that's what she fears
most of all
because, alone in this world,
she knows it's not
the truth
& that maybe I'll
decide to appear some day
to show them just
how real I am
aye just how fucking real
we Fogartys can be
when we take the notion
& I wonder what Rutherford
or anyone fucking else
would have
to say then
thinks Una, trembling
when she looks up & sees
what Tanith Kaplinski

&
the rest of them knew
& had experienced
so many times

with
the unexploded shell
that's ticking
away deep inside her
yes, tick tick
ticking away
there, unseen
awaiting its opportunity
glowing green
pulsing slow

D
A
N
G
E
R

U
X
B

he is

P
R
E
S
E
N
T

Because, back in The Bedford
they all knew how real I was
all right.
Back, you might say,
in Old God's time
when Paddy Conway had

been the guv'nor,
a good many years
before the Nigerian barman
came along,
decent skin that he was,
and an authority on Mr Exu.
'Sure, I knew Dan The Blackbird!'
you would hear Paddy Conway
the guvnor say,
'That's what we used to
call him!'
&
No wonder, too
for he was
a queer old bird
an odd one, for sure
Dan the doppelganger
aye, shifty old Fogarty.
Paddy, he says, to me this night,
Paddy, he says,
I wonder did I ever tell
you how
I was never really right –
that is to say,
never actually
properly born.
A queer thing, isn't it
to be saying
to someone
with the only thing
being
that he looked so unhappy
so at a loss sitting there
Dan Fogarty
sitting there all alone
in the middle of the day
that, to tell the truth,
I actually believed him.
One day I remember him
catching a *hault* of me by the collar.
Ah here now, Dan, I says, let me go
like a dacent man,
for you can't be doing the like
of that.

& I was a little bit afraid
for I knew he'd been mixing
concrete up in Norwich
& there were rumours of things
that had happened down there
regarding a fracas with a canteen
manager
& a cat whose head had been
mysteriously stove in
with a spade
well when I mentioned this
didn't he start to make light of the whole
thing & chortle
aye and then starts apologising
& backtracking profusely
aye, sitting there in front of the counter
and when I look again, what do I see

only a pair of large *deora*
yes, big fat tears coming
coursing down his cheeks
& what do I see him doing then
only standing up there on the rostrum
flailing his arms
with the two eyes locked tight shut in his head
& him dancing a jig like he hadn't so much
as a care in the world
aye, stomping away there up and down
the *flure*,
with these great big black laced-up brogues
he used to wear
I'll never forget the fierce exertions
he put into it
The 'Killiburn Brae'
it'd be called,
that tune,
maybe you've heard of it
but he isn't finished yet
ceilidhing even faster
& he blathering away
spitting and kicking
in Irish

aye, no end of gibberish
& it pouring out of him.
Like some fit or
affliction had suddenly
come over him
with him spitting,
as I say
& swearing to high heaven
waving his fist
as he let out all these
scrakes
&
yowls
calling down the rain of heaven on anyone standing as would ever
'fucking' dare to slight the reputation of the Fogartys
even though no one had so much as uttered a murmur in that
direction.
Then, glory be:
The little drop of the Father
On thy little forehead, beloved one

The little drop of the Son
On thy little forehead, beloved one

The little drop of the Spirit
On thy little forehead, beloved one

To save thee, loved one
From them as might wish you ill.

Now, that put the fear of God in me when I heard
it, I don't mind telling you,
Paddy Conway continued, and he
fiercely fretful,
rubbing the palms of his hands
in a parallel motion up and down
the length of his off-white apron,
& the reason for that is,
more than most I know it to
be a song unique to the *craythur*
that is known, in folklore, as the
gruagach.
I'm not telling you a word of a lie
they can just as suddenly fling a crock

of fire water into your face,
aye and scorn you as they're doing it again.
& then when you look,
sight nor sign of him will
there to be seen.
It is often remarked
that there is another
even more wicked side to the breed,
a fondness for abducting innocent human
childre, preferably unbaptised.
It is often expected that
he arrives in a gust of wind
some night when you least expect him
& that what you'll be looking upon is
an ugly wee runt of a man in a
skirty coat
aye, a coarse runty fellow
& he burned up by the sun
wearing a pair of old brogues
that no tinker
would be seen in.
With not so much as even a hint
of malice initially.
But, make no mistake, that will
come later.
& he indulging himself in the
pelting of innocent individuals
with stones and rocks,
or causing burning peats to
fall from the fireplace, injuring both humans and animals.
Aye, and singing no end of bawdy songs,
or disclosing
scandalous things concerning visitors to the house,
from secret locations around the rooms – the chimney, maybe,
or the ceiling. They could even break windows and cause
apparitions to appear – invade people's privacy
as they lay there asleep – perhaps even cause their beds to
levitate alarmingly.
As could Dan The Blackbird by times
all got up in his Sunday-morning best
a dicky bow, even.
& he, all the while underneath,
like some shadow with no face
a repugnant entity in a cowled jerkin,

with sharp fang-like teeth, through which he
spits brazenly,
scorned crumbs of The Sacred Host.

Paddy Conway seemed pale, and for a bit it looked
as if he was on the point of abandoning the story.
Before raising his hand and shuffling towards the
washbasin in order to fill himself a glass of tap water,
sighing protractedly as he downed it in one swift gulp.
Before proceeding, as before.

Then he comes, the barman resumed,
aye back arrived Dan The Blackbird
& started rambling and
raving to himself about this and that,
little of which
I could make any sense of.
Regarding the poor misunderstood gruagach,

them that had the misfortune
to be placed on earth
against their will
midway between Paradise
and the Infernal Regions
at every turn to be low-rated, slurred & slighted
never to know any proper home,
reviled in the body of a three-
year-old child,
only with the face of a three-hundred-year-
old man.
Whose only distinguishment in this world
is the quality of malevolence,
when they're not invading innocent people's
dreams
for that they will do
& make no mistake
& turn milk sour
overnight, prevent hens from laying,
inflict terribly incurable
diseases upon households,
make cattle fall ill & sheep break
out of their pens.
As their armies, on horseback,

cry melia murther!
To the sound of Bonnie Sugrue,
aye Red Jack's daughter,
& she sweeping with her fiddling bow,
changing speed & tempo as all of the gruagachs
of the world get out on the floor
lepping and foot-stomping spontaneous,
uninhibited, with sharp lilting phrases
accompanied by a series of syncopated handclaps
striving for all they're worth, for ecstasy
Jig
Jig
Jig
& *Jig* again!

&

Whoop! Hurrah!

&

Listen to me boys!

&

If you're wan of us
come on in here
because there's a welcome waiting
but of course there is,
you cursagod wet-eared
spawn of the afflicted devil!

May the kidneys of Christ
slung there on his crosstree
any day now fair burst open
& slather you moist,
as you weep beneath
The Cross Of Jerusalem
Aye for maw-hir
&
your mother
&
the red blood
of

Inishfall
for
bad cess
to you
all
who ensured
that I, Dan Fogarty,
was never proper born
no, never
do you hear
ever fucking
rightly
birthed
are you listening
do
you
hear
me

you had better
for this night
may the red blood
skies
of The Apocalypse
on the hills
overlooking The Holy City
may they &
the black-eyed
panther
& the leopard with
the wings of an eagle
consume your souls
above water
already on fire!

'And so that's how it was –
that's what he had to say,' Paddy
Conway sighed morosely.
'Only when I looked,
Dan Fogarty was gone –
with no one remaining in the bar but myself
& an old lag, name of Crossan
who'd been there the whole time.

Did you see Fogarty leaving just now?
I said.
& to which he replies: I seen no *Fogarty*!
What Fogarty?

With not so much as a sound about the place
after that,
only the curtain lightly blowing
& the *childre* at the circus
below in Roundwood Park
chanting out songs
I remembered myself
from the fair long ago.'

I'd been in the middle of
recalling all this from The Bedford
when I looked around and saw Connie
arriving with the trolley for tea.
'Ah, here's The Princess,'
says Butley as he rubs his hands
but then turns around and suggests:
However, please don't stop on my account!

Even though nobody had been saying anything.
Please – pray continue! – Butley urged.
Continue with what? I said,
as Una comes ambling over.
I was wondering, she says, sitting herself
down beside Butley Henderson,
I was wondering what happened to
Mott the Hoople.
& then starts telling him
about how it was me
who made her steal the children
in broad daylight
one Sunday in Queen's Park.
Because believe you me,
it wasn't me who did it, she insists,
as a matter of fact, I might as well
not have been there at all,
that day in the park,

Mr Henderson.
O no, but of course not, sister,
I heard myself laugh,
because you, as always,
are guilty of all charges
especially those of
capturing *little birdies*.

But I'll never forget the look
on the faces of Bobbie & Ann
when she opened her purse
& showed them her miraculous medal.
You really should have seen their eyes,
especially those of little Ann.
A true and absolute wonder,
it was.
It really was.
'*An Scáthán Solais*, is what it's called,'
Una explained.
'And which is also known as the *Mirror Of The Ages*, depicting
past, present and future. Anyone can look into it, children, this
extraordinary mirror – thereby laying their eyes upon the faces of
their ancestors and all their many achievements. Even when the
Pyramids were raised it was old. *Anois, nach e sin rud deas iontach?*'
'Isn't that really something, *páistí?*' she said,
'I've got lots more magic things the like of this
at home
in my house.'
At Home With The Fogartys –
would you both like to see?'
And little Bobbie and Ann, they
most enthusiastically agreed that they would.
'That's all settled then,' she said.
'So let's all go home to
lovely *Knocknanane.*'
Meaning, of course, our nest,
'The Hill Of the Birds'.
A *proper* nest,
yes, a special home
for our own little wee *éiníní,*
our 'birdy' house.

'Gosh! This is so exciting!' I remember little
Ann saying
as they laughed and joked & made their way
across the park, through the gate
& out among the cars.
Before finally arriving at
the back door of Brondesbury Gardens,
now, of course, entirely deserted.
'Welcome to a *real* Nirvana!' she stammered,
'Yes, at very long last
a perfect, proper Paradise!'
only then, of course
almost the second she'd closed the door
behind them
began quaking and crying
& apologising to the *childre*
& generally making a fool
of herself
what she would do without me
I just don't know.

Not that I've received much acknowledgement
over the years
especially not here in Cliftonville Bay
in spite of the fact that
no matter what hour of the day or night
it might be
I'm always here to hold her hand,
the poor woman.

Poor woman?
What on earth am I talking about?
Just try telling that to any of the guests in here.

Who, as you can see,
are eating out of her hand,
every single one of them.
To such an extent that, ever since our arrival
back from London, I think she's been considering
abandoning me altogether.

Not that she hasn't tried that before
which is why I've tended to keep my distance
in case of anymore violent disagreements
because I can't, to be honest,
bear the thought of
anymore scenes.

As we had the other day
when I mentioned Tom Padge McGurran
Padge who used to
sing in The Bedford
what a great old character he was
God bless him.
I remember the pair of us were laying cables
down in Rochester.
Ah, the heart's a wonder, Padge, I says,
give us a bar of a song, will you
craythur?

As he leans on his pick
&, with not a bother on him,
off he goes,
because that was always the way
with Tom Padge McGurran
of Killaloe.
And which is why I had absolutely no hesitation at all
in recommending one of his celebrated
favourites for Una's now-imminent
World-Famous Capers!
'Ladies and gentlemen!' I pronounced,
'I'd like to introduce a very special
guest!'
as the pair of us launch into singing:

Hello there old Ireland
diddly die-dill machree!

When, glory be to God,
don't I find myself receiving
an almighty wallop
across the face
before looking across to see

not so much my sister
no, not what you might
call our Una at all
but a complete and utter
harridan
shaking like a leaf
with all her bits and pieces
thrown around her
as she screams
& I mean screams:
'He's a liar!
That's all he is,
a lousy, selfish,
manipulative liar!
& always has been
for there's no Tom Padge
& never was!'

Then, after that,
starting up the same
old dirge
insisting it was me
who'd been responsible
for all her heartbreak
down the years
& how
never in a million years
would she have me in her show
telling lies the like of that
because there is such a thing as
a bad angel, she says
whether he goes by the
name of the gruagach or
slinks around favelas
in Nigeria & Brazil
attired all in white
which
is the colour of purity
ha ha ha
the one they call *Mr Exu*
the sly one
with his polished white loafers,
buttoned waistcoat & ponytail,
insinuating himself

into the recesses of people's minds
spreading lies about how
he doesn't exist

& then what happens?
Her whole body goes rigid
and she knocks down
the great big potted palm
beside the door
as Rutherford, white-faced,
comes running over
along with Connie.

As, professionals that they are,
they somehow succeed, against the odds,
in calming down the whole unfortunate
situation.

So, it's a grand old station.

With that, more or less,
terminating the possibility
of any further rehearsals
as they lead her by the elbow
along the corridor towards the bathroom
where they tidy her up
& she does that laugh
with her narrow shoulders
o yes
& old Una
Magoona
she keeps on repeating
Yes, I am Una
Una Fogarty
daughter of Dots
who had the misfortune
to fall in love with
silly old Troy
yes, tumble head over heels
i ngrá
in love
with McClory
the Scottie

yes, fell for him so bad
all them hundreds
of stupid years ago
o look
at him now
in your mind's eye
smiling like he used to
do you see him
sister
do u want
to maybe do the
mickey-jump-jubbly
with him
as of old
well, do you
want to
or not?

Aw!

O how beautiful
it sounds
that long-ago
Scottish burr
& it debating
all about how those
two wee childre
they got stolen
with the police
now
like slaters
crawling everywhere
around Queen's Park
in every nook and cranny
of North London
in fact
with their radios spurting
& blue lights revolving
as the officers
they make
one-to-one
house searches
with photofit sketches
of the two little

babbies
vanished
pouf!
like a plume of smoke.

O come
away
o
human
child
to
the waters and
the wild –
you can hear it plainly
on the breeze
on the wind
you can hear it

& yet, what do they still
go and do
o Lord aren't people so foolish
they turn around
&
say that there's
no such thing
as

the

g
r
u
a
g
a
c
h,

o but there is
you see
there's a *gruagach*, all right
just as sure as there are
lambs that gambol
out there in the rolling fields

of Kent
& the white surf of Margate
breaks daily
upon that sandy shore.

With poor sweet Connie,
Rutherford's lieutenant
looking edgily,
like she seems to do
does so often now
looking out through
the high window
at the front
fidgeting and twisting,
chatting absently
to her superior.
With The Princess,
to be honest,
this past while
getting nearly as
bad as our Una.

Asking repeatedly
what are we going to do
not only about our Una
but as regards her own private life
& being reassured
by Margaret
on a daily basis
who tells her not to worry about Una
for now that they've changed
the electronic codes on the door
there's little fear of her scarpering
off to London again
we're lucky we kept our jobs
says The Princess
looking like she's about to
break down herself
on the spot, poor thing.

With Butley & Roystone
the terrible twins
coming along to cheer
up for a bit
or so they seem to think
with some North London
stories of an entirely different type
the Sunday-morning jazz
in otherwords
which were held
each and every Sunday morning
without fail
says Butley
in the Done-Our-Bit Club
with not so much as one cloth-eared
Paddy to be seen anywhere
about the place
causing rows and disputes
& no end of unnecessary dissension.
No, not so much as a single soul
from the so-called 'old country',
that rain-drenched land of self-pity
& sentiment
where the two gentlemen
felt comfortable
paying homage to the talents
of Messrs Coltrane & Thelonious Monk,
or anyone else of the 'bebop' persuasion.

'Cloth-eared though they might be,'
muses Roystone, 'I have got to
be honest and acknowledge the fact
that Pat & Mick,
for all their failings,
they have generally
never, in my experience,
been anything other than civil.
That is, of course, when they
weren't engaged
in blowing my beloved city
to pieces around me!'
'Yes, that's true,' Butley interrupted. 'There was in existence
a certain contingent who made our lives a misery – not that

they were representative, and not for a minute would I
suggest otherwise.'
'Uh-huh,' Roystone nodded, 'I expect they mustn't have laws
of their own – certainly no grasp of anything approaching a
civic code was in evidence. Not next door at any rate – why
there were times in the night when I'd wake up to the sound
of what I took to be a wardrobe falling down the stairs.'
'Yes,' said Butley, 'A wardrobe filled with bricks, indeed.'
'Going to change the world, by all accounts. With their
idiotic music and spurious, half-baked philosophies.'
'They used to filch our electricity willy nilly & call us names
– *The Pokey Men*, if you don't mind. Although in retrospect, I
have to say I find it amusing.'
'Nonetheless, there had always been something unsavoury
about the place. Chilling, even. Even yet it can get to me.'
'Make you sick even to have to think about it.'
'I'll never forget the night we broke in. Although I
knew we shouldn't have.'
'But you were disturbed. You said you could hear a woman
weeping.'
'Yes. Weeping and wailing and screaming.'
'Yes, screaming relentlessly: *Don't hit me! Dan, Dan,
please don't hit me!*'
'Whoever Dan was – gives me the shivers. We shouldn't have
ever gone near the place...'
'I nearly died when you knocked over the milk bottles. Such a
state as those layabouts had left the place in...to be honest, I
wanted to get the hell out. But it was already too late...'
'Old torn letters, empty food cartons. An old rusted
workman's lamp, a ragged old curtain hanging from the
window – a great big giant butterfly on the ceiling...'
'All I wanted was to get the blazes out. But it was already too
late...'
'Perhaps we imagined it...'
'WE DIDN'T IMAGINE IT! WE'VE BEEN THROUGH
ALL THIS BEFORE – I KNOW WHAT I HEARD!'
PLOC
PLOC
PLOC
'That's why I wanted to sell up and get out. Yes, get the hell
away out from No. 45 – indeed as far as humanly
possible away from the Kilburn area!'

As up arrives Rutherford, just as he's
finishing off his story
with this knowing smile like
she's been listening all along.
with her kind eyes
twinkling
as she catches a hold of
him by the sleeve
& says to Roystone:
you wouldn't by any chance
be telling *little birdies*?

Reminding me as it does
of the question
I'm always asking
why do birds sing?
Cén fáth a channan siad?

I mean, there's thousands of them
who come up here to the door of the hotel
every day
& such a racket as the rascals make!
With the question remaining: *why?*

Yes, just why does it exist, this chorus of pathetic notes
repeated five or six times, afterwards prolonged with an
entirely new accent?
Perhaps the robin might give us some advice, with its
succession of infinitely varied phrases – indicating that he
alone is in possession of the territory and that he intends to
remain master there.
For singing, to a bird, is to issue a challenge too.
Before the timid finales, rivals habitually affront each other
with their voices.
Chaffinches ceaselessly toss each other their triumphal
refrain, as if they were seeking their last breed of adversaries.

Over the fields and woods, the males' boasting rises thus, loud
or discreet, sweet or harsh, repeating from place to place.
But then are they to compare with the song that is produced
by that uniquely majestic species, the great white bird that is

the whooper swan, silver son of the sea god *Manannan Mac Lir*.

With his strong voice mastered at full octave, resounding fiercely, triumphantly as his wide sailing flight brings him close to his mate.

To hear him sing, Aunt Nano used to say, is to forget everything one knows and to remember everything one has forgotten.

'For that's the way that it is, do you see – with us queer old birds, that is from the times way before now.'

And I know what she means.
For all I ever wish whenever I wake up
to greet
the sun
not knowing
whether it's it
or the moon
I'm looking
at
is to recall at least
a portion
of so many of the things
I've forgotten
bombed away
without trace
in my mind
yes,
entire houses,
whole streets
erased
as the whistling stops
&
V
V
V
down they come
again
the consequence of
lumbering, advancing years
& with no way of knowing
when an even more

powerful
UXB
might turn around
&
take a notion
yes
phléasc!
go
B
O
O
M!
& leave you standing
on waste ground
annihilated
gawping into
the steep ravine
of
yourself.

What a way to end one's days
& o how I wish
it could have been otherwise
more like the way
my sweet young sister
wanted
with us both acting roles
in our very own version of
the fairytale
'Children Of Lir'
soaring high above the rooftops
in the company of our lovely little *páistí*.
God only knows
it would fair break
your heart
even thinking about
such things
but as Una says
you still have to go
on
no matter what it might be
that ails you
as Una says

on and on
we must go
for we Fogartys
as always
what choice do we have
but to get up & go
& go on
&
on
&
    on
        &...

I mean, you really do have to hand it
to her for courage
& for absolutely everything she's done
in order to make, once again,
her annual Cliftonville Capers
happen.

& which look, at last, like they're ready
to go.

Not, mind you, that you can ever be entirely
100% certain

that, at the very last minute,
just before curtain-up,
she won't go back
to her auld troubling ways
like she did last year
one minute to showtime
when she took into blaming
me publicly &
with tedious predictability
– I mean it really is a whine by now! –
insisting that I was, & always had been,
the sole
cause of her enduring *imní*,
or anxiety and depression,
as they call it now.

Well, holy God
some of the things you have to put up with
when you do your best
to make someone happy
only to find it turning out
that all you are to them is an
óinseach
not only far from the best
but in actual fact
the worst in the world.
A fret,
a cur-dog,
no use either to man or beast.
Yes, that's all the thanks you'll
get for your efforts.

But then, where's the surprise in that – when, as is often the
case in old Erin, God bless her, your closest, aye your blood,
them turning out to be the most ungracious of all.

Although my sister
– at least
most of the time –
doesn't actually mean it
& as well as that
it's understandable after
everything she's been through.

But still, all the same,
I don't like her doing it,
turning against her very own brother –
calling him all the foul names
under the sun
& sometimes, in her vehemence,
coming close to harming
herself
once punching herself
in the eye
&
spitting

Dan
Dan
I hate
you
Dan
why did you have to
ever get born
& which of course
is the greatest laugh
because everyone knows
or should do
that I *wasn't*,
of course,
at least not like
any ordinary mortal.

Another time she threw
scalding water on herself
which of course was meant
for me
but fortunately she missed
although you should have heard the
shouts of Butley Henderson

whose head she just missed
that great big bonce
that looks like a duck egg
sculpted out of lard,
with goggles on –
bloody hell!!
he says
did you see that
bloody hell!!

looking a bit
like a terrified Billy Cotton
who in his time
had presented
Variety Bandbox.

A subject on which
the very same Butley Henderson
considers himself
something of an authority
indeed in more recent days
has my poor sister
tormented
with suggestions from
that very same programme
yes, driven up the walls
entirely
with every time he sees her coming
runs over to annoy her
Capers
Capers
Capers
that's no good of
a name for any show.
No!
Variety Bandbox
is what it has to be
Variety Bandbox
Variety Bandbox
yes
yes
yes

to such an extent
that the other day
he succeeded
in reducing
the poor girl to tears
because what does she care
about Billy Cotton
& does she not have a mind
of her own
but still he keeps at it
Variety Bandbox
Variety Bandbox
Variety…

& then when she doesn't accept his
suggestion
starts spreading all these rumours

and veiled imputations
regarding her musical competence
& suitability as director
going back on everything he's said
about harbouring a certain degree
of tolerance towards the Irish
now running down the family name
the same old claptrap
all over again
yes, there they go,
the cloth-eared fools
the Fogartys
aye,
the Fogartys
what would you expect
ah, the poor thing, she's hopeless
hopeless
she is
& that's all there's to it
but then, after all
what would you expect
whenever it's the name of the
Fogartys
you're dealing with.

Yes – that, I'm afraid
is what the silly fellow said.
So there's nothing for it
but I shall have to have a word.
Because, as I've mentioned before
& I'll say it again
it simply isn't in me
to stand by

   &

&

watch

    our good name

                                    slighted

& scorned

no, not again
I'm sorry to
have to say
once again
so
FUCK HIM!

He's nearly as bad as
Troy McClory.

Ah, but all the same
there are times when
I really & truly do
absolutely regret
the way it all
worked out
between myself &
the Scotsman
because, as I've acknowledged,
there really were times
when he could be funny
yes, very amusing indeed
so he could
a terrific raconteur
& that, I suppose,
at least in part
was what our Una
was probably
attracted to.

With that poetic turn of phrase
he had
& the capacity to relate a story
from beginning to end
hold the attention of
an audience around
a table
with, at his best,
something of
the *shaman* about him

a distinctive word-weaver
& spinner of yarns
with a lot of it inherited
from his old mentor
Douglas McVittie
&
which I think we would
have to
acknowledge that by
& large
it's a skill that's
fast disappearing
or at least under threat
in these contemporary times
of digital explosions
& fibre-optic
overload
where
throughout this past decade
there's been
an unprecedented blitz of information
& without maybe realising it
we are living underneath
the punishing weight of endless data
&
noise
&
social media
soundbites
&
selfies
the almost
unbearable burden
of immediate &
proximate stimuli
but not Troy McClory
o no not
the Scotsman
from the nineteen-seventies
when all of this would have
been the stuff of fiction
which even The Professor
Mr McVittie
could not have even

begun to dream of
crinkling up his eyes
as off went
that good old Scottie
again
yes, Troy McClory
waving the joint
as he swore blue-blind
that this latest yarn
he was spinning to them
was true
& which he could
assure them of
because none other
than Ray
Davies of the group
The Kinks
had told it to him
yeah, man
I swear this happened
when their band had been coming
from a gig
up in Leeds
driving along the M1
with Ray still dressed
in his *Bozo* hat
& bells
yeah, man,
I swear
still with his face-paint
got up as a clown –
baggy trousers, turned-up
shoes
same as he'd been
wearing onstage,
when – *I kid you not!* – what
goes and happens
doesn't he go and get a heart
attack
you've go' tae get me tae a
hospital says
Troy and what a joke
that was, with the singer
on the table being

examined, in his circus
slap
I'm afraid we may be going
tae lose him!
says the surgeon
& that's where the famous
song originated, you see
Troy McClory
continued to explain
but no' only tha'
picked up his guitar
and started to charm the
birds & our
Una
& indeed everyone
who happened to be
present at the table
that morning
swaying from side to side
with his song
about clowns
& runaway circus fleas
it was a terrific rendition,
it has to be said.

It's just a pity
that a certain person in
particular hadn't been there
to hear it
this would be Sandie
I'm talking about
a young girl called Sandie Greene
originally from Hull
who hadn't lasted very long
unfortunately
only two or three weeks
in all
because she had
absolutely loved The Kinks
and boasted proudly of
owning all their records.
Why, she had even more than
Tanith Kaplinski,
she said,

who had loved them too –
and, as a matter of fact,
whenever they got stoned
the pair of them
would always link arms and
sing that very same tune
at the top of their voices
coming along Brondesbury Road
in their cheesecloth shirts
& ankle-length wrap-around check
Madras skirts
before dissolving into hopeless laughter
whenever it came to the
part about the runaway
fleas
& the circus ringmaster not cracking
his whip anymore
let's all drink to the death of
a clown…

You know something else about Tanith
that I forgot to tell you?

She absolutely adored The Everyman
Theatre in Hampstead
& to which she used to go
frequently with Jo.
But on this particular occasion
she had decided to go on her own
this time she was on her own.
There is no such thing now
– well, there wouldn't be, would there,
in this busy age of
information technology
Netflix, Amazon and all the rest of it
no, no such thing as cinema double features,
whether of the horror film or anything else.
But back in those days
you could see one every afternoon,
if you wanted, far
from this big Babel bubble
of crackling digital mayhem.

Actually, Tanith was singing about 'bubbles'
along with some of the infants
in the school where she'd been
giving a performance.
But all of that was forgotten now
as she reclined, like Sexy Lexy
in the middle row sipping her juicy
sweet Kia-Ora.
Blinking away furiously
because for the life of her
she just couldn't stop it
remaining rigid in the fish-grey light.

She spent four hours in The Everyman that day
& then went home.

Making up her own words to a song by Sandie
Shaw about the rain pouring down as she flew
out of London all the way to gay Paree
and as Tanith Kaplinski murmured it softly
that very same night in the deep drifting
heart of her dream
she couldn't have been happier
as she came strolling along the leafy
avenues and canal banks with her stripey
umbrella held high,
feeling absolutely
free as a bird.
Until, suddenly, still in the dream
night came down really quite unexpectedly
& she found herself becoming a bit confused
having wandered down a dim-lit side street.
Where she could hear the bells of the city
clanging out
before becoming aware
there was someone behind her.
But not only that
it immediately dawning on her
that this wasn't Paris, in fact, at all
no, not the capital of France
but the water-lapping city of Venice!
And it was then that she heard it
the most subdued & awful chuckle
as she looked behind her

to find in front of her
a truly dreadful figure
tiny in stature
stunted
not much bigger than a three-year-old child.
Attired in a shapeless red duffle coat
with a hood
its sloped shoulders hunched as, very slowly
it began making its approach,
gradually pushing back the pointed hood
to reveal its
knobbled, disfigured countenance.

Only then did she see
the implement that was upraised
a blade abruptly flashing
in the silver-pale light
of a moon suspended
between two spires
'Top of the mornin', ma'am!' it said
brutally and swiftly
with a single swift, well-aimed blow
opening her neck
as she awoke
to find herself utterly
drenched in sweat,
calling out Jo's name
but then remembered
that Joanne Kaplan
her closest friend
& artistic fellow traveller
had gone home yesterday
for the weekend.

& such was the degree of embarrassment
she experienced on her way to college
the following morning
I can't tell you
when she remembered the silly little
innocent song which had acted
as the soundtrack of her dream
why, it was 'Monsieur Dupont'
by Sandie Shaw, of course!

& o how she laughed
as she found her mood becoming
increasingly more lighthearted
as the day progressed
reassuring herself
with the thought
Ha! Don't Look Now!
how harmless that actually sounds
about as threatening
as a children's playground game
eventually enjoying the
most wonderful day at work.

&, afterwards, over time,
becoming more and more convinced
yes, almost completely certain now
that everything was going to be fine
absolutely fine
yes, she thought.
Indeed, beginning to wonder
how she could ever have possibly
thought any different?
Pouring scorn on the fantasy of
the double-feature she'd been
brooding over for the
duration of the entire previous day
with her more frivolous
self now, thankfully, restored.
As she wheeled her bicycle
along the 'boulevard'
of the Killiburn High Road
in the process almost knocking over a
stocky-looking man
who she took initially to be yet
another Guinness-quaffing itinerant
labourer
but then she noticed how well he was dressed
in a neat two-piece black suit and crisply
starched white shirt
Na éiníní!
the little birdies,
she heard him whisper
forcing himself intimately
up against her ear

you see what they're trying to do
is communicate?
The anxieties of our ancestors –
warn us, he went on,
& I suppose I ought to know
for don't I record them in cemeteries
all over London
I'm Joe Meek, he said, extending a hand
which she instinctively declined
I am the one and only
guardian of lonely satellites
friend to the sprites & spacemen
all those drifting souls that come to me
mad to leave their mark so they are
Miss
small wonder they'd say
that I'm out of this world
ha ha, he scoffed,
& ha ha again
as he tossed back his quiff
& bade her goodbye
I'm off home now
to the Holloway Road,
he whispered invasively
into her other ear,
yes, back to Holloway
where bereft,
fragile voices are eagerly awaiting
my arrival
wailing through the graveyard trees.

As Tanith Kaplinski shivered,
groaning just a little
as she sighed and shook her head
thinking to herself
what odd characters you met
in places like the Kilburn High Road
continuing on her way
past Kilburn Square
down to the end of Salusbury
Road
shouldering the back gate of
Brondesbury Gardens open.

& then who should she see, standing
on the landing by the upstairs
window, blowing a kiss
as she gave a little wave –
why, Sandie of course!

But not Sandie Shaw, sweet-voiced
chanter
of 'Monsieur Dupont'
but the other one
yes, Sandie Greene, all the
way from Hull.

Who had arrived in London
been hoping to break into acting or dance
but had left suddenly, without
even bothering to say goodbye.

It's been suggested
that the singer Sandie Shaw
was not unlike her contemporaries,
the actresses Rachel Roberts
& Rita Tushingham
who had featured in so many of
the early sixties
black-and-whites.
In the sense that what she
made you think of
more than anything
were those carefree out-of-town
beatniks to whom something happened
that always made them seem tragic.
Maybe getting pregnant at seventeen
and for the rest of her life acting
out her private, unspoken tragedy
– you could see it in her eyes
all the disappointment of girls
outside London, looking in.
Sandie Greene was a bit like that too,
thought Tanith.
But she really had been so fond of her,
her friend 'the lonely girl from Hull'.
Becoming so excited now in her enthusiasm

to get back inside to talk to her friend
that she almost knocked over the caretaker
standing outside the tool shed,
furtive in his overalls.
'Oops! I'm sorry, Mr Gordon!' she apologised.
But Moody Alex didn't answer.
Not that she'd expected him to.
No – just muttered something about
'bikes being left unattended'.

But Tanith didn't care about any of that
being far too exercised by
the prospect of chatting with Sandie
& hearing all the 'goss', as they
called it
in a somewhat uncharacteristically
really quite old-fashioned way.
'Sandie!' she called,
ascending the stairs
the half-flight first
leading towards the small landing
with its oval window
from which you could see
straight through into the
house next door
the exact equivalent of
landing and half-flight
scarcely three feet away
where Butley Henderson's shadow
passed fleetingly
hello, she called, *are you*
up there, Sandie,
Sandie is that you
pausing to catch her breath
on the second flight
rather exhausted
when she could have sworn
she heard her name
just as Butley commenced his descent
on the exact equivalent of landing
and half-flight next door
as she released from her lungs
another delighted cry: *Sandie!*
propelling herself forward

& flinging the door of the
apartment open
only to find
– why, in actual fact,
nothing.

No,
nothing at all.

Because Sandie wasn't there.

She searched the house from top to bottom
without success.

No sign of Sandie.

Working herself into an extremely agitated state
before, in the end,
persuading herself there was
only one thing for it,
& that was to call her number
the only one she had.
'I'm sorry,' said the voice on the
other end of the line
'I'm sorry but I'm afraid you're mistaken.
Sandie's gone to America,
and has been for quite some time, in actual fact.
Who is this? Are you one of her London
friends – is that who you are?'

She decided it must be her mother,
replacing the receiver
& returning to the spot
where she just *knew* she'd seen Sandie.
And stood there for a while,
idly plying the toggle of the blind.
& it was just at that point
she heard it again
top o' the morning to ye, ma'am
ah aye, top of the morning to ye, ya
wee bitch
only this time
to her surprise
finding herself

almost absurdly calm
as she made her way
towards the source of the
rustling noise
which appeared to be coming
from the direction of
the air vent
remaining there quite still as
gradually the sound increased
then, remaining quite composed,
sank to one knee
as she reached out to touch the
pleated white metal grid
but then, of a sudden, the
rustling noise stopped.

Outside someone was calling
across Queen's Park
as she waited and waited
quite certain there would
be a recurrence
of the whispery-ish susurration
that made you
think about grasshoppers.

There wasn't, however.
No, nothing at all until
much later on
she found herself awaking
in the quiet, small hours
& wondering how could it be
was there any explanation
she could find for the rustling
and, as well, for what was
happening now
something that might, in some
small way,
relieve her
by providing a reason
as to why a grey mist and the sound
of lapping water
should somehow appear
in the early hours

before her eyes
yes
in the pre-dawn
murk.

Gradually forming
in her mind
at first
so unthreatening
in its own way beautiful
like a rudimentary cut-out
from a shadow-play
child's cartoon
at least
until the barge, for that's what it was,
came gliding ever nearer
so close, eventually,
that you'd even fear for your life
until you were distracted by the sight
of three figures
all of whom were attired in black
like marble statues, one of whom
was veiled
& which provided her with a great
deal of relief, at least when the lace
covering was raised
because she knew she was recalling
a Winter scene from the Venice of
Don't Look Now
& which was saying: *so beautiful*
until she realised that what
she was looking on was not the
face of Julie Christie
but that of her dear departed father
Adam 'Addie' Kaplinski
& that the funeral barge was
not carrying Donald Sutherland
laid out in black crepe
with orchids
but *her*
yes, none other
than Tanith Kaplinski herself

who now heard her estranged mother
moaning softly,
with bitter regret,
as a tugboat hooter sounded in
the distance
& she heard her mother sobbing
to no one other than the gulls
an abyss opens up between
you & your children
you may try to bridge it
but then you realise
it's already too late

just as it was for the convulsing
figure that was Kaplinski
as she reached out now to
touch her mother's hand
in recognition
& remorse
finding nothing
however
only vine-slender tendrils
of a mist already almost
entirely dispersed.

as her eyes slowly closed
& she saw herself and that
very same funeral party
standing in silence
around a grave in Willesden
Cemetery
as a priest with an Irish
accent read out her name
pronouncing it
incorrectly,
as Tanith wondered
just what on earth he was
doing there
for she wasn't Catholic
or Irish or nothing
so, someone had to be arranging it
she thought
directing her there for the purpose
of their own private sport and amusement

there beneath the swathes of soft
North London rain
in what she knew because she
could feel it
had to be the future
when along came the incomprehensible
celebrant, muttering
with his muttonchop whiskers
seeming a double for Peter Wyngarde
if that could be imagined
his thin lips softly murmuring now
a song she remembered from o
so far away
from where she did not know
& which went:
o willy waly
beneath the weeping willow
and he giving the black-and-gold crucifix
a gentle little kiss
as he bowed his head and began,
now with a baffling, word-perfect
lucidity:
we are gathered here today
to say goodbye
to Tanith Kaplinski
& the summer in which she once lived
so please will you join me
in a decade of the holy rosary

& that was what they did
except that the words which they
uttered were different
as was the water that he shook
down over the coffin
and the man in the trench coat
like a silent-movie ghost
stepped forward to mumble a brief prayer
& even though he had no face
yes, even though under his trilby
you couldn't make out any features
at all
she still knew it was her father
who whispered she could have been anything
you know

our Tannie
but lacked application, like her mother
so goodbye my love
& the Summer Of Love that could have
been
but never was
between you and I, I mean –
yes, say goodbye to Addie,
he said,
with the rusted gate creaking behind him
as he left,
the Irish priest concluding the service
as he stepped across the roll of fake grass
which the diggers now took charge of
with each of them gripping one corner
as they set to work
now confining her forever
to an eternal Summerless darkness
yes, the last day of Summer
thought Tanith as she drifted
galactically
down along a tunnel
of darkness
on what she knew
was now
the last day of Summer
now
&
forever
&
ever,
Amen.

The skylark
The skylark
The skylark
The skylark tends
to vary his combinations
composing, improvising
and on the simplest thread

achieving great art.
The skylark is, traditionally,
a symbol of frolic –
and I hope that
explains why my dear sister Una
has selected it for her
logo
in all her advertisements and
promotion for the forthcoming
Cliftonville Bay Capers
& which Butley Henderson misses no
opportunity to laugh at
saying what would you lot know
about drama you'd be better off with a
leprechaun cor blimey or maybe an old
shillelagh.
& which you expect to be echoed
by his partner in crime
Roystone Oames
who is rarely at a loss for something
smart-alec to say
you could always rely
on him to come up with something
but unfortunately, he doesn't appear to
be here anymore.
I think, in fact, he may have died.
Gone off to visit,
David Bowie
maybe.

Anyhow, the skylark, as I was saying
traditionally in the Royal Navy the order
'Hands to Dance The Skylark' was made
if the captain deemed that the ship's company
needed livening or cheering up
perhaps on an uneventful ocean passage.
& I have to say that on many occasions
&, yes, in spite of our many arguments
and differences of opinion,
that's what my wonderful sister reminds me of
at least when she's left to her own devices

& permitted to run the *Capers*
on her own
without any slanders or interference
from Butley Egghead.
I mean, you really ought to see her
at her best
with the other day her pretending
to be Irene Cara out of *Flashdance*
flinging away her walker and doing
the splits right there on the carpet
much to the amusement of Rutherford
at least for a while
What a feeling! she bleats
& there might have been a glitter ball
rotating splendiferously over her head.

I do miss Oamesy
though,
I really have to say –
because, unlike Butley
Polish-The-Noggin
Henderson,
he did at least
make some attempt to join in
& I think, to be honest,
was a much better musician
with his trademark rendering
of 'Bye Bye Blackbird'
made famous by his hero Miles Davis
now almost shockingly absent.

But I guess that's the way.
& the show, as Una always says,
it simply will have to go on without him.
Polish-The-Nog, of course,
he could do it if we asked
but, to tell the truth,
I just wouldn't please him.

& if you ask what's the nature
of the ongoing quarrel
well I think it ultimately

comes down to respect.
Because I have absolutely no
difficulty at all
with people, how shall I put it,
who disbelieve
even brazenly flaunt and give voice
to incredulousness.
But it's a different thing entirely
when someone
with whom you've previously
got along fine
as I did with Butley
elects to scorn not only your race
but casts aspersions on the dignity
of your sibling
who walks like a donkey with its
hooves in a bucket
I overheard him muttering
one day in the kitchen,
behind her back.
Not that being slighted
is anything new to either her
or the Fogartys
as I said when I comforted
her
because she does, I'm afraid,
take these things bad
& always did
which is why I told her
to give as good as she got
& call him
Specky Four Eyes Dickhead
the next time she happened
to meet him
in the corridor or
wherever
& after that, then,
to spit in his face
not once
or twice
but three four
five
times
maybe even more

if she fancies
& to ask him then
how
does
he
like
that
yes
how
do
you
like
that
Mr
Henderson
a nice little
gallyogue
of saliva in your
eye
does that feel
good
yes, I hope
it does
I wonder
maybe
will
that now
soften
your
cough
a little

only when she did it
– *phlupp!* –
right into his phizzog,
what does that old Butley
do
start to cry & sob & sniffle
until Connie The Princess
hears him & comes over
what what what

& what happens then
Margaret Rutherford comes
rushing over
& has to pull our Una off him
& so earnest did old
Rutherford look
that I have to admit
I swear to God
I near broke in two
with all the laughing
as I hopped &
skipped
all around
the *flure*
(deep down, quite unseen,
inside her mind
as I'm sure by now
God help us
you must have guessed).

Aye, fishing around
for all these auld jokes
which the English
in Albin
have always liked
&
you could tell
by her súile
aye by her eyes
you could
tell deep down
that Rutherford
was no different
to Butley
or any of
the rest of the
Sassenachs
for, when the chips are down,
it'd be in the
breed of them
with the truth being
that they just

can't help it
come here to me now
says the barman to
Paddy
if you're able to guess the number of
buns I have in my bag
aye, tell me how many I've got
then, as God is my judge, Paddy
you can have them both,
ah ha ha ha ha ha ha ha!

With Rutherford, God bless her
still standing there, anguished,
wringing her hands.
Before asking Una to come in
into the kitchen
& have some tea
with her
& starting then to ask her
all about the childre
aye, talking away to her about
little wee Bobbie & Ann
who went missing all those years
ago
I mean – were you even *living* in Kilburn
at the time?
wonders Margaret,
thinking that Una is talking a load
of disordered old doodlebug raiméis
& that all of this about the children
is on account of her imní
& all the various other
disappointments she's been subjected to
throughout her life.
Well such a laugh as our Una
let out when she heard
old Rutherford suggesting that
the whole thing
about our little birdies
was fiction
O, that old Ruthers!
she sounded so – *English!*
so reasonable as she gave her
version of affairs

that our Una, God bless her,
was making up the whole
blooming Queen's Park affair
& blaming
herself over nothing
with it being all I could do
not to go over and give old Ruthers
a bit of
a tweak on the titty.
As Una decides to play along with
it all,
concluding, ultimately, that it just
isn't worth her while
no, that's right, she agrees with Ruthers,
it was all a load
of silly old nonsense
concocted by the press
who have to sell papers
because anyway I was working
in Middlesbrough that weekend
& couldn't have taken them
even if I'd wanted to
no, I couldn't have kidnapped the
children
I think I'll leave that to the gruagachs
she says
as Rutherford smiles, that faint
weak-water smile
before tapping her my sister on the hand
& saying
thanks for all your hard work
on the play
because I really am looking
forward to it
we
all
are, actually.

I think it's going to be the best one yet,
says Una,
I really do.
& it was great to see
the pink bloom returning
to her cheeks

So it's full steam ahead
with The Cliftonville Capers!
says Margaret,
gently closing the kitchen
door behind her.

Next stop the West End!
you can hear Una laugh
all the way down as far as the library,
where Murphy is resting at Todd Creedence's
feet, staring at his slippers,
as everyone gets ready for – guess what?
David Attenborough and his notorious iguana!

Let's get him a part in Miss Fogarty's
Capers! laughs Todd, tickling
the Afghan's floppy ears
as Murphy's eyes just open and
then close.

As regards old Oamesy,
you remember I was telling you,
checking out to
visit David Bowie – well it
turns out that he's not, in fact, dead
after all.
Although he will be shortly.
Because he's got cancer, by all accounts –
and is just returning briefly
to pick up a few things.

With Una, I'm happy to say,
almost entirely back to herself,
having decided to take on a lot
of the parts herself
not because she's better, as she says,
just simply because she, obviously,
would instinctively know
the characters more
their motivation, etc.

& which is why she was singing
King Crimson
the way she had heard him do
at the top of her voice
the other day in the lobby
with Connie sitting
on the window seat beside her
giving her a morale-boosting
bit of applause
when she was finished
but with Una,
in spite of that,
as is so often the case
no matter how well she has
directed or performed
pulls away anxiously at
the threads on her sleeve
&, looking up at Connie,
screws up her face,
before announcing,
with the fiercest conviction
that, in her opinion,
Ian Hunter is a bombastic
has-been
& that, anyway,
all the young dudes
is
          no
fucking
                    good

yes, a useless

          whingeing

fuck

          of
                    a song
& that

'In the Wake

of

Poseidon'
                    is

at least

one

        hundred times

more better.

With Consuela Gomes
the beautiful Brazilian Princess
from São Paulo
this time saying nothing
just slumped there
listlessly
on the window seat
looking drained,
as she has done
these past few weeks, I've noticed,
pale as the lilies that some
confused and heartbroken
relative has left
on the counter.

Subsequent to which,
no matter how poor Princess
Connie engaged
or did her best
not a great deal of
what my sister said
made sense
as regards the *Capers* or anything
else

[415]

as she ground her gums and
reached out and kicked
& pulled at the curtain
knocking over a container
of mash that had been put beside
her fuck that
she says
screw that my brother
& begins, yet again,
the whole exasperating,
tedious routine
of blaming it all on me
just like always
ho hum
here we go
I don't like that do
you hear me, Dan Fogarty!!

So why my brother
won't you protect
me
instead of jeering &
thoughtlessly tormenting
me
for your own cruel gratification
&
telling everyone
bréaga
&
lies,
whether about *birdies*
in Queen's Park
or anywhere else
not to mention
slandering Troy
yes, doing all you can
to blacken the poor fellow's name
because I loved him, Dan
more than anyone, I, Una Fogarty,
loved Troy McClory
oh shut up
I said
knowing how emotional she can get

if you're foolish enough
to indulge her in the slightest way
so just get on
with the play, I said
aye, ar aghaidh leat leis
an *spraoi*,
away with The Capers,
I insisted
then she starts to bawl
as Connie leans over &
shoves a spoonful of
warmed-over stodge
down her throat.
As I shake my head
& give her a poke
laughing as I tell her
do you know what Una
if you don't show some
signs of perking up
I'll maybe have to act
the whole *Capers* show out
myself.

& what a sellout that would be
ladies and gentlemen
the West End presents
The Miraculous Medal
featuring Dan Fogarty.
Yes, the bold Dan Fogues
& his poor dead mother Dots.

'But she wasn't always
that way!' I'd say,
standing in front of the
microphone,
in my great big brogues
& bright green leprechaun's
floppy hat.
Begod and isn't it a
quare privilege, too,
I'd chuckle,
to be standing here
before ye all,

yes, all the Lords & Ladies
of the land
& me only poor auld Dan
Fogarty from the mountain
Dan The Man that's late
of Currabawn
like so many of me countrymen
with barely two ha'pence to rub
together
not long, God help me,
off the emigrant boat
to be permitted
to regale ye all here
in the warm velvet
plush
of this
magnifico
London theatre
for the purpose of
telling you all about
the life and the kind of it
that was lived by us all back then
in 1974
when Mike Yarwood was at
the height of his fame
and Clockwork Orangies
were kicking Irish tramps to
death
late at night
in underpass shadows
doing a dance
on the poor man's broken head.
Back then when the rats
were moving in
& bin bags piling up
gravediggers striking
& no-warning bombs killing children,

when the fifties
at last had come
to an end
o yes for sure
just ask Butley Henderson.
No, no more

Billy Cotton
going full swing
with his *wakey wakey!*
& rows of plumed
dancers parading jiggy-jiggy
across the stage
where Billy wants to know

here look my man
how many feathers are you
to find on a thrush?

as a cheeky young girl
a-whirling and spinning,
waves her bejewelled baton,
singing no end of songs
from the London Palladium
& Variety Bandbox.

Ah yes, boys o boys
it sure was a happy time
those old fifties
with the war at last over
and not a single
V-1 in sight
& a far cry surely
from those
ancient
uncivilised times
they had
in Ireland
in the little
unremarkable
village of
Currabawn
where
the Fogartys
were born, yes
furst saw the world
in a little whitewashed cabin
where Friesian heifers
looked over the door
at the family seated
all together around the fire

with the smell of bread baking
& the clock going tick
& the clock going tock
until the door burst
open and the butt of a flaming
torch was thrust with a vengeance
right in front of the face
of old Mogue Fogarty
who knew immediately
these men concerned
were no other than his neighbours
yes, a rogue masked band
on a night long ago
when all the world turned black
and a terrified exclamation broke
from the lips
of the teenage girl shrinking
fearfully into the chimney corner
shadows
for she'd recognised Felix Clohessy,
one of the intruders –
help me, Mammy!
she pleaded as they struck her
aye and did it again
for you seen nothing
they growled at the child
divil the bit of
recognition did you make
with only being
more of your inbred
Fogarty falsehoods
it's only on account of
you being a bitter-born
liar
a fabricator
like all of your lowborn kin.

Aye then, says the priest,
& he arriving with a storm lamp,
for it's long been well known
what's been proceeding
behind these walls –
the greatest profanity
maybe of all

& that craythur in the corner
with a stomick on her
like a bag of grain.
& 'tis you, her father, Mogue Fogarty,
as is responsible
& no other!

Before the priestheen,
lifting his staff
lit on him, emboldened
A curse has come upon this land,
he vowed,
stabbing the air
with the stick at the child
as she trembled there, on her knees
on the flagstones
that trembling Doreen-child

She will be taken, warned the priest,
yes, at first light, forever,
this innocent taken away,
for it's all been arranged –
the nuns will come for her.
And, as for you, Mammy
Fogarty,
may God have mercy on your soul
that you allowed it to come to this!

And with that, they were gone,
the scent of tar still lingering
acrid and accusatory
on the air.

But Mammy Fogarty, with all
the strength she could muster
from within every remaining
fibre of her being,
she did her best to compose herself
and pack the few little biteens of things
they owned inside of a bag
& before long were trotting
towards the station in Bat Noonan's

sidecar
a hackney-man as wouldn't have
them abandoned in their time of trouble
being ferried by train across country
towards the port
where they would board
as so many before them
passengers and exiles
emigrants, aye,
& bade goodbye to the small
townlands that they loved –
including Moondice & Garradrimna
but, most of all,
o
most
most
most
of all,
sweet Currabawn.

On which, as now they well knew,
they would never be privileged
to lay eyes ever again.

& soon were
faraway out to sea
which looked so unlike water,
more like a bath of lead,
huddled together
like the hunger-babes of old –
until Liverpool
arose
with its temples
& smoky towers
&
after which
they did not live long
with Daddy Fogarty passing
not so very long after
& Mammy at forty
expiring in a home for
indigents

with poor Doreen, God help her,
being parcelled
off to a home
for troubled teenagers.

How nice it would be
so heart-warming
to think of Little Doreen –
that is to say,
'Dots' Fogarty,
as something
akin to Margaret Rutherford
in the way we all like our mothers
to be
soft and matronly and smelling
of buns

but she wasn't, sad to say
instead a skinny little thing
resembling a *kippeen* or a
bit of a stick,
a fragile and always moving
chain-smoking bundle of
nerves
who wouldn't so much as say boo to a goose
so it really was fortuitous
that, quite by chance, when she got
to London after leaving the
child-home,
she found herself
taken under the wing of Auntie
Nano,
who also hailed from sweet Currabawn
although she had been in Albin
for decades
& who assured her that all she had to do
to turn her life back around where
it ought to go
was be 'nice and charming
to discerning gentlemen'.
'That's all!' explained Nano, 'and soon you'll
be rolling in no end of buttery coins!'

Now that all of London was hers,
really that old Dots,
she had found herself falling
quite in love with it.
'Because I'm yours, my gel'
the big neon board beside SKOL seemed
to blink
right there in the heart of Piccadilly
as here she came again,
sauntering along and swinging
her bag,
in the Coronation year of 1954 –
lingering by Eros as she popped in
to purchase a newspaper.
Sigh! she moaned, perusing *The London Evening
News*
& imagining the likeness of her very own self
on its cover,
announcing her position as 'London's premiere
hostess!'
O how she had beamed by that newsstand 'Up West!'
Amidst all the magic of Pall Mall
and Shaftesbury Avenue…!
What wonders for Dotsy – why, I think, o goodness! –
upon this hour, I shall surely faint!

       *BOVRIL
  *EL PARADISE   *NIGHTLIFE!

  !!!!   *THE BLUE ANGEL *MAX FACTOR
   *NON-STOP
*FUJI   *JOHN MENZIES
       *SKOL
  *BRYLCREEM
    *DOUBLE DIAMOND   !!**
!!!!! *WRIGLEY'S   !!!!

*HADES   *SHANGRI-LA
    *LOVE IS MY PROFESSION

*COLONY   *SHOWGIRLS
   *LA BOHÈME

& what, do you think,
in her sprightly, fevered mind,
was she wearing on the front cover
of that London evening newspaper?
Why, only the most gorgeously cut
sequined sheath gown in silver, as she
plied her elegant tortoiseshell
cigarette holder,
& explained how, once upon a time
yes
once
upon
a time
there had been an innocent young
inexperienced Irish girl who had liked
nothing better than to stroll in the evenings
all along the length of Shaftesbury Avenue
where it cut the stretch of road at Cambridge Circus
a wonderland alive with its flotilla of
fruit and shellfish stalls and hot-chestnut braziers.
And where
further along were The Tatler News Theatre
The Phoenix Theatre and The Astoria Theatre
always adorned with colourful, hand-painted posters.
Having derived her customary quota of enjoyment from these
sights, the malnourished-looking young girl with the buck
teeth and freckles made her way up the staircase of her
dwelling house and let herself into the sparsely furnished
room which contained an enormous ancient gas fire, a single-
ring cooker and an ominous-looking meter.
Yes, that was all
that was to be found there
in Doreen 'Dotsy's' bedsit
but for what stood on the table
a thick china cup and saucer, two plates and assorted
items of cheap metal cutlery.
Nano would probably have laughed
her elderly head off
if she had happened to be there
to see
her new girl protégée
undressing
vowing that this was a state
of affairs not destined to

last very long
because soon Dots Fogarty
would be lying under
oceans of
appreciative gentlemen
&
as a consequence
literally rolling in
gold & pennies

as Dotsy
unzipped her frock
& gingerly stepped inside
this new creation
which Nano had gone out
& bought for her that day
the material was a black brocade
woven all over with tiny sprigs of silver roses
it had a high collar that plunged to a low V-neck.

There were no sleeves to speak of
and the main feature was a sort of overskirt
in the same fabric
which was caught up in a bunch of formal
pleats on the hip.
After she had succeeded in zipping herself up,
Little Dots Fogarty slipped into
her patent-leather stilettos and practised
walking around the room.
In front of the mirror, she turned around
with one hand on her hip and
gave an exaggerated flutter of her false eyelashes.
O! Nach iontach an club oíche éinín mise, I really am
the voluptuous nightclub swinger!
Then she donned her precious scapular
and holy medal.
Our Lady conceived without sin
Pray for us
who have
recourse
to thee
And that most certainly
would have made Auntie Nano laugh

just the same as Troy The Scotsman
with neither of them believing
in God anymore
God said Troy
ha ha ha ha
yeah, a big man with a beard
check it out
man that's fucking weird
& Nano, after her many years in
London
she was of the very same
cast of mind.
But, of course, Troy
being a Scot from Edinburgh
he had actually been
raised a Protestant
& used to express some degree
of amazement
at the beliefs and behaviour
yes, of Catholics and their ways.
Man your holy medallion
he used say to Una
you been wearing that
all your life?
My sister used to laugh when
she heard him saying
that
swear tae Christ
it really
does
blow my
mind.

But that, of course,
was, as yet,
a very long time
into the future
as
Dots locked the door of her
bedsit behind her
& walked down the stairs
feeling really like a princess
discovering that it was slightly different
when you got out into the street

where the combination of high heels
and tight skirt necessitated a mincing step
but all the same, she nonetheless felt like royalty.
And a long long way from that
dump of an orphanage.
'O my my! Why, you have turned into the
proper little dolly!' cried Auntie Nano
the very moment she saw her,
whispering confidentially into her ear,
'I've an Italian actor who says he'd like
to meet you. He's waiting for you over
there, yes go ahead, dear
beyond there, in the alcove.
He's positively loaded,
luvvy, so try and be nice.'

So that was the beginning
of a new career
for Doreen 'Dots',
alias my mother,
Fogarty.
But it's not the only piece of
news I have
& God bless the hearers
I hope you'll be listening
to the piece of news I have –
I mean, talk about people's
personal History Of London?
Iris Montgomery, eat your heart out!

With Doreen arriving back home
that very night
in the early hours,
when all of Killiburn
& Brondesbury Road
was fast asleep
& her with a pile of money
in her fist
but already wondering
in spite of herself
if this was all there
was ever going to be to it

meeting blackguards
the likes of Slack Timmoney
(who had also left her
ag iompar clainne, with child) –
sitting there all day
alone in her bedsit
with that old fireclay heater
dispersing flickering
shadows &
her
out of nowhere bursting into tears
& that was even before giving
birth to Una and having to arrange
for her to go into care
the very same as herself in the old days
& that is even before
I myself appeared
whatever little pieceen
there might have been.
Bit-Of-Dan!
I suppose you could say
that wee part that trickles
and goes *ploc ploc ploc*
with nobody even being
any the wiser
& which you mightn't have
even thought she had in her
a miscarriage I mean
seeing as I've said
all she was was a piece of a thing
who was lucky to have
recovered at all
from her botched abortion
aye, that ginmhilleadh olc
which clatty-fingers Mannion
had visited upon her
that rainy day one Sunday
in Clapham
o Lord above
such a *phléasc*!
of a thing to happen
&
above all
on a grey &

gloomy wet Sunday Sabbath
when it always
seems to be the colour
of an out-of-focus
picture on the telly
a telly, that is
in the long long ago
the sort you would see
on Sundays when it always rains
that is to say
smoky
wintry
grey
long before iguanas,
Saigon or anything else.

And which really did have
a profound effect on Dots
even though to Clatty-Fingers
Mannion
it mightn't have appeared
that way at the time
with Dots, in fact, enjoying
a nice cuppa tea
& a biscuit at the time
yes, she seemed fine
but the more she kept thinking
about what had just happened
that wasn't the way she was
thinking at all
for what did our mother
go & do then
took the cup & fired
its contents
right across the floor of
Clatty Mannion's kitchen
&
then started screaming
much to the abortionist's dismay
& then flying off away out the door
just managing to make
it to her bedsit
knowing that this Mannion

business
it wasn't finished –
with a small bit of me,
do you see,
inside of her yet.

But it was just too much.
With the truth being
that she couldn't
face it anymore,
just couldn't find it
in herself to face it
& which is where
our little play gets its name –
The Miraculous Medal
which she strung around her
neck
along with the scapular
of St Anthony Of Padua
with her reaching up, drained,
as far as the bathroom cabinet
out of which she picked a small brown
bottle of Tuinal
& told herself, swallowing
that never before had she felt better
in her life
as she turned up the wireless
& left it going, full blast.
I'd like to go a wandering
Upon the mountain track
Val-de-ree
Val-de-ra!

Before giving her medal
one
soft little valedictory
pogue
&, with luscious abandonment,
flung herself before the dawn.

O, Lord save us and bless us,
talk about the History Of London?
Faith, I could easily write a dozen

books on the subject
& which was what Dots Fogarty
had been thinking that night
before she ended her life
in the attic
yes, what she had been thinking
as she walked that night
making her way back home
as she sighed with regret
because she knew she wouldn't ever
live in it again
London town
this city with all the marvels
that she craved
& always had
at least before it had all gone uafásach
yes, really badly wrong.
Horribly so, and no mistake.
All because of that stupid Mannion! she hissed,
that useless, good-for-nothing
Clatty McFuckFingers!

But that had been so long long ago
when none of the grunting
of the men
had as yet succeeded in getting to her
not yet –
& when all she'd had
was a sparse but beautiful room
not far from the gleaming white marble of St Paul's
where, on Mondays,
one's day off
she could busy herself
with her easel and paints
some day
somehow
daubing away at the little chimney pot
that she'd placed at the top
of the golden thatch
of that little whitewashed cottage
where one day she would live
with her own little family
all your own wee *béicil páistí.*

Whose laughter might help her
do away with even the smallest
hint of the trimmlins
which in recent times had
come to unsettle her in
the night
No. No *tremblings* at all.
Just a sweet falling
wave of calm
coming wafting down
from the hills
of Currabawn
dream-townland of
her memory.

But, knowing in her heart
that the laughter
and jollity
of it all
that all of it,
in reality,
was imagined

&

whenever that happened, Dots Fogarty
would just tear off the
little smock that she had sewed herself
& flinging her brush and her palette
just sit there in the armchair, looking
as if every drop of *fuil*
had been drained, there and then,
from her body.

Screwing her fists in her eyes
as she swore
&
stammered how she didn't
any longer
fear those stupid trimmlins
or the imní either
& how they could
do what

they jollywell fucking liked,
hee hee.

Except that her bedsit
began changing all around her
yes, that humble little bedsitting-room
it ever so slowly & tormentingly
began to empty itself
of all its colour
robbed of everything
assuming the very texture of *nothing*
the virtual essence of absence
stripped of everything that had
once distinguished it
now a grey
&
wintry place
to all intents & purposes
nothing other than
a featureless rectangle
with the bright bowl of fruit
she'd painted recently
now reimagined in form and line
in contrast & in shadow.
its stark black and white
like archive-reel footage
an X-ray of all that was
left of a soul.
How she dreaded the trimmlins now
imminent as she knew they were
in this place of removed colour,
with the space all around her
suddenly appearing so vast
with everything heretofore ordinary
now replete with chilling menace
&
intent.
It appeared morally barren.
Even the bells of St Paul's had grown silent.
Outside, all
was a dead exterior.
'I might well be the last person on earth,' she murmured
regretfully, 'a tiny figure in an immense conspiracy.'
And that was more or less the reason,

combined with her experience
across the city
with her little bag
on the Killiburn Brae
why she eventually went upstairs
to the attic.
And feeling immensely relieved
as she did so
that she had finally taken
the decision.

So, there you have it, *craythurs*,
that's the story of
Dots & The Miraculous Medal
for you –
& that, more or less,
is how it all began,
in that very same cubbyhole
of a grim, narrow attic long ago
high above the roofs of good
old Brondesbury Gardens.
Where our poor mother, God bless her,
remained for days, undiscovered,
beneath a lattice of creosoted
rafters
lying there surrounded by
various inquisitive francaigh.
In otherwords, rats –
but not just them,
all kinds of pests – including
beetles, indeed,
ambling indifferently
across that marble-pale brow.
Yes, all of God's wondrous mini-beast
creatures
they all, in the end, made their way
up to the attic.
Wondering what small little biteen
of her
they might snack on
or ferry away
to their homes under leaves
in Queen's Park

behind the Killiburn Road
– a long way, surely,
from the very last memory
of this world as our
mother had perceived it
in those last few seconds
before she departed to meet her Maker
& where, in full glorious colour,
she saw herself
as just about the happiest
little girleen in the world
aye, as ever had been given life
to stroll upon the soft green swards
of this golden earth
aye, and the warm green fields
of Currabawn in particular
where she imagined herself feeding
hosts of birdeens by the river.
Yes, all the thrushes and sparrows
and blue tits
as they wheeled awhile and
then came finally in to land
on the boughs of the rowan
reaching out across the bower.

Why, then, do little birds sing?
Is it to transfigure?
Or, perhaps more cunningly, to deceive?
Which begs the question – might it be, perhaps,
that, like hares, they're
simply another species of
gruagach in disguise?

Ah would you go along out of that,
Auntie Nano, in her cups, used to always
say,
sure there's no such thing as
gruagachs,
or what is wrong with you –

have you lost your mind?
& then give you this
wink
&, whatever way she did it
faith, make your fuil
run cold, so it would –
as if she knew, all along,
that there was indeed such thing –
& that only a fool or a pure-bred
ommadawn
would ever dream of doubting the fact.

Like on a night
when the whole blessed
schkale
of the Fogartys ended,
or perhaps began,
on the grey wet slopes of
what is known as
The Killiburn Brae
ironically located
on the far distant side
of the city,
by the water, further to the east

where, upon those lonely slopes
what, in our time, would have been
called a *brae*,
a sloping bank,
Doreen 'Dots' Fogarty
cast away all she owned of
me
just the littlest mawla bag
containing a small caubeen
& pair of sweet velvet britches
stitched in green
& a pair of buckled black brogues
for a babeen that never was
to be,
not
        properly,
                anyway,
                        ha ha.

Val-de-ree
Val-de-raah! `
she whistled all the way home –
the happy wandering tune of
a *little bookil* who never got properly born
her would-be son
with his schoolclothes arranged inside in a bag
tossed right across the side of a bridge
beneath the coastal lights of early morning –
lying, in unpeace, at the bottom of
'The Brae'.

So that was the end of Dots Fogarty's
career in Soho –
yes, Doreen Fogarty's
own personal *History Of London* –
The End.
No, no more early mornings
blinking in the daylight
making her way through tall Georgian townhouses
along darkened alleys where cigarette butts
and empty packets littered the cobbles
where the wind liked to sharpen itself
between the old brown-brick walls
and where on Sundays
it always, ha ha, seemed to rain…

But that wouldn't matter anymore
now that she was finally gone
& where for a long time
they would still often speak in puzzled
whispers of the Irish *mystery girl*
& who she'd really been
because the mysteries
in those times
they were the colleens who had no
proper names &
came and went, without ceremony, in the night
the housewives
the part-time nurses
like phantoms
coming & going
on buses

not full-time
pleasurers like themselves
at all.

Ah, The Mystery Girl, they would fondly sigh,
recalling the nights
when she'd tipsily ascend the stage
in Nano's –
at first a little shyly
& then, when she got going,
singing her pretty little heart out
becoming ever more
emboldened.
& how boisterous &
rowdy
the clientele would become
when she'd raise her dress
just that little bit
above her knee
aye
& shake her hair
and along came three middle-aged
men onto the tiny platform
alongside the rows of wine barrels
as they tuned their instruments
more in preparation for a funeral than a party
it seemed
but oh how wrong you would be
thinking that
with their evening dress
white shirts
& ready-made bow ties
one sporting a jet-black toupee
the drummer with a pronounced limp.
as the leader, melancholic
& exotically quiffed
attired in a two-piece black suit
& spotless, stiff-collared white shirt
continued with the process
of attaching a cumbersome contraption to the piano –
ingeniously transforming it into an electric
fairground organ.
& then giving Dots her long-awaited

thumbs-up
As the 'Mystery Lady' once more
assumed the stage
& launched into her showstopping
signature tune, one she had learned
from observing Johnny Dankworth:
about those little bebop mouse-rascals
which never failed
to bring the house down
that impertinent little novelty jazz tune
probably because she put her heart and
soul into it
because that was how she felt herself
that all her life she had been toyed
with,
solely there to provide amusement
for someone, or some
thing.

Before disappearing into the Soho night
is that you Doreen
Doreen Fogarty
is that you
Dots
come back here Dotsy
Dotsy Fogarty come back here a
moment
splashing through oily puddles
with a headache
& then what happened
didn't she go & break a heel
Mary I'm sorry
for doing the dance
I'm sorry for slighting you
and your father
I'm sorry for entertaining
doubts & wicked thoughts
O Mary conceived
without sin
pray for us who
have recourse to thee!
With a tear in her eye
as she folded her fingers

around the silver
miraculous medal
yes, the very same one
which Una, to this very day,
wears on a string
of blue wool
beneath her vest.

Screams,
indeed,
if
she's
left
without
it.

Yes, if my sister happens to be
deprived in any way
of that sparkling little oval
which consistently,
even to this day, brings her solace,
here in the afternoon quiet of Cliftonville
fingering that polished little escutcheon
as she murmurs, giving it a kiss:
O Maria concepta sine peccato qui ad te
confugiumus
O Mary conceived without sin
pray for us who have recourse to thee –
and which can explain
that faint, distant smile of
gratitude
you can often determine
on her countenance
when she's sitting by the
window eating her meals

or by the high window,
staring off into space
when the rest of us are watching
Planet Earth with
Attenborough,
or *Emmerdale*,
or any of the rest of
the programmes which are
on during the day.

The plucky iguana,
nonetheless,
remaining the all-time favourite
of everyone sitting there,
as Todd Creedence lets
out his trademark cheer
& goes clambering across
the chairs as he lifts
his closed fist and hollers:
'Motherfucking sumbitch diamondbacks!' –
meaning the reptiles, of course,
who have been lying in wait all morning
outside the hatchling's egg
which then cracks open
as off he shoots like a bullet
and against all the odds
manages to leave the slimeball
predatory fuckers of snakes behind
as he stands there triumphantly
on top of the ridge
grinning away as one of the wrigglers
goes *ahhhhh!*
& loses its balance
& tumbles away
         down
              the
                   side
                        of
                             the
                                  ravine

towards infinity.

& which is good
she really enjoys that
although I have to be honest
& say that
even since this morning
I don't think Una,
God love & guard her,
that she is looking at all well.
I only hope she makes it as far as the show.

Although, to be perfectly honest,
I haven't been feeling all that well myself,
with all this reminiscing
maybe not doing me the good
that I'd hoped it would.
Because a lot of the time I find
I keep getting these headaches
& don't have the patience I might
have once had with Una
even if I admit I was never
at any time a saint.

It could be my background,
of course,
growing up on the side
of a wet mountain
in a valley far from
any proper code of manners
or civilisation,
with things not helped
by the invasion of a vindictive
clergyman
& his platoon of fellow-travelling
landlords' agents
who made out to be affronted
by the subversive prevalence
of lax morality
in our homestead
but who, all along,
had wanted nothing
only the little biteen
of land that we possessed
yes, every one of those grabbers,

whose descendants
are still to be found in Currabawn today
& which is why, perhaps,
I had that dream
in which I saw Felix Clohessy,
descendant of the landlord's agent
coming whistling, it seemed
without a care,
along the road
& I says to him: ah there
you are, Felix, my man!
cén chaoi ar mhaith leat do tóin le hagaidh caubeen?
– how would you like your arsehole
for a hat?
& what does he see looking at him
when he starts & turns around –
only the perkiest little blackbird
yes, a smooth-plumed wee *londubh*
standing perched in a bower
& it whistling its heart out

although in a manner most
unusual, it must be conceded,
proceeding: *skrik skrik! Skrik kraik!*
just as the ambulance
– an ambulance, I do declare!
comes tearing around the corner
at high speed,
and ploughs right into the
trína chéile –
that is to say, discombobulated
poor Felix,
leaving him stone dead
there on the road.
Dead, surely
which is bad
but not one whit to compare
with what happened to the local
priest, a youngish curate
& one as wouldn't be
inclined to believe in *gruagachs*
not, at least, until he woke
up, having given birth to a hare,

& which, after a portion of time
had elapsed,
he succeeded in attributing to
his indulgence in too much
wine the night before –
before looking over
& there it was, in the corner
watching, large as life –
with the sheets of the
leaba
completely saturated in blood
& it stock-still, not moving
a muscle.
Yes, the giorria
the hare,
with not even so much as the slightest twitch
perceptible in its ears.

The very exact same entity,
or manifestation as had met
the eyes of Troy McClory
one night, long ago
towards the end of that summer
of 1974
when he had done
his share of dreaming too
after a beautiful day
they had all enjoyed in Hampstead
when everyone had been drinking
bicycling and catching
butterflies
yes, pretty fluttering féileacháin
laughing away up there on
The Heath
& even though now it was
the middle of the night
& he knew he was still stoned
yes, very very stoned
and indeed drunk as well
he really ought to have known
that it wasn't just
any old ordinary

dream
no, not at all,
& that what he was experiencing
in fact
was a premonition
no, no brionglóid
no
not a chance
not a fantasy
not any kind of dopedream
or night-time random wayfaring of
an overstimulated mind
as he heard:
'May the curse of Calvary
and the seven rancid kingdoms
light upon your brow
this night,
Troy McClory
& any amadán
who is slow-witted enough
ever to attempt ill-rating
the Fogartys!'

& it was then he awoke
to see something
scuttling across the floor
something which he could not
quite make out
& which made a rustling sound
like grasshoppers.

But which, just as suddenly
as it had appeared, was gone.

Troy McClory flicked on the light switch.

It was like someone or something
was reaching down inside his brain.
With matters not being helped one bit
by the fact that
not only had he been drinking & smoking

but had ingested considerable quotas of *speed*.
In an alternate world, it might have been
amusing,
lighthearted & funny.
Yes, *greannmhar* perhaps,
possibly even hilarious.
Like something, conceivably, from
the popular BBC television programme
Monty Python.

Way out.
Too much.

But not now, however.

Because right at that moment,
Troy McClory felt truly ghastly.
& couldn't quite understand it,
for hadn't their so-called
spiritual decontaminator,
their exorcist,
The Fumigator,
given the building
a clean bill of health?

All he could conclude
was that Mitchell,
yes Phil Mitchell,
aka Donnie Butterworth,
that he must have been wrong
– or worse still, had been nothing
other than a fraud
a charlatan, yes
who didn't know what
he'd been talking about.
Anyway, this was it,
pretty much,
Troy's own personal jaunt
up to Calvary –
how it began.

With every type of sound
now arriving in the night
with no other purpose
at least that he could determine
other than to trouble him
to torment him,
aye, and give him a serious
dose of the trimmlins.

Except not only
in the middle of the night
but just as often
in the early morning & middle
of the day.
SHUT UP!
implored Troy,
hands
pressed against his ears
knowing in his heart
he was only making
things worse
with that, once, in a fit
he had raced across the
room and delivered a swift
& mighty blow of his foot to
the cheap little stereo still playing

T
U
B
U
L
A
R

B
E
L
L
S

in 9/8
  7/8
time
plinka
plonka-a
plinka plonka
plinka plonka
plink
before realising just what he
had done
holding two sections of the broken
record in either hand
just staring down at them
like he'd forgotten what
they were

which is sad
yes, a pity
& none of which
need ever have happened
& indeed more than likely
probably never would
but for the day
that he decided to publicly
disrespect my sister.
Although, admittedly, not
without the assistance of others,
who can accurately be described as
both eager & willing.
Yes, certain other 'psychic cosmonauts'
who, purportedly, had been her friends
all Summer
& whose number
obviously
would have included
Iris,
Joanne
&
'The Duchess', Tanith Kaplinski
dancer extraordinaire
& would-be award-winning star of
Sadler's Wells Theatre

Sometimes also, though, the boys would
join in
especially if they happened to be *ar meisce*
drunk, in otherwords
or out of their minds on amphetamines, ethyl
alcohol, or even STP.
& which was why the police had all laughed so
much
when representatives of this raggle-taggle band
had arrived into the station in Queen's Park
and reported that they'd been hearing
well
various noises.
Noises
noises
what kind of noises
music
they
said
that kind of
noise
muffled music
like drums
&
sometimes
this weird kind of
rustling sound
rustling sound
said the cops
yes, like grasshoppers
the kind that maybe grasshoppers
make
ha ha said the cops
maybe it might
be some of your pals
from the IRA
your bombing friends
no they
said you have got
to believe me.
That was a good laugh, said the policemen
that was a good one, eh
a flat that's haunted by IRA
grasshoppers

that really does get me going.
Anything else
the cop said to Jo
yes, she said
Rumpy pumpy
Rumpy pumpy, said the cop
Rumpity pumpity
Rumpity pumpity, said the cop
And bumpity bumpity,
a wardrobe filled with bricks
falling down the stairs.
I have fucking had it
said the cop
so have I
his colleague
agreed
throw these time-wasting
morons out
& inform the lot of
them they're lucky
they're not charged
with wasting the time of the police
you're lucky we don't charge you
with wasting the valuable time of
the police
rumpity pumpity
fucking bumpity

With it just being unfortunate
that the Birmingham bombs had happened
around that time along with
some other, less spectacular
outrages
so that not all that many people
would have been very favourably disposed
towards the likes of Troy
& his pals, at any rate
what with the country
seeming to lose its shape
a place in desperate
need of discipline
with shortages, blackouts
& certain catastrophe seeming
to be looming

We'll see what we can do, the senior policeman said, in
disbelief staring at the jottings he'd made:

Rumpity pumpity
Rumpity boom
&
what sounded like a wardrobe falling down the stairs
& then went off to get his tea.

There were those
who contended that the
'continuing disturbances'
they might be attributable to
as the antiquated plumbing system
which hadn't been touched in over fifty years
according to said Alex Gordon
the ex-services caretaker
so I mean what would you expect
he kept on saying, impatiently hoking leaves
from a maddeningly blocked drain
although, you ask me mate, I reckon
it might have helped
if the lot of them in there
hadn't spent their time injecting themselves with
needles
& suchlike.

& who knows –
I mean, who can rightly say?
That Sexy Lexy – that the former
serviceman,
Moody Alex,
– that he wasn't right?

Although I definitely did
feel sorry
for Troy
Well, maybe not all that much, but definitely a
little – certainly on that particular night
when he found himself waking up yet again
all sweated up
but at the same time
ice cold
& imagining himself being addressed by, can

you believe it, a coin
or what, at first, he had taken to be one –
an old sixpence, in fact.
But, as it transpired, was an old-fashioned miraculous
medal, shaped like the cutesiest little oval moon.

I have never really seen him in such an awful state,
with it making no difference in the wide world
at all,
him closing his eyes or pressing his hands
ever so tightly against his ears.

Such a sweet voice,
to make him feel so
terribly afraid
to invoke such an enduring
state of *imní* in the already profoundly
troubled student.
To be worried about a medallion,
just like the one he had sung about
to his adoring girlfriend on the heath
namely my sister Una

when he'd strummed his guitar
& sung her Bob Dylan
when they'd been up in Hampstead
squatting there by the pond
listening to the bees
humming in the very same key,
Troy laughed, as he sang a Dylan
song all about beauty.

Yes, those were the words
he had used, serenading our Una
my Una
my lady with the sad eyes
you are all mine,
he said,
yes, that was exactly what Troy
had said
neglecting to add
the other bits that he was thinking
namely

I mean you do believe that
don't you, Fatty Fogarty.
you do believe every word
I'm saying
tell me, Fudge –
assure me that you do,
hee hee.
Cor, wot a laugh.

& now here it was
that very same shield
gleaming in the Kilburn moonlight
as it dangled there in the
pale milky light
yes, ever so slightly
swaying back and forth.

Coincidentally,
the same one which had provided such
enormous amusement for some of
the others in the flat
including the human matchstick
Miss Iris Montgomery-Carew.
With all of them finding it
soooooo
amusing
when they'd been dressing our Una up
to make her look 'presentable & cool.
Real cool.'

Because they were all attending
a concert, you see
& Una had been afraid
she might look out of place.
So they'd all agreed to 'style' her.
Look at her little holy medal, they said.
She wears it to protect her from coming
to any kind of harm in England.
O Mary conceived without sin
pray for us who have recourse to Thee.

The Mother Of Christ will protect her, it says.
Ah, the poor thing.
Yes, poor little fudgy Miss Pudgy McFudge.
Let's doll her up and make her look presentable.
Turn her into a seventies groovy chick –
trying out all these different types of sunglasses
to make her look like *Nico* from the *Velvet*
Underground
Tee hee!
What a scream.
Fudge McFogarty, Killiburn's own version of the
Goodyear Blimp.
Ha ha.

By now, naked and shivering
by his bedside,
in the Killiburn gloom,
Troy McClory, whether it was
the dope or not, with all of this
he really was finding himself
becoming quite dazzled.
Not having anticipated that the coin,
or medal, rather,
that it could possibly have known
so many things about him –
such an amount!
It did, however,
it certainly did.
As the silver rays bathed &
overtook him completely
swamping him, yes
though not entirely unpleasurably,
as they shimmered and glowed
and the little moon seemed to
smile, telling him a story
of the kind he used to so long
to hear
in the newsagent's shop of
his best friend
in the whole world
Professor Douglas McVittie
where after school they would dream

[455]

up more inventions
including invisibility cloaks,
ice-bullet telescopes
& capes that when you swooshed
them
covered the world in magic
dust
something like you'd see,
maybe encounter
in the Land Of Rupert
Yes, Rupert The Bear
somewhere along
those verdant slopes of Nutwood
among those bonny
banks and braes
Wheer are ye,
mah clever little friend
where could you possibly be gone?
laughed Doug,
ye olde Professor from Morningside
long ago.

Troy wondered
what the scientist might
make of this
magic shield
this mirror of the ages
a circling silver
shiny polished moon
a magic coin that could talk.

O how he wondered
over and over again
till it started up again
the by-now familiar
pain in his head
that went *rrrrrrtt!*
Which was
when he heard the muffled
sound that made him stiffen

poker-stiff
because there it was again
the exact same noise being

repeated
a soft swishing rustle
of the type that maybe
grasshoppers might make,
the softest whisper

why do birds sing,
the susurration wanted to know
though it wasn't scary
at least not initially
more like the voice
of a little boy or girl
from a way back
why do birds sing
he heard it enquire again
because a bird is rarely silent
sociable creatures though they are
they are generally highly strung
perpetually on the alert.

Why is it they do it, Troy
is it the joy of being together,
of having the same plumage
the exact same life and the exact same soul?
Or is it, as your friend
Professor McVittie used to say,
if you remember,
that they simply have no choice
other than to liberate themselves,
through nature,
of the vital bursting plenitude
they harbour
within themselves, Troy
within themselves
yes, within themselves.

Then the distinctive rustling &
the voice itself fell
silent.
As the silver medal turned
first this way and then that.

Why did you call my sister names?
Why did you disrespect her,
a fresh voice queried,
why, Troy McClory,
did you go and have to do
a thing like that
& use her to stick your *bud* in
whenever you wanted
any time the desire would
overcome you
& she was available
because that is not a nice thing
to do
no not a very nice thing at all
anymore than calling her
a Goodyear Blimp
or Fatty or Fudge –
I don't like it at all.

But why do birds sing
that is the eternal question
that is the question
which remains,
& with your brains
you really ought to know.
Unless, of course, as in so many
other aspects of your life,
you are really little more
than a faker,
yes, a fraud, Troy McClory,
because if you weren't
&, in actual fact,
were a proper musician,
not to mention artist,
why, then you would know
that musical art is born of satisfaction
the satisfaction which a being
experiences in expressing his life
by a sound.
The golden fly, Troy,
buzzing, loves the noise of his wings
the cicada, in the ecstasy of his vibration
forgets the enemy watching for him.
Do you know what I mean, young McClory,

a bird enjoys the note modulated
by his throat.
So, open your mouth, Troy.
Yes, there's a good boy
open those dry, cracked,
trembling lips.
Maith an bookil, attaboy Troy,
now take this holy communion and be sorry
do penance and repent for what it is
you've done
& Troy McClory did as he was bid
almost folding his hands in supplication
as the miraculous medal's metal
touched his hot fevered tongue
&, in that instant, its true radiant glory
enveloped him
&, just at that moment, he saw
them both exactly as they had been.
Yes, Troy & Una, my lovely sister
Nunie, my beloved sister & Troy
on that very first night
when they'd gone to
The Marquee
The Marquee Theatre
where all the best rock groups
in town could be enjoyed
& saw there for the very first
time
Troy's favourite,
Robert Fripp & King Crimson
who were playing their album
in its entirety,
none other than the
'magnificent opus'
as Troy had often referred to it,
IN
THE
WAKE
OF
POSEIDON,
whose 'dark, enduring majesty'
he so admired.

And which, prompted
by the fond reminiscence,
he was about to place on the
stereo turntable
when the phone rang
abruptly.

With
Troy McClory
stubbing his toe
as he crossed the room
doing his best
to extricate his foot
from the carpet on which
he'd just snagged it
before falling sideways
& banging his elbow
before eventually
succeeding in righting
himself
stumbling over
the debris of sleeping bodies
anyone who
happened to remain
because the majority of the occupants
by this stage had
gone
just a Dutch student
&
some couple
from Cornwall
then making it, with some effort,
into the hall
where the instrument
was still urgently ringing away

Hello hello
said Troy – *hello?*
Hello who's that
he didn't recognise the voice
but again, it sounded
like that of a child
maybe a boy
or it could have been

a girl
but it didn't matter
for Troy had become
a block of ice
Professor McVittie
tonight he's going to die
it said
& so he did

Troy got the news the following morning
at nine
a car accident
just a mile or two
outside Glasgow.

So things, as you can see, they
weren't improving.

& not so very long after that, there
came the pending interview with
The King Of Cavan
Macaulay 'Breffni' O'Rourke
who had long since been under
suspicion because of his
friendship with Blind Owl
Frank
yes, Frank Olson who'd been
kicked out of training
college along with him,
acid-fried Blind Owl
blissfully wandering in
his own private world
behind those black, thick-framed
spectacles
& Macaulay too.
& this is where it had led
as the quivering King Of Cavan
began muttering
to himself
already, in his own mind,

shrinking hopelessly in size
from six foot two
to five foot nothing,
asking himself repeatedly
why did I ever stop in that place?

As he sat behind the table
& the sergeant walked around
a different officer this time
different officer
different station
So you're telling me, he said,
that your name is The King,
– that that's what you're known as
by your friends and associates?
Yeah. That's right, officer. That's the deal.
And that's it?
Just The King, man.
Macaulay O'Rourke, The King Of Cavan.
But they weren't convincing,
either his charm or
braggadocio, that is –
no, not anymore.

I want you to look at a couple of photos.
Do you think you could maybe do that for me?
Or are you already too out of your fucking head?
Easy, man.
Hey, man. Jeez!

& so commenced:
The Paddington Inquisition.

Very well then
I hope you are comfortable –
are you comfortable?
Yes, I am
but don't worry about that
because all you're going
to get out of me is

the truth
so you can take it easy
and relax, my brother
because I got
no problem with anyone
no, none of my fellow man
whether *fuzz* or not
nope
no axe to grind with
society
nothing
just answer the questions
if you wouldn't mind
if you please
I'm sorry, officer
I beg your pardon
so describe to me the hovel
that you live in
if you would
let's start from the top.
It's nothing, man
it's just a place. To us it's home,
it's love
it's a den.
A den
I see
love
yes, I see.
Your neighbours have supplied us
with valuable information
regarding the type of
behaviour which one might
expect to encounter there
yes, at No. 45 Brondesbury Gardens.
Ha ha, laughed The King,
I know who you mean
when you say our neighbours,
those two freaks next door
The Pokey Men,
as Troy likes to call them
ha ha.
Well, they got no damned business
spreading lies & rumours
no, no damned business

harassing us, officer.
You think this is a proper way to live?
said the officer.
Then, at this point,
the photos appeared:
the old worn blanket
hanging in front of the window
the grave in the garden
where they'd buried Mr Jones
the deranged Airedale
to whom someone had
heartbreakingly
administered a tab of acid.
The garden, said the officer
that's the place
for one of God's creatures
wouldn't you say
those innocent animals
with whom you say
we share the planet
That was a bad vibe,
officer
a bad suss, really
we don't know who did it.
And, ever so softly, Macaulay
O'Rourke
began to weep.
Have a look at this,
said the sergeant then
crushed cans & debris
orange-crate ashes
filthy mattresses
&
ashtrays filled with roaches
with a sign on the wall
FUCK
THE PIGS
UP
THE IRA,
The King Of Cavan said
I want to make a statement
you have arrested one of my comrades
he said
& intend to charge him with conspiracy

to commit murder
you say he was planting
bombs
but I happen to know for a fact
that he wasn't
because, you see,
he was with me at a gig
to see Mott the Hoople.
He was with you at what?
the officer said
He was with me at a gig
Mott the Hoople
in The South Bank Poly
at the very same time that you
say he was someplace else
& if you don't believe me
well then, officer, you can check
yes, check in the bar directly across
the road
because he will tell you
yes, the barman will tell you
he'll tell you exactly where he
was
yes, & Frank Olson too
he will tell you where
my comrade was,
because he knows.
Comrade? said the officer
yes, comrade
why did you call him that
call him comrade
what has that got to do
with anything?
I think it was you
you who administered the drug
to Mr Jones
No, he said
no, The King said
stop it
don't say that
with the truth being
that he wasn't sure
not entirely certain
because it could have been

might possibly have been
because, after all
they had been so out of it
that night when they'd
arrived home from
The Hippodrome
what a crazy night
that had been
woozy so woozy
with oil projections
dancers
flashing lights
&
Alpha Waves
like
gravity-defying water
coming flowing
down along
the walls
Answer the fucking question!
demanded the sergeant
answer the fucking question
when you're asked!
Comrade.
Irish Republican fellow traveller.

And that was when Macaulay saw it – whatever
it was
standing there watching him
in shadow at the back of the room,
with small arms folded.
He started crying
softly at first
but then, gradually, uncontrollably
as the policeman sighed
and flung another
file on the table in front
of him
You had better keep quiet about this
he said
because the people we have for this
already

they done it
and no one else
so make sure and keep your
mouth shut about alibis
because if you don't
if you so much as breathe a word
about concerts
or Mott the Hoople
then every word of this
will be printed
he opened the file
already two convictions
for possession of LSD
expelled in disgrace
from teacher training college
The King started weeping again.
Here, said the officer
handing him a hankie.
membership of The Anti-Internment League.
What's this? said the officer.
Macaulay's skin crawled
& then crawled some more
he could see it, smiling
tapping its toe
making that same, barely there
sound like rustling
ah but begob you're a mighty man,
Cavan,
it said in a suppressed whisper –
the gruagach.
With his face all of a sudden
breaking into a broad, cheeky grin
as he tapped his toe
& went *rumpity*
with his fingers,
the sergeant remaining
really quite oblivious
as, of course, was the
express intention
as he smiled again
& went rumpity boo
& the poor King Of Cavan
that helpless old Macaulay
O'Rourke

Lord bless us –
talk about trimmlins!

Here's a health to you, Father O' Flynn
Sláinte and sláinte and sláinte again
Powerfullest preacher, and
tenderest teacher, and
kindliest creature in auld Donegal!
he heard.

Then it halted & there wasn't
so much as a sound
– not a peep.
Are you okay? asked the sergeant.
What is it you're looking at?
As the strangest calm seemed to overtake
The King Of Cavan.

&
the officer was impressed
for a while, at least.

But then his suspect offered:
it's *them*, you know.
Tragedy is, that once upon a time
in fact, they were angels.
Did you know they can sometimes appear
as a whirlwind of dust?

& that was as far as he got before
the sergeant on duty
rose from the table to be relieved by
his colleague
a gruff Yorkshireman in his fifties.

Who didn't even bother to look in the suspect's
direction.
The poor hippy-monarch who was now in
the middle of talking to himself
hey dudes
where are you
I wanna hear you

nervously chanting
the words of Mott the Hoople
a tune of theirs
that you often could hear
Troy McClory singing
but what does the name really
mean, laughed The King,
ha ha
what does it mean
what does Mott the Hoople
actually mean
he kept repeating
when they were finally
locking him in the holding cell
this is the question
only then realising
that no one was listening.

No one, that is,
except the small, crouched
effigy
sitting there waiting for him
in the corner of his cell
with the pointed hood
of its jerkin
tugged forward
so as you couldn't
rightly catch a glimpse
of its eyes.

With the only one, ever,
to be told about this
being the editor of a book of
poems, ironically
by the self-styled King Macaulay
'Breffni' O'Rourke
who had been the only one,
really,
from The Temple
who, ultimately, amounted to anything
much.
& this was many years later
at the beginning of the nineties

capturing a coveted award
for his acclaimed slim volume
in which he'd described
the greatest trauma of his life
the gruagach there, waiting –
demonstrating all the conceivable
patience of the world
through eyes that seemed truly infinite
in their depth
so chillingly resourceful
in the gruagach's capacity
& appetite for vengeance –
its hand stretching out,
the colour of clay.

Thus, then, concluded the
adventures
of the 'New Society' in
No. 45
Brondesbury Gardens.

With the house pretty much
deserted
with no one ever dreaming,
not at that time
that one day it would become a modern
motel.
Namely, of course, The Rambler's Rest.

To which I had made my sacred
pilgrimage, something
which I do not regret
in spite of the degree of danger & personal risk
which it brought to Una, as much as myself.

All the same, though, I'm glad that we
made the trip up to London.
Because I just knew that the
sacred little oval
miraculous medal
that it would still be there –
even after all these years
& just what it would mean to Una to get her
hands on it once more.

I could feel her heart beating as I brushed
away the cobwebs, and found it right there –
in the exact same place that I'd left
it,
over forty-five years ago now.

When a small excavation had revealed
its presence
o how our hearts had leaped!
for there it was
that very same little greyish ball
of cotton wool
slowly unwrapping the wad
of cotton

o heavens
how it shone!
As Una went dancing around the room
before kissing the inscription
underneath The Virgin's feet
aye, giving it the greediest *pogue*
as she squealed, sweeping her skirts:
O Mary conceived without sin
pray for us who have recourse to thee!
she wept
& it was worth it all
just to see that
even if she'll never give me credit
for bringing her there
slandering me and saying that
I don't even fucking exist.

But then, that's our Una
& you just have to accept
that's the way things are.

What a miracle!
I could hear her say,
mo dheirfiúr dílis Una,
my ever so good-natured
kind-hearted sister Una,
sensing her closer to me now
than ever
even if I might have imagined it
as off
the pair of us went
on a sightseeing trip around
London
to celebrate
a place so changed
you could scarcely imagine
now that we'd reached
the year of our Lord 2019.

But still so wondrous!
I exclaimed, as we cruised
& I held her hand tightly
on the upper deck of a

cherry-red Routemaster bus –
Just
like
old
times!
Una giggled gaily.
& which indeed it was
in a strange kind of way
like as if you could make out
the X-ray skeleton of
the old town
somewhere deep in your memory
as on we
whizzed
with our fingertips folded
lovingly around
the lambent shield of ages.
Hooray! we both squealed,
as my lovely sister
she gave ME
a pogue,
resting her gentle warm head
on my shoulder
as on we sped
through the streets
of perhaps the greatest city
in all the world:

*SNAPCHAT   *TDK   *GOOGLE

*BRAVIA   !!!!   *PANASONIC
                              !!!
*FOX ROLLING   *SAMSUNG

*FACEBOOK   *TWITTER
          !!!!   !!!

  !!!   *HYUNDAI   *REDDIT

*YOUTUBE   *INSTAGRAM
              *SKY

continuing on our journey
making sure to keep it safe
that glowing scáthán
glistening magic mirror
in which
everything that ever had happened
to the Fogartys
was contained
but most of all
events in Brondesbury Gardens.
However, all of that was history now
thought Una, as one we sped
past
*Costcutters!
*Sports Direct!
*Vodafone!
      &
*Cash For Gold!

chugging along in the warm-seated bus, Una
sat upright and patient
as a small girl – beaming
as it made its way through Knightsbridge
& then
on to Hyde Park Corner
before arriving in the heart of
Piccadilly
where she disembarked,
waiting to cross at Burger King.
Tourists and Londoners streamed
around Una Fogarty
none of them knowing for
one single second just how successful
her trip to The Rambler's Rest Motel
had actually been
and just what an age-old treasure
she was
holding in her hand.

Such a babble on all these mobiles,
she thought,
sensibly avoiding the raging currents
of Shaftesbury Avenue
then cutting up the backwater

of Sherwood Street
beneath the Bridge Of Sighs
at the back of the Regent Palace Hotel
where homeless kids lay
begging in blue sleeping bags
& right into Brewer Street.
Feeling free as a bird
to be at last away from
Cliftonville Bay
as she spent the whole afternoon
singing her heart
out as prettily as any swallow
or blackbird
throwing her head back
in gloriously ecstatic pose
& breaking into spontaneous performance
in short sudden bursts
singing the song of what must
surely have been
existence.
The real – and perhaps *only* reason – why the
sweet little birdies in the trees
perform at all.

Having just enough time
to buy some presents for Connie and
Margaret Rutherford
before hailing a taxi and speeding off
to Victoria Station
& thence back to her home-from-home
in Cliftonville
after the most magnificently satisfying day trip
ever
making her way back to the only home she
knew
after the collapse of Troy McClory's
aspirant empire
the only one she was ever likely to have
with all her friends
at the legendarily hospitable
Cliftonville Bay hotel.

With the station being crowded
because she'd gone and forgotten that it was
actually the August bank holiday weekend
&
all the carriages
were stuffed from end to end.

With excited páistí everywhere
& all of them running
hither & thither & yonder
yes, up and down the aisles
the way that little childre always do
blowing these multicoloured
streamers out of little cardboard tubes
before having to be warned
by the conductor
a thin and grey-haired man in his sixties
who looked, Una considered
not at all unlike
Alex Gordon
yes, Moody Alex
as they used to call him
God rest his soul.
It had been a long time since she'd
thought about him, she sighed
as a middle-aged lady caught
her attention
optimistically indicating
the seat directly opposite
& being immediately given the go-ahead
from a more
than accommodating Una,
as she sat herself and her two children down
I'm forever blowing bubbles one of the
bright-eyed páistí was singing,
encouraged by a fellow in
a tracksuit
opposite.

Who had the exact same thick neck
& bristled, bullet-style head
as a certain person she had known

in the past
yes, which reminded her so much
of Phil Mitchell
self-styled so-called
spiritual decontaminator
from all those
many distant years before,
Don Butterworth.
Who knows where the time goes?
Troy used to sing,
Una remembered,
the old Sandy Denny song.
& straight away
saw him in her imagination
with that great big frizz of
lion's mane
unwashed
blondie hair
that leather jacket
& his Ian Hunter
aviator shades
preparing to recite his favourite poem
& which, incidentally,
was particularly important to her
what with it being the one he had
recited to her personally that day
beneath the sycamore
in the middle of Queen's Park
not so very far
from the sandpit
where,
heartbroken,
after the fall of Troy
& his broken empire,
nervous but overjoyed
she'd, quite miraculously,
encountered her own little
future family –
yes, her own private páistí
Bobbie and Ann
who everyone afterwards
insisted that she'd
kidnapped
& in some kind of mental delirium

made them
her own private birdies
sneaking them secretly
into her nest
like her own private,
personal
Children Of Lir
two little birdies
who, somehow, had been
magicked
into swans –
yes, two lovely white ealaí
that was what they had said about
her and the páistí
Una and those lovely little
kiddies
Bobbie beag
&
sweetest lickle freckle-faced Ann.

& maybe, yes, that's what it had
looked like
but with the truth being
she hadn't done any such thing
no, not kidnapped anyone
only just wanting to save them
& give them a home

Anyway, just like
Troy's dreams for The Mahavishnu Temple
the whole thing had ended in complete disaster.
But she didn't mind any of that,
no, not now so much.
Not now that she had her
miraculous medal
once again in her safekeeping
and through which
she could see
their *little birdie* faces
yes, any
old
time
she
wanted,

she smiled –
permitting herself to indulge a
luxurious little shiver.

Because she had no intention
no, absolutely no intention of
permitting even the slightest
hint of shadow to fall, at any time,
across their pretty faces
or any other unwelcome &
clearly mistaken memories
from that wonderful
Queen's Park day, no matter
what anyone else
had thought about it.
Na páistí goidte!
Kidnapping, pah!
What balderdash & poppycock,
truly.

No, had solemnly vowed to keep it
the sacred relic
close to her heart
for, heaven knows, quite enough of
her treasured remembrances
were disappearing fast enough by the day
with whole streets of houses falling
down in silence
as effective as the Luftwaffe
dropping their payloads
in the film
Green For Danger.

You go to the shop
& then when you come back
you're not there
& neither, as a matter of fact,
are your loved ones
either
or the house that you lived in
once upon a time
mummy
daddy

kings
& queens
entire populations
civilisations
ancient and modern
there they were
as Auntie Nano used to say
there was your history
all of it gone
city and country
all being erased
now that
Baron Von Richthofen was on the loose,
with his assiduous tail-gunner
strafing everything visible that
remained
ta-rat-ta-tat!

O dear, said Una,
shifting about on the seat of
the train
digging her nails into the
middle of the holy medal
but still giving a broad smile
as she went on twisting it
this way and that
before turning
to the little boy
opposite
& smiling, even more broadly
this time,
remarked
to the little chap:
O but yes!
and make no mistake!
Because that is what he will do,
The Red Baron!
Because that bloody rascal
you can be sure he'll
show no compassion
O
absolutely
none
at

all!
she insisted.

Then, finally, somewhat hoarse,
she appeared to relax,
settling her handbag on her lap.
Her cheeks were flushed &
all she kept thinking was
that she hoped they wouldn't start up again
waves of words and unconnected thoughts
coming surging like a great big
green-and-white Margate wave.

We're going to *Dreamland* –
the amusement arcade,
the little boy told her,
we're off for the weekend
with our buckets and spades.

Yes, and then it's off to the beach!
interrupted the little lady,
& maybe
if it's warm,
with a bit of luck,
go in for a swim
and duck our wiggly toes,
ha ha!

Their grandmother smiled and
offered Una a choice of sandwiches.
Flattered, my sister opted for ham.

They really are such wonderful children,
Una told her,
& in case you might think I
would harm them in some way
kidnap them
or anything untoward
like that
well, let me tell you
I most certainly would not
so you have absolutely
no need to be worried
on this trip or any other

because I, absolutely, would never
lay so much as a finger
on them or any other
páistí
because it wasn't me, you see
it was the gruagach.
&, after that, through no fault of her own
Una Fogarty was off again
as the crashing imagined
Margate green-wave broke
& words went scattering like
pebbles
some the size of pigeons' eggs
others large as ostriches'
all over the shingle of the beach
she imagined in her mind
sweet stalls, she said
as the children chortled.
Yes, hooray for Margate!
cheered Una Fogarty
as on she went
beach cricket, she suggested –
maybe, like Troy and I,
we could all have ourselves
a little game of that
outside one of the souvenir shops
that we're going to see
along with
yacht races
cotton dresses
motor launches
esplanades
&
not to mention
fish suppers
canvas camp chairs
& stretching yellow sands
scented with salt and seaweed
with rock pools
hidden away
where maybe we can engage in
some naval manoeuvres
what do you think
eh kiddies?

ha ha!
Ha ha!
That would be good
wouldn't that, yes, be
good—!

Then the children's grandmother
winced – just a little,
as she smiled & said
yes, perhaps,
responding to my sister
with one of those tolerant smiles
which was
the very exact same –
faint & lonely, Una thought
– as those that she'd seen
in black-and-white photographs of
her very own mother.
Where she looked
a little like the actress
Googie Withers
Una remembered from a
matinee on TV
one that she'd seen called
It Always Rains On Sunday,
ironically on a wet weekend
afternoon.

& which was why
she leaned across
the table and said to the grandmother:
Googie Withers, yes.
It always rains on Sunday, madam.

I'm sorry? she heard her fellow
passenger reply
but not in an unkindly way – just
because she was a little disconcerted.
As Una coughed hoarsely and explained
exactly what it was she'd meant.
Rachel Roberts
Rita Tushingham
even Bless This House, she said,
with Diana Coupland

it's often on
immediately after *Planet Earth*
it's a kind of crushed loneliness
you often find in English eyes.

Uaigneas an tSasanach,
Nano would have called it
although not for one moment
am I suggesting that it's any
particular preserve of the Norman
or the Saxon
for the old imní,
meaning anxiety or
depression,
Lord knows it comes to us all.
Irish, she sighed,
English
Chinese –
doesn't matter.

Yes, life is hard
agreed her fellow passenger,
it certainly can be difficult at times
even with these two little monkeys here
I have to remember to be on my guard
at times
already they have way
too much screen time
as you can see
as Una nodded
and the kids went on
staring at their smartphones
before sighing again and
shaking her head
& going on to explain
a bit more
as her counterpart listened keenly
and the telephones continued going
blip blip blip.

I wouldn't have so much as laid
a finger on those childre, explained Una,

it's all to do with Dan, you see –
only for him
it would all have been fine.
Yes, just fine, I really think it would,
except that he kept on
transferring his own private
bitternesses to me
& saying how he had never
got a chance
never had a proper start in life
that, whatever else,
at the very least I'd got born
& that was why he made me
do things
constantly interfering
making judgements in my mind
I mean what did he think
that I was only just this little stupid
mouse
there for him to perform his experiments on
ha ha ha
because that's all I can think
that that is all I represented to him
a silly little old mouse of a woman
that he could turn around and do
what he liked on
just the very same as my mother
& all the women and ladies of
the world
mice ha ha to be experimented on
just like in the song
ha ha
will I sing it
no because I can't
it'll only remind me of
her,
my mother Dots.

But, yes, that is the way
those are the facts,
that and his
impossible behaviour
none of the bad things
might ever have happened.

Although, in a way,
I don't entirely blame him,
never having been
adequately raised –
not even properly
born, as he says himself,
smiled Una Fogarty,
but he didn't have to turn
into an enemy
did he.
& which is what he did in the end
swearing and cursing
& calling me all sorts of names
you have no idea of
the kind of temper he can have
even now, she said
even yet that's true
right up to this very day
if you understand me.

The lady passenger nodded
as Una swallowed hard
and went back in her
mind to the memory of her own
flamboyant Troy
& the way he used
to stand on the stairs
as he read his verse
or sometimes even ascend the table
shaking out his curls
chewing intensely
on the stem of his shades,
after stammering a little,
shedding his triumphant stanzas,
declaiming a great big chunk
of Allen Ginsberg,
Pablo Neruda, maybe,
or T. S. Eliot –
not entirely dissimilar to this or
or any of my own other
Miltonesque epics
rendered in the style
so popular at the time

the ubiquitous Ampersand
oscillating between celebration
&
the
most
awful
catastrophes
imaginable.
With it just such a pity
that *Poguemahone*,
one's own unique concordat,
uncompromising account –
that it hadn't yet, unfortunately,
been fancied into being.

For what, I ask you,
is verse at the end of all,
if not art's apotheosis
whether scratched upon the
unblemished page
or across the breadth of firmament
unfurling before the sun –
yes, out among those clouds
exuberantly scrolled by twinkling
gruagach Gael,
or brown-eyed, platinum-haired
Senhor Exu.

Then, all of a sudden, Una jerked –
releasing a little cry
as Troy McClory's
expressive, handsome face
it dramatically and unexpectedly
fled from her mind.
As, in her frustration, Una Fogarty
grimaced and covered her
ears:
    Ka!
    Ka!
    Ka!
she heard him cry.
All the little birds of the air,
can you hear them, man –

those tireless voyagers,
what can they be trying to tell
us?

Before she felt his
strong arms around her
coming right back
out of nowhere
& kissing her
hard & passionate
on the lips
right there
in the kitchen of
The Mahavishnu Temple
right there
in front of everyone,
even Joanne and Tanith.
Maybe most *especially* Jo and Tanith,
to make amends for his
rotten behaviour towards her
along with them
that day in the bed
& not just because they had
called her names
such as Fudge
&
Fatty
&
Goodyear Blimp.
No, there were an awful lot
more things than that
to contend with
such as that night
when they'd agreed to
'make her look like Nico'
the legendary singer
& chanteuse from Lou
Reed's Velvet Underground –
who she really hadn't heard of
to be honest
& knew absolutely
nothing about
not that it mattered
because when they had

got her
completely stoned
they covered her face
all over in makeup
& then found this stupid old
Hollywood-style
lime-green trouser suit
& a pair of oversized
boxy glasses
& succeeded somehow
in convincing her that she looked
'real smooth',
a description which, mesmerised by their
effusiveness,
she had already begun not only
to accept but actually
revel in,
to the extent of even dropping
the occasional name
chiefly for the benefit of Troy McClory
such as: Syd Barrett,
Van Der Graaf
Generator,
& on one occasion,
Robert Wyatt of
Soft Machine
which she could see
had really impressed 'her man',
as she thought of him now,
in spite of everything.

Even, after a while,
trying out a few
little lyrics herself
strumming the ukulele
having become convinced
that, finally,
at long last,
she was
truly one of the
inner circle
& not just Ten Ton Tessie
from the bogs of Ireland

who had somehow wandered
into the commune by mistake

It was a lovely memory
&, even better, it had
remained intact for some
time
allowing her to luxuriate
properly
before once again vanishing
across the horizon of her mind
like a runaway flea
taking leave of the circus.
But she didn't mind
because at least it had stayed
a lot longer than was usual
although why that might be
she couldn't really say
& which provided the reason
why she cried suddenly, forgetting
that she was still in the train,
on her way to the seaside:
probably that fucking stupid
brother of mine, up to his tricks!

No wonder she was smiling,
she thought,
being able to give now
just as good as she got,
with the little boy across from her
in the carriage beaming
fondly back at her
hey Nana! she heard him say,
hey Nana
as his grandmother said yes
& he said Nana
I want to play
Angry Birdies!

& when she heard
that what could Una
do only smile
even more
doing

her best to blot it out
yes

not even
for so much as
a second begin to
dwell on it,
that lá uafasach
yes, that truly
awful, utterly appalling
day when, quite by chance
she'd arrived home
early
& what was it she found
yes, what did Una find
only Troy and Tanith
& Miss Joanne as well
enjoying a threesome in
the back bedroom
of Brondesbury Gardens,
with Tanith's slim bum
and it bouncing up and down
as she kept on repeating
Troy do you love me
Troy please say you do
as he held her tight and
plunged right into her,
groaning & groaning as
the perspiration splashed.
O my Tannie do you like it, say yes,
like what your hammer-man Troy has
to give you, do you
huh
do you, babe
huh
huh
huh?

And it was at that point,
just as the train began approaching
Herne Bay
that Una decided that she needed
a little support
just a small bit of encouragement

[491]

because that had been a hard
thing to remember,
perhaps the hardest one of all
something she'd been keeping to
herself all these years
just as she'd been doing with
her 'item of support',
the little doll which
she now produced –
her own *wee babogue*,
as she called it,
the one Auntie Nano
had given to her mother
& who, in turn, had passed it
on to her.
The Doll Of The Fogartys!
she smiled as she sighed,
unclasping her handbag
still smiling as she popped it out
her own little private
babbie baby bookie
ickle Bobbieann
the bestest Fogarty babeen
ickle bean-bag doll
a compendium of
her own little children
that never properly were
yes, a mixture of Bobbie
from Queen's Park
but also Ann
this is my little family
she said to the kiddies
and their gran:
Ann
&
Bobbie,
Bobbie
&
Ann
please will you say hello to them,
childre.

Bobbieann! cried
the páistí
momentarily setting
down their phones
hello Bobbieann!
they bleated,
as Una Fogarty smiled
yes indeed, my *childre*
on board the train along
with me to Margate
or Watertown as me and Troy
used to call it
long ago when the pair of us
we came here
for the day
Watertown, said the little boy,
why that's a good name
yes, all aboard for *Baile Faoin*
Uisce
with all of the Fogarty family
look here, do you see
here on top she's
got a boy's green blazer
& then
a girl's plaid
kilted skirt
isn't it nice.

A boy that's wearing
the kilt of a girl
said the little fellow
don't be cheeky, admonished
his grandmother.
As Una smiled
& said
no that he was right
for Bobbie had
indeed been sporting a blazer
when she'd met them
that Sunday afternoon
in Queen's Park
& asked them home.
Yes, showed them her medal
& asked them would they

like to have some treats
at home in her house
in The Valley Of Knocknanane

That means the *Valley Of the Birds*,
she explained to the childre
O, said the páistí,
already losing interest.

Not that she was in the business
of blaming them
no, not one bit
for what use is a kidnapping
which turns out to be nothing other than
a 'borrowing' –
why, it isn't a kidnapping at all,
for heaven's sake!

Anymore than a 'home'
which turns out to be a joke,
or a parody of one.

Suddenly, out of nowhere,
Una Fogarty burst into tears –
as her opposite number hastily offered
her a Kleenex tissue.
What did you say her name was again?
asked the little girl
tenderly placing her hand on Una's forearm.

But she wasn't really capable
or didn't feel she was
of making any reply
envisaging it all
with a clarity she'd assumed
lost to her
with a vividness returning
to that glittering weekend afternoon
when she'd returned from
Queen's Park

back to Brondesbury Gardens
with her heart in her mouth,
to a house now completely deserted
& abandoned
except of course for her glowering
brother Dan
o how she wished
they hadn't started arguing
the way families do
when they haven't known
true & proper love
do you know what's going to
happen, he said
for Christ's sake do you,
don't you know they're watching the house
& what do you do, you bring childre here!
Bad fucking cess to you for a sister
may God curse the day
that ever we shared a womb!

& if she lashed out and struck
her so-called brother Dan,
that snarling, glowering
Daniel Fogarty,
then what of it
for all he ever was,
yes, all he'd ever been
was a liar
swearing as he'd look out for her
& protect her
& all the time being an enemy
an adversary inside her head.

Una was sobbing intermittently now
dabbing her eyes with the scraps
of the tissue
as she thought
how even in the worst of times
she had never argued in that way
with Troy
No, never even in the most awful of
times
What a pity the Luftwaffe wouldn't
strafe him

yes, obliterate her so-called brother
with their machine guns
& bombs
and reduce that whole particular
street of memories to rubble
for the rotten way he had made her
feel
Not once but twice lifting his hand
to strike her
You óinseach! he'd hissed –
I rue the day!

With his face twisted up like
that of a loathsome *gruagach*
as why wouldn't it be
seeing as that's what he was.

How she wished she could have Troy back.

And all those wonderful times
that they'd had together.

Back in the days when
there hadn't been any
rustling
no sound of grasshoppers behind
walls
or eerie music proceeding out of vents
not to mention what sounded
like wardrobes falling over
or chests filled with bricks
being trundled downstairs
in the middle of the night.

none of that
& everyone wondering
whether it might be the demon
Pazuzu
that they'd seen in
The Exorcist
how else to explain the
fogged-up mirrors
the strange dreams
not to mention the

tragic suicide of
Tanith Kaplinski
a ballerina with such promise.

EYE
AM
WATCHING
YOU, read the words
underneath the enormous
eyeball,
crudely painted above the
mantelpiece,
as Dan Fogarty swore and kicked
over some more furniture,
at least you were born
born
born
born
which is a hell of a lot more than
I was ever going to be
the most traduced and isolated exile
of all
fated never to know so much as a hint of love
or to ever be within so much as the roar
of an ass of it
no, not even, God help me,
from my own dear sister
listen to me, damn you
when I am speaking
yes, listen to your own brother,
damn you!

& that was more than enough
for Una
more than she could find the strength
to withstand
& which was why, all those many long
years ago,
she had been overcome by the greatest
episode ever of the trimmlins
and, as a consequence, had begun to shake
and quiver herself
as well as shaking the two terrified children

to whom she apologised for
ever bringing them anywhere
near what was really her absurdly
impractical, hopelessly imaginary
home.

Insisting that it would be OK
& that now they wouldn't have to go back
to go anywhere near their awful mother
who was a heroin and cocaine addict
visiting her adulterous lover
in nearby
Carlton Vale
because from now on
she was going to be their mummy
yes, here in the Valley Of Knocknanane
but that was before Dan had got drunk
& started roaring and kicking
tables & chairs – even, good heavens! –
knocking over a wardrobe!
& when they saw him
& realised that this might be their future
they had started to cry because they were
afraid.
& which had then got to Una
who started also to scream,
& that was when her brother had
taken to slapping & beating her
& shaking the poor craythur
like she was nothing more than a *babogue*
herself
& threatening to pull her head off
saying listen
listen do you hear
&
what are you doing
shut up
shut up
dún do bhéal!

It was supposed
to be a home from home
a valley of dreams
that would show

all those fools
Troy McClory
included
just what a proper
new dawn
a whole new world ought to look like
but now
it was all over
so she hadn't any choice
no, none but to take them back
to the very same sycamore
by the sandpit in Queen's Park
to the very exact same spot she had
found them
& where the place was already swarming with
police
& who if not for me would have caught you said
Dan
me that has always been there
to guide you
for all the thanks
I ever received

After which she had put
their coats back on
& left them back at the corner
of Iverson Road
not a stone's throw from the
entrance to Queen's Park
& the majestic
overhanging sycamore

Goodbye, she had said.
Slán libh, a pháistí!
with it breaking her heart
to do it.
Knowing she'd never
have children of her own
whether with Troy or anyone else
& that this had represented
her very last possible chance.

No, no more birdeens for Una!
she exclaimed, all of a sudden,
leaning forward across the table
in the train,
divil a bit of éiníní ha ha
for me, old maid Fogarty!
As the children blushed a little
but, nonetheless, still smiled.

'It's the loveliest little dolly ever!'
exclaimed the little girl, blinking her eyes.
'The best I think
I've ever seen, actually!'
'May I shake hands with it?' enquired the boy
as Una lifted the doll's small hand.
'Look! She's got a lovely necklace
too!' exclaimed the girl.
'It's a medallion,' explained Una,
a sacred relic. Or, if you like, the Mirror Of the Ages!'

Wicked! said the little boy, angling his head
to inspect his reflection.

As the train once more began to
gather speed
shunting forward as the trolley lady stumbled,
doing her best to count out
change
for Una
who now insisted on treating everyone to cakes.
Danishes! she beamed,
holding Bobbieann by each arm
& swinging her gently to and fro.

Because Troy had always loved them,
Danish pastries,
just like Bobbieann!
she explained to the kids
at which point,
her fellow lady passenger,
the children's grandmother,
she began doing her utmost
to change the subject
being just that small bit afraid

that Una might,
in her excitement & enthusiasm,
come out with something which mightn't
be appropriate for the children's
young, impressionable minds.
'Ah yes, Margate!' the lady
began, unexpectedly.
'It won't be so very long now
till we've arrived
and will be passing by
Dreamland & the Winter Gardens,
which was practically a second home for
my husband and I
in our youth. And to think
that they've gone and opened it all up
again after all this time.
My, o my, who would have thought it
you think that the past it is gone
and then one day you wake up and
it's back.
I just can't wait to see it again!'

'Yes, Dreamland!' agreed Una
'I know exactly what you mean
& in some small way, now
that I think of it
it's responsible for the establishment
of my
own little troupe of performers
humble though they may be.
Oh yes.'
Performers? quizzed the lady,
pivoting a tiny crumb of pastry on her
little finger, I'm not quite sure I
understand.
We're going to see *The Good Dinosaur*
cried one of the children enthusiastically,
as the other one beamed,
dissolving into a bout of protracted
giddy laughter
covering most of her face with her hands.
Margate, continued the lady,
Margate has always had three natural
advantages as a seaside resort

& has done
right from the earliest Victorian times.
Because it's got good sea bathing, salubrious air
– and, of course, its admirable and beautiful situation.
Yes, and there's special trains
interjected one of the kids,
with lines and lines of lovely beach huts.
Yellow sands, the little boy said.
All them birds got cold feet
in them puggles, his sister giggled,
peeping out through the gaps between
her fingers
excited by the prospect of further laughter.
Watertown is the place for me
said Una Fogarty
for me and Troy
& our old friend
the great God Poseidon
ha ha.

The woman smiled faintly,
as the children enquired
where do you come from
wondering did
she come from Margate.
No, replied Una, you see
I'm from Currabawn.
Currabawn, the little girl mused,
that's a funny name.
I know! chuckled Una,
that's exactly what Troy
used to say,
that's a funny name
that's a funny name, love
he always used to say.
As the little girl laughed
shyly
Tee hee! She giggled, did you
hear what she said – she said *love*!
And Una could understand
why she might have found it amusing
– even unbelievable, perhaps.
That someone the likes of
Troy

yes, someone such as Troy McClory
should have ever considered
addressing her in such a manner.

But he did, as a matter of fact,
she then went on,
even though
I know that you probably won't believe it.

By this stage she was addressing
herself exclusively to their chaperone,
their by now quite discomfited & profoundly
concerned grandmother.
'However,' went on Una,
'if you listen to me carefully,
you'll see that everything I'm saying
everything that happened
in the end,
it all makes sense.
And that it should come
as no real surprise that
even at this late stage of my life
I might find myself in a position to do what
has always been my heart's desire.
That is to say,
to produce a harmless little revue
which is, to some extent, based on my life
& which, now that my business
in London is, finally,
concluded
I fully and unreservedly intend to do.
So – *Cliftonville Capers*, here we come!'

'You were attending to some business
Up in London then, were you?' probed the granny, glancing briefly
towards Bobbieann,
who my sister now had stood on her head.
Quite, agreed Una
because I knew I had left this *figary* behind me
But now that I've found it, safe and sound...'
Figary? puzzled the woman
as Una produced her medal
& folded her fingers
lovingly around it.

What I mean is this precious heirloom,
she explained
or, if you prefer, the Mirror Of The Ages
– call it what you will.
Our Lady conceived without sin
pray for us who have recourse to Thee! she
intoned.
'That's funny,' said the kids all together,
'it really is funny the way that you talk.'

Now now, reprimanded their grandmother,
where's your manners, boys and girls?
I know what they mean
smiled Una warmly,
because Troy, God love him
he was always saying the same,
I declare to God.
The way that you talk
it really does get to me, he said
& I think that may be why I love you,
Lady Ocean.
She said it again: *love!* the little girl squealed.
Yes. Lady Ocean of Watertown,
you see, is what he meant,
said Una.
I love your voice, the lilt of your Irish accent.
That was why he first asked me to come, she
added, to come along.
& then waited for a moment
staring directly at her visibly stiffening
fellow passenger
plucking away as she did so
at the little strands of thread
protruding from the sleeve of
Bobbieann's pullover.
Asked you to come along? the
lady said. I'm afraid I don't
quite understand.
O that's quite all right, said Una,
laughing
I mean to this place in
Putney that he and the others
were instrumental in setting up

[504]

an arts & performance space
part coffee bar, part arts centre
part flophouse I suppose
& which they'd intended to
be a multi-purpose venue
mixed film shows
variety
a centre of avant-garde performance
they'd started renovating.
That's nice, said the lady.
I like to go to plays.
O, it wasn't anything special
explained Una
but Angela Carter
came in one night.
Angela Carter?
Yes, with Tanith & Jo
to see a show
Joanne had directed
loosely based on some of her own
works.
I didn't know anything
about her
to be honest
no, not the first blessed thing,
in actual fact –
but Jo &
Tanith
filled me in
& taught me everything
there was to know about her.
Can Egbert Poltergeist
Defeat The Great Plague
Of Walking-Sticks
& Reach True Maturity?
What? said the lady,
as the kiddies stared empty-eyed
o that was just the name of another play,
one of the ones that
Troy produced himself,
Una explained.

I'm afraid I don't go
as often as I should,

to the theatre I mean
the lady responded,
because I find it hard to get the time
with these two little chipmunks here
she laughed
as did the kids
but Una by now, she wasn't
really listening,
I'm afraid,
having become preoccupied
with the way that Jo and
Tanith used to go on
whenever people like Angela Carter
were around – doing their best
to get themselves
noticed, using big words they barely knew
the meaning of,
& when the famous author had
said she actually really liked
Tanith's dance piece
Les Oiseaux,
in which she had played the mechanical doll –
c'est magnifique!
was what Angela Carter had actually said –
after that,
things had really started going to Tanith's head
& she'd begun to think that she was in
possession
of some kind of otherworld 'aura' or
something – some sort of
special 'artistic' glow.
& which was probably why
all the rumours had begun –
that I had grown envious.
Yes, insanely jealous of her, in fact.
& which was why
I'd pushed her out
the window.

Window? stammered the
children's grandmother
straightening, abruptly,
in her seat.

But, by now, Una Fogarty
was listening even less
staring abstractedly out the window
as the lush green countryside of Kent
rolled past.
The Magic Toyshop by Angela Carter
magnificent choreography, *Time Out*
had written,
with Tanith Kaplinski being
singled out as:
definitely one to watch.

&
after that
Una didn't say anything
no, not a word,
for a long time after that.
The train had stopped for quite some time
at the station in Herne Bay.
Then, when it finally picked up speed again
as if there had been
no pause whatsoever in their conversation,
Una began turning
Bobbieann upside down by the ankle
& smiling, not just at their gran
but the children also, as she continued:
Because, you see, *páistí*,
at the time, fringe theatre in the suburbs
was booming
& I know that that
might be difficult to understand
now, but at that time everyone wanted
to help and do their thing
& you didn't have to ask anyone twice
with so many different people
coming and going to the flat
o, over and over,
from morning yes until night,
open door.
She began to count them out on her fingers.
 1. Big Peter Hanlon
 2. Luke Powys
 3. Maddie Lynam
 4. Sandie Greene

5. Jenny Venus
6. Frank 'Blind Owl' Olson
7. Maggie Breen (sometimes)
8. Lord Offaly Of Down, aka Dessie McKeever
9. Johnny Winter
10. Shuggie Otis
11. 'Red' Bonnie Sugrue
12. Macaulay 'Breffni' O'Rourke,
    aka 'The King Of Cavan'.

&, of course
there were also the old reliables
Iris Montgomery, Joanne Kaplan
& her soul-sister & lifelong
friend, o the wonderful Miss Kaplinski.
caitheadh amach an fhuinneog i?
Thrown her out the window?
All I can say is
I'd have a lot to do
to be going around doing that
with the truth being
that I admired her enormously
I really did.

Yes, I really and truly did,
she sighed.

Then she grinned
from ear to ear
& sat there embracing her babogue
fondly, gazing longingly
out the window.
Ah yes, they were great old times
all the same, she said
except I realise that it's really
quite impossible for anyone
now to imagine.
What with power cuts,
refuse strikes,
work-to-rules
& all the rest.
But oh what fun we had, I swear
you ask Tanith
yes you go and ask her

ask the world's most magnificent dancer
go on, ask the girl
that they said I didn't like
which just shows how much they know
because no matter what she might have done
bheith ag marcaíocht le Troy
yes, riding my boyfriend behind
my back, as a matter of fact right
there in front of me.
O my goodness! came the response
as the childrens' chaperone looked
out the window
with Una paying no heed at all.
Yes, I really did respect her,
Tanith,
they heard her continue,
& not so much as for one
second am I going to do it
yes, criticise someone as sensitive
& intelligent as Tanith
please, said the lady –
but again, no response.
Except: 'Irrespective of who she fucked!'
Do you know how many people
were there that night
in The Putney Arts Centre
go on, guess
she said to the kids
go on, go ahead
but just remember it's a tiny theatre
so come on now, *páistí* –
but they said they couldn't.
& then it was Una's turn
to let out a little giggle
& turn Bobbieann up and then
right again down
as she raised her shoulders
and held up four fingers.
Four, she said.
isn't that a laugh?
Laws-a-day, I was so embarrassed!
As she began to sing at the top of her voice
much to the amusement of some
sunhat-sporting beer drinkers down

at the other end of the carriage:
Les Oiseaux Dans La Charmille,
the opera which she had been thinking
of adapting herself, she said
making it about two other little birdies
a pair of the sweetest children who had, magically,
been turned into swans
ealaí!, she screeched. do you hear me
ealaí!, taken by the fairies and their shape
altered into that of swans
with no choice but to abide
for twenty-score years
on the shores of Lough Derravaragh
amn't I telling you
The Children Of Lir
do you hear what I'm saying?
The Children Of Lir
na páistí goidte –
the stolen children,
will you listen to me!

By now, however, she seemed
absolutely and completely exhausted
before leaning forward and,
to his astonishment,
giving the little boy facing her a sharp pinch
on the cheek
Ow! he squealed suddenly,
with his sister insisting that she
thought it was fun
pinch me too
she said then to Una
I want you to, she emphasised,
so please will you do it
as their grandmother turned away
really looking quite horrified.
Why do you think,
began Una in a different tone,
why do you think it might be that
birds sing?

Before waiting for an answer
providing what she considered
one very possible &

plausible reason
Perhaps it's to liberate
themselves of some vital plenitude
within
which, they find, they can barely contain.

Then, with her index finger,
she rudely poked Bobbieann in
the eye
It's all your fault! they heard her accuse,
Your fucking fault, do you hear me, so it
is! Do you hear?
Because you were supposed to save my life
& for the first time provide me
with warmth & love & shelter
& instead what went &
happened?
I HATE YOU, DAN! wept Una Fogarty,
plunging her face right into
her fists.

As the woman got up and said
I'll go & see if there's a nurse –
but, just as dramatically, Una
already appeared to have recovered.
& was sitting there, smiling,
implacably serene,
stroking the back of Bobbieann's head.
With the children
as children do
appearing to take it all
in their stride.

Then Una began laughing as she told them
all there was to know about Troy.
Or should I say
'my Scotsman Sea-God!' she
giggled, a little shyly.
With the páistí just continuing to
gaze blankly across the table at her,
as she continued.

I don't mean to boast
they heard her explain,
but, in another world,
some universe where
all things are equal
& opportunities are
not being denied
my Troy, without fail
he could have been
a professional performer
A professional performer? the little girl said.
Yes, replied Una
not for one second noticing
how profoundly agitated their
grandmother was
actually becoming
looking everywhere
for a nurse
so far without success
chafing her hands
as though only now realising
just to what degree
she was, in fact, out of her depth.
A fact which
was scarcely surprising,
in the circumstances.

I would definitely say the West End
yes, for sure.
I was in the West End before, said the girl.
But Una wasn't listening to a word that
either of them said
leaning back in her seat
turning Bobbieann
upside down and righting her again
steeling herself, privately,
against the lurking dread
of the dark blinking neon
green for *Danger*
UXB
that was always there
at the back of her mind
a shell at any moment
threatening to go *phléasc!*

doing her level best to smile
as she wound the arms of
the little dolly
this way & that
taking a deep breath as
the train suddenly lurched forward
wagging her finger as she shook
her head and said to the children
in an almost perfect Scottish burr
you do not, my girl
have tae worry your heed
for I love it so much
your angelic face
fair turned me sideways
up and doon
so you have – I wisnae ready
tae be smitten,
Una Fogarty frae Currabawn,
what've ye gone and done?

They'd been up at the heath
again that day
enjoying a picnic
before heading back out to
Putney.
It's-A-Two-Foot-Six-Inches-Above-
The-Ground-World
was the play that Troy had been
directing at that particular time
& he had promised the actors
not to be stoned.
Nae so much as a drag shall
pass these lips! he had promised them
without fail
the day before in The Bedford
but already he was late
& was showing no signs of great concern
about it,
as he and Una lay there beside the pond
with fingers entwined
listening to *King Crimson* on the
portable cassette.
You are my consort, the lovely *Amphitrite*,
he had smiled

tickling her nostrils with a
long stem of grass
& I shall always be your Poseidon.
Before climbing into the fork of a
tree and delivering, for her benefit alone,
his *pièce-de-résistance*, by Edward Thomas
For you and all the birds of the world, my lady
when the first ray of sunshine brings forth
joyous notes from their throats
the sensation of well-being
of wings still moist from
the bath spread out to the light
the joy of being together
of having the same plumage
let them know
that I remember Adlestrop
&
all of their kin.

As back down he came
& the pair of them sighed
as they lay there on their backs
finishing off what was left of the food
observing them closely
those heroes of the air
making successive oblique dives
toward the ground before
finally rebounding once more into the sky.

Why do you think they sing? he
whispered
because they have to, Troy, she smiled,
or maybe they could be trying to
communicate
warn us, maybe, he suggested,
somewhat vacantly,
no, rejoicing, she insisted
as he forgot all about it
& kissed his Lady Ocean
You'll never leave me, said Una
as she smiled.
'I'll never leave you,' vowed Troy McClory
chewing on the stem of his Ian Hunter
shades

turning over
yes, turning over on the picnic rug
on his side
because for us
there is but one
abiding kingdom
Poseidon &
Amphitrite
together
in their
u
n
d
e
r
s
e
a

k
i
n
g
d
o
m

My one and only love
Una Fogarty
Queen of Currabawn,
both now
&
forever.

Then Una said to the páistí
in the train,
using Bobbieann to illustrate her words
& it was after making that commitment
which we both knew, even in those times
of free love & no possessions
to be the absolute and unvarnished truth
that the following weekend
on the very same train

we made our way out here
to Margate
yes, to the private wonderland
of our own precious Watertown
there to store up memories
which we knew would sustain
the pair of us forever
the pair of us forever
yes, the pair of us forever
lying there on the golden sand
the golden sand
of the glittering beach
of Watertown
where nothing
in the universe
would ever bother
either of us
ever again
as he took them off
his Ian Hunter shades
& looked right into my eyes.

All the things I remember
that he used to say
Sew me a shirt that doesn't have a seam
wash it in a well that will
remain forever dry.

The impossible realised, she said
to the children
who, this time, neglected to make any comment
having been discreetly dissuaded
by their chaperone.
Angela Carter, went on Una,
she died too
just when her dream was only beginning
later on giving birth to the most
beautiful infant
but then isn't every infant beautiful
said Una
yes every little babogue in the world
possessing its very own special &
unique magic

isn't that right, childre
childre don't you think –
nach bhfuil an cheart agam, eh?
Eh?
ha ha ha ha!
Tossing her head back &
laughing even more robustly as the train
now at last pulled into Margate station
& all of a sudden, she started
furiously leathering the table with
the doll
& shouting at the top of her voice
first at Bobbie
& then at Ann
bashing it this way & then
the other
until she was really
quite hopelessly out of breath
as she searched her bag for
another piece of tissue
or a napkin,
anything
to wipe her brow
because she really was
out of sorts
&
all of a-dither
as she twisted her face up
and rasped hoarsely at
the babogue
now, it has to be said,
looking more than a little
the worse for wear
what are you looking at
Fogarty, she said
what are you making those eyes
at me for
do you hear me, Bobbie
Bobbie do you hear me
& you too, Annie
yes Miss Madam
listen to me whenever I
am talking
because I really do feel

that you two, both of
you have caused quite
enough
              trouble

              yes given me

more
        than my share
                    of *trioblóid* ha

    ha

                    phew

      o

          boys

                God in

                heaven

                I
am

                                tuirseach

          yes I am
          o but I am

          o yes yes
          very *tired* indeed
soooooooooooooooooooooo
        exhaust.........

          as the train idled into Margate station.

& sprightly Miss Una Fogarty
for all the world like a spindly brown twig
made her way towards the foreshore
of Watertown
skipping & singing
&
swinging dolly as she went
come along babogue
yes, come along
really quite amazed
by the numbers
that she found
waiting for her there
by the esplanade
just as she came around the
corner
with the world & its mother
seeming to be present,
colourfully sprawled
in front of the beach huts
with their buckets & spades
as a brass band oom-paahed
& fairground organ music eddied
from a great big candy-striped
marquee
pitched on the Oval Lawns
as a megaphone barked
'allo 'allo 'allo
why not purchase a nice tasty whelk
fresh from the waters of the sea
here in Margate
indeed why not bring one home
for your tea?
Not right now
I'm sorry but I'm busy,
replied Una.
Tripping awkwardly on a piece
of driftwood
& going & spilling
all her money
yes, all the coins that she
had in her pocket
& then having to bend down
damn & blast

to make it her business to pick them all up
with Bobbieann looking up
as if to say *silly*
o keep quiet you *thrawneen*
laughed Una
counting the pennies out
one by one
yes
one
two
three
four
five
six
coins
right
back
inside her purse
where they belonged
did you enjoy
the trip
said Una to Bobbie
the trip my dear
I hope you did enjoy it
& you, lickle Ann,
what about you
enjoy it did you
but the páistí said
no because it had
made them too excited
& that was why they had to go away
& Una said I know what you mean
however because you've been
good what you need is an ice cream
so come along now, páistí,
let's youse & me go over there
to Peggy's Ye Old Pavilion Tea Shoppe

As through the door
they sashayed like royalty.
Peggy Norton had been running
her little refreshment shack
Ye Olde Tea Shoppe
her pride and joy

she said,
for years
O years & years
she gonizing.
Why yonks,
she smiled,
yes it's true
reminding
Una as she spoke
of the actress Irene Handl.
A right old busy bee
& no mistake
just like old
Margaret Rutherford
God knows
another no-nonsense rogue
always insisting how she'd
brook no slapdash work
& yet, all the same, considerate too
yes, kind & thoughtful
in her way
in spite of that flinty exterior
and dependable too.

So Una reckoned
on being able to trust
Miss Handl
& as a result
she just could not
wait to get chatting
to busy bee Peggy
the proprietress
but then she became aware
of a shadow, of half of one
very like the one she had sensed
while buying herself & the kiddies
an ice cream
that day in Queen's Park
but then she looked again
to her immense relief
the shadow was gone
maybe she had only imagined it,
she thought,
& then what did she see

why, her heart nearly stopped.
Yes a great big sign
a huge painted wooden board reading:
MOTT THE HOOPLE
DREAMLAND 12 SEPT 2019
GRAND REUNION GIG!
with
original members, inc.
IAN HUNTER
& there he was
right there on a great big coloured poster
just as if they
had never parted
their lead singer
the rock god
with the exact same blonde hair
and trademark mirror shades
chewing gum, cocky as you
like.

Troy! she cried abruptly,
with her legs nearly buckling
underneath her,
as I live & breathe
do you see who it is
she said to the proprietress
wiping her hands behind the counter
of Ye Old Tea Shoppe
nearly fainting as she stood there
as Peggy Norton the proprietress
said in her voice that was the same
as Irene Handl's
yes, by all means, dear, please
take a seat
& I'll be down to you in a mo'
to attend to your needs
& that is exactly what Una Fogarty did
pull up a chair and sit down
by the window,
out of nowhere remembering

Troy as he'd held her not twenty yards
away, out there along the shore,

putting his tongue down her throat
& talking about King Crimson
& Fritz The Cat
& Rupert Bear
& The Flamin' Groovies
Edward Bond
&
the two Angelas,
Davis
&
Carter.
Who are you
really
she could hear him plainly say
almost as clearly as if he were
standing right beside her
there in the tea shop
I don't know, Troy
because all I do is clean silly offices
that was all she could think to
say
not that it mattered
because already he was taking
off all her clothes
and removing the King Crimson
album from its sleeve

to put it onto the stereo
handing over the joint
as she lay there
I adore you, Lady Ocean,
said Troy
to Una Fogarty
& to which she
was going to reply
thanks very much
but
who
            was
                        that standing
there

            just
                        outside

                    the window

yes, directly outside the window

                    of the tea shop
standing

looking in

          was it a shadow
                    or a policeman

could

                              it

                    be
well, let it be
The Fuzz
if it wanted
because she didn't care
as she took the arm
of Bobbie
& then the arm
of Ann
& ever so softly
began to sing
especially for Troy.

How beautiful it looked
that old Margate strand,
stretching away beyond the window
thinking of those words
those very same sentiments
spoken by her lover Troy
that day when they'd taken
refuge in the concrete shelter
along the seafront
as all of it came rushing back
you could even see the excitement
in her lovely dolly Bobbieann's eyes:
Sweet stalls!
Sand!

Cotton dresses
&
the teensiest
pebbles.

Pebbles as small as pigeons' eggs
Troy had written
somewhere in his notebook,
pebbles coloured
the blue
of heaven
in this New Arcadia
where
ferry boats
shuffle
in their slumber
past the
breakwater.

Did you ever hear of *The Waste Land*,
my love?
She remembered him saying
as they sat there,
under cover,
sheltering from the rain,
perhaps you've heard of it
it's really quite famous,
ha ha, she had replied
as she threw back her head
and looked right up at the sun
or was it the moon
o I wouldn't know
not being from around these parts
she had chuckled
as her lover had
laughed
&
then laughed
again
just like they'd done
that morning in the
fairground on

The Waltzer.
When Troy had
christened her
Lady Ocean Of Watertown
& even after their day out
had kept on calling
it to her
making some others
in the flat a little jealous
ha ha that was it
wasn't it
because they didn't like that
how can she bear to
listen to such tosh
she had overheard Tanith
complaining one day to Iris.
Yes, replied Iris
actually I find it so
embarrassing to see
her fluttering around him
like she does
but then, I suppose
you can't really help it
when you're in love
can you Una
Una, well can you?

& Una said yes
that was right
& even in spite of all
that had happened
anything she'd give
to be back there where
they'd been again
to be that person
now blown up
with The Baron and
his bombs & all his Stukas
having strafed what remained
of all those rickety memories
& which was why there were
tears in her eyes
deora which already
had begun streaming down

[526]

her face
as with all the defiance that was left to her
in spite of the shock
that she saw on Peggy the
tea shop proprietress's face
she flung the dining-room table back
and, cursing violently, hurled Bobbieann
across the room against the wall
demanding to know what had
happened to Peter Sarstedt
or the girl in his song.

Yes, *my lovely*, she began crooning,
gradually calming down,
tell me everything that
is in your mind.
But, you see, that is
something that I really
cannot do
because there
isn't anything left
in there
not now
that it's been carpet-bombed.
I think you
understand what I mean
don't you Peggy-Irene Handl?

Yes dear, the owner assured her
as the doorbell rang and a
Knight Of Malta officer,
attired in his official uniform,
came in,
accompanied by a female
police constable,
disappearing behind some laminated menus.

After they had got back
from Margate that day,
recalled Una,
they had parked their
bicycles outside a pub
looking forward to
seeing King Crimson

at the Marquee
where they were
scheduled to perform
their latest work
the album called
In
The
Wake
Of
Poseidon.
She just couldn't wait!
She enthused to her lover,
no I just can't wait,
squeezing his hand.
Did you know that The Beatles
once played in Dreamland,
he told her.
No I didn't, actually, Troy
yeah, one summer as
a matter of fact
'65 maybe
how can he possibly
find me attractive, she
wondered,
when I resemble a donkey
with its hooves stuck in a bucket
ah yes, sad Fudge
poor old Goodyear Blimp
to this day not knowing
which of them had invented
the nickname
but she suspected Tanith
knowing her to be covetous
for had she not confided in Una
that she didn't blame her
for falling under Troy's spell
sharing all his bountiful knowledge with her
telling her all these things
he knew
Allen Ginsberg
& T. S. Eliot.

Who, of course,
had written his famous verse

here in Margate
like Troy had explained
writing all this famous
poetry
long ago in the very same
concrete shelter
where she and Troy McClory
had taken refuge
from the drizzle,
watching children as
they played on the beach.
Just as the poet had,
Troy explained,
& the gonizing exercises
of injured soldiers from the war.
Troy McClory had read
from *The Waste Land*
to her,
& then had suggested,
taking her hand,
as the rains began clearing,
let's you and me
make our way to
our undersea kingdom,
that OK, Lady Ocean?

Peggy-Irene Handl
was busy as a bee, wiping
& cleaning and, at the same time,
mixing smoothies.
Which she didn't normally do,
she informed Una
it was just that there was
some kind of reception
she explained,
as she chatted away with
the officer and the Knight Of
Malta
occasionally stealing
glances over at Una
and her dolly.

All the things I have to do! Sighed Peggy,
there's no end to it
no, no end in sight
at all, she said,
I mean, look at this banana,
look at this banana, she said
with a little cocktail cherry on top.
That's a nice one too
– pink stripe and all.
& I like this tasty fellow
gumball gelato.
He's a good chap.
Any views on our Peppermint Friend?
White-and-green all down along the side.

It was one of the greatest days of my life, said
Una.
As Peggy came over, bending over the table.
Just pop a little sprig on here – &
there we are! She beamed, standing back.
Smiling at Una, whose chin rested on her hand.
The Magic Toyshop, it was going to be called,
she informed Peggy.
The play that he'd cast me in, I mean.
I was terrified, really and truly I was, Una said.
Literally terrified –
never having been in a play before.

But Peggy, to be truthful, wasn't really
listening very attentively – being much too
preoccupied with her own affairs.

'And now, this orangey fizz!' she exclaimed,
'I think I'll just pop that in the middle!'

As Una continued.
'Troy had gone through the whole thing
the night before
By the time he was finished
I had a lot more confidence.
He kept on saying: *be cool, Una babes,
Stay cool!* & by the time that you get up on that
stage…

you'll be ready
my love,
prepared to enter
another world.
And I was! Una moaned,
thanks to the book you gave me, Troy.
Angela Carter – I love her to bits.
A *shaman*, Lady Ocean,
that's what Angela was
& I knew, in the end,
she'd inevitably see you through.

Because, in a way, she's a lot like you.
Lives in a fairy wonderland also.
I think you could be a very good actress
he said.
You wouldn't believe that, would you –
Troy McClory saying the like of that –
to the likes of old clattery-bags
hooves-in-a-bucket
Una Fogarty.

But he did.
He had.

He *had*! cried Una,
pushing back the table
again
& this time knocking over
some crockery
a side plate and a saucer
and the startled proprietress along
with them
as she stood there
upright.

Do you think I look like Judi Dench?
she asked Peggy.

Who, coincidentally – Judi Dench,
that is, not Peggy! – had appeared
onscreen in the darkened movie theatre

[531]

at exactly the same time
as Alex Gordon had undergone a
severe cardiac arrest in the back row of
the Soho fleapit.

Without uttering so much as a word of
complaint, sliding down onto
the grubby carpet,
with the very last smell he remembered
on this earth
being that of congealed
Kia-Ora
wafting densely up
from the carpet.

'A juice you don't seem to get any longer,'
remarked Peggy casually
during the course of their
conversation.
'Yes, that's right!' agreed Una.
Orange, said Peggy
because everything changes
& now it's all smoothies.
Not Kia-Ora, agreed Una.
No, not Kia-Ora, nodded Peggy,
that has more or less been
completely forgotten.

Just like a former member of
the British Army,
with Moody Alex
remaining there,
undiscovered in the aisle,
as the very next feature
began relaying high above him,
entitled *Come Play With Me*
starring Mary Millington.
With numerous nurses
running around, semi-nude,
oblivious of the fact
that poor old Alex Gordon
former corporal in The Signals,
in Aden

he wasn't wondering any longer
just what was the secret of the sexy Playmates
or whether the bristols on that
might do the trick
as there on the screen,
a corpse-complexioned butler
came careering down a winding
staircase, aghast at
what he'd just witnessed.
Before pressing his hand to his lips
as he rolled his eyes, exclaiming
ever so hoarsely:
Well, blimey O'Reilly
if
that
don't
take
the
corker!

Una was enjoying the gobstopper
the proprietress had just given her
because she used to enjoy them all the time
she said.
Did you dear, said Peggy Handl,
nodding discreetly towards the policewoman at
the table
I'll bet you did too, she laughed
as both the constable and the Knight Of Malta
smiled.
But then, once more, became concerned &
drawn
stealing furtive little looks over across at Una
I'm sure you liked your smoothies too,
said Peggy,
or did they not have them when you were
young?
But by now the Knight Of Malta
appeared to be way too busy
chatting urgently on his phone

with Peggy losing interest
& taking no notice after a while
just like her gobstopper-munching customer
Miss Una Fogarty,
aka Judi Dench
now laughing away
heartily to herself again
tickling Bobbieann underneath
the chin
as the little babogue smiled
& smiled,
looking up with those two lickle
button eyes and her little legs
splayed.
Just as, through the great picture
window to the front of the shop,
what did Una Fogarty see go drifting past?
Why, only a great big stripy
balloon, no less,
coloured blue and red,
cruising at low altitude
veering in the direction of the Cliftonville
cliffs.
& reminding her as it did so of Troy's
favourite story about a
cartoon character
when he'd been a boy
that is to say, Rupert Bear of Nutwood
& how he'd invented
a flying machine that was invisible
in which he and his friend Professor
McVittie
could come and go, willy nilly.
Yes, travel to any foreign country
of their choosing, wandering
unmolested to China & Russia
& even to special lands
which they, personally, had invented.
But might just as easily have been created
by Angela Carter.
There is a revolution coming
my love,
said Troy in her mind,
but if there is

it's every bit as much an
insurrection of the heart
as it is the redistribution of
money & wealth & power.
It's like flying, Lady Ocean
yes, gliding across the skyline
before finally attaining
that Holy Grail, the one
we call inner peace
because that's what the quest is for
much more than for anything else
& that's why you and me have
got to be the first
the very first piper
at the gates of our own secret
golden dawn.

Such was his passion
it was more than she could bear
as she shoved back the table –
the very same as he used to do,
& climbed right on top of it,
waving the dolly
as she trembled,
bawling her heart out
to the drifting balloon & the swaying
sea of Margate.

Ah want tae paint!
she erupted in a
somewhat unconvincing Scottish burr,
the children of Amphitrite!
I want to paint:
a thousand
coloured birds!
Enough to
block out
both the sun
&
the fucking moon!

And I am the woman to do it,
Bobbieann, she giggled, shaking
her head as she sat down again.

Because: sin é an fáth.
Because that is what I was
put on earth to do,
don't you understand?

She tugged down her skirt, almost in
the manner
of an old-fashioned schoolmistress
& then, primly & demurely, shouted
into the limp puppet's face:
DON'T YOU UNDERSTAND, MY
BABOGUE?

At this, The Knight Of Malta
who, of course, had followed her from
the train,
having closely observed her
all the way from their stop at Herne Bay,
closed his phone smartly and
looked directly across at his companion.

As the constable dropped her eyelids a little,
considered for a moment and then shook her head.
With Peggy arriving over to
treat Una to a refill,
draping a teacloth across her knee.
'Been up to London again then,
'ave you, dear?' she said.

Yes indeed, there's no doubt about it,
Peggy Handl agreed, most emphatically, with
the Knight Of Malta
as she refilled his cup in the failing
light of the late afternoon
not so much as exhibiting the slightest
indication of surprise as the
mild-mannered official
continued lamenting the number of
times he had been delayed on that line,
and indeed, as a consequence, was
actually considering giving up
travelling by Southeastern Rail.

As Una continued
insistently snapping her fingers,
shouting both at the dolly and
assorted members of the cast
of Cliftonville Capers.
(Who, of course, were not present,
except in her mind.)

Because that will just fucking not do,
I told you! she snapped.

Before looking up
& finding herself momentarily
irritated
by the fact that, up until now,
she just hadn't realised
simply how alike
The Knight Of Malta
&
'Blind Owl' Olson
actually were!
Like twins, for heaven's sake!
What a coincidence.
With those very same
spectacles –
thick, black-framed
the very very same
yes, just the very same
as
of
old.
How wonderful!

Yes, Frank 'The Blind Owl'
Olson,
she explained to the gentleman,
making it her business
to introduce herself
to the mild-mannered
official.
Joining them at their
table, in actual fact,
excusing her 'bad manners'

in front of
the very nice constable
but then, of course, it's
possible that you know it,
officer, she said,
The Mahavishnu Temple,
because we did get into a little
trouble with the police
over bombings and such
even though none of us was ever
actually involved in anything –
you, especially, Blind Owl.
So how are you Frank
how have you been all these years
wasn't it terrible
what happened to The King Of Cavan
were you there that night
at the South Bank Poly
when Mott the Hoople
were playing

& who you know Macaulay loved
so he definitely had been there
& not involved in any conspiracy
to cause explosions or anything else
no matter what those detectives said
but all of that is a long time ago
just like Linda Blair and *The Exorcist*
yes – so if you, I'm afraid, think
that I'm going to start all
that nonsense about bombs
or anything else
then I'm afraid, my good friend,
that you have got it wrong
yes way way wrong,
I am sorry to have to say.
Then she sneezed, leaning back
precipitously on her chair
as she called out over their heads to Peggy
you're probably wondering
what the name of it is as well, are you
Irene, the name of our next production,
I mean?

Without bothering to wait for a reply
You're thinking probably, more than likely
it's an opera, yes?
Maybe *La Traviata* or something like that
but that's where you're wrong, you see
for the decision, I am proud to announce,
it has already been made
& the Cliftonville show for this
coming year is going to be called
Watertown.
Yes, that's it
with most of it based
on my own experiences
yes, me & Troy
here in Margate, of all places.
Were you aware that Poseidon
had over a hundred children?

No dear, I didn't know that, said Peggy.

Amphitrite – that was his lady wife's
name
Lady Amphitrite
the undersea goddess.
She gave birth to Triton
under the sea
the very same as I did
myself.
That's nice, agreed Peggy.
Then Una turned back to
the so-called 'Blind Owl'
with it being a long time
since she'd looked on that
twinkly, wise old face, she thought.

Oho, Blind Owl
Blind Owl, she repeated,
& then tweaked Bobbieann.
Yes, gave her a poke
right in the middle of her face
& had herself a laugh while she was doing
it.
So who am I, childre, can you tell me
what's my name? Is it Meryl Streep

or Judi Dench?
Because I can't seem to make up my mind –
isn't that funny?
Yes, it's funny, she said, and tickled her
again.
Although not as funny, she continued, as Troy
climbed up on the table the way he used to.
Go on then, Bobbie, do it for us, will you?
As she made the little babogue perform an
energetic jig between the utensils.

Look! she cried,
as the dolly continued to lep and kick,
why, glory be to God
if she isn't the spit of Auntie Nan!

But with, thanks be to God,
she explained to Blind Owl,
all of them old problematic trimmlins
being vanquished, yes, now long gone at last.
Kaput, yes, and make no mistake!
Sea – ná déan dearmad!

Emitting all these protracted, luxurious
sighs
now that she was enjoying herself
stroking the soft spongy hand of
her best and closest little doll-friend
the privilege of being
once again close to Troy
with no evidence at all
of that old rascal
Mr Death & his Friends

Because against all
the odds we've found it,
Blind Owl, she said assuredly,
just as Troy always promised
we would.
Hy-Brasil, Frank, do you know
what I'm saying?
That inner peace

which those lovely
little birdies in the trees want to
tell us all about.
Which is why they sing, my old friend –
to affirm the very
joy of existence!
&
it was at that point Una herself commenced
her attempt at a coloratura-style oratorio
although it has to be admitted
that it fell somewhat short
nonetheless singing her heart out
giving it everything she had
over & over again
carolling away at the highest
pitch possible
as she swung Bobbieann
proclaiming herself so absurdly
& blissfully happy –
How contented I am to be back here
in Watertown,
but, more than anything, to have met you,
Frank!

& continuing in that vein for some moments
more, until inevitably,
as is so often the case whenever she becomes
that little bit overemotional,
she was consumed by a violent episode of
the trimmlins,
collapsing, crying, off her chair
& looking up to see
Rutherford & Connie
through the big picture window
hastening across the carpark
in the company of an
elderly police inspector
who she knew was that
because he looked the spit of
Inspector Cockrill
played by Alastair Sim
in *Green For Danger*
as

D
A
N
G
E
R

U
X
B

the stencilled label on the shell began to glow
just like she'd always dreaded it would

& then

went off

                    and roofs

& windows

                    & Una Fogarty went sailing

          off
into the wind

                    like a hot-air balloon

                    deflating as it

came down from the air

                              punctured perhaps

               by Baron Von Richthofen

                              in his loop-the-loop
red biplane

               laughing

with everything around her
collapsing in silence

till she lay there

prostrate

as the first diamond-beads
began splintering against the window

&, as so many times in her life before,
she found herself wondering
why does it always

seem

to

rain

on

Sunday?

With the Knight Of Malta
seeming a little apprehensive...
but he needn't have worried
for everything now was under control
as together they marched
– as united and determined a little platoon
as had ever appeared on Margate sands –
in the direction of the ambulance,
where Irene-Peggy and Miss Rutherford gently
and patiently assisted Una into the vehicle.

So, that was it,
I suppose, more or less.
With Meryl Streep, as she
has lately come to insist on as
her 'correct' and 'most appropriate'
persona,
being unfussily
reassigned to her quarters
where her health and condition
appeared, initially, to be coming
along quite well indeed.

At least until
a number of short weeks later
when her nurse Consuela Gomes
aka The Princess Of São Paulo
confided in her reliable superior
Margaret Rutherford
that, regrettably, she'd
once more discovered
a putrefied haddock
stuffed haphazardly into
the bottom of a
laundry bag
under a pile of residents' socks
&
blouses

& if that wasn't bad
enough
the next Monday morning
being greeted by the inscription:
E
Y
E

A
M

W
A
T
C
H
I
N
G

Y
O
U

N
U
D
E

D
I
S
I
N
T
E
G
R
A
T
I
N
G

P
A
R
A
C
H
U
T
I
S
T

W
O
M
A
N

elaborately scrawled across
the tiles of the bathroom wall,
in the thickest lipstick of
fire-engine red.

Poor Connie had been really
quite taken aback
at the time,
& in the process of her delivery
describing to Rutherford
a number of equally unsettling
& very similar
sensations which she herself
had been experiencing of late
– Auntie Nano, of course,
would have diagnosed immediately
what she was describing as a
a condition of incipient imní,
the trimmlins, in otherwords.

As The Princess went on to
elaborate to her superior
exactly how this 'feeling'
she'd been experiencing,
the manner in which it reminded her

of something she'd once felt as a child
after enjoying a beautiful day in the market
when the normally fish-smelling, foetid
air had all of a sudden seemed scented
with roses
returning then to find
her mother and grandmother
clutching one another, in complete hysterics
with the body of her father stretched out
under linen, across two lintel chairs.

With her keeping on going on
about it, Connie,
until every intimate detail possible had
been disclosed
& went on about it
that day & the next
until poor old Rutherford,
I mean you know the way she is
being completely no-nonsense
& practical in every way
a traditional old empirical
rather unimaginative Sassenach,
much as she liked Connie
& thought she was sweet
she just couldn't endure anymore of
these over-the-top histrionics
especially when the 'sweet little'
Brazilian started
explaining how
recently
she had begun to feel
this sense that
not only was she being 'watched'
but, intermittently, in the nights,
that she was somehow
being *interfered* with.

Why do birds sing, The Princess
Consuela Gomes
murmured abstractedly to herself

why, for all sorts of reasons,
I suppose, she decided
– but, maybe, do you ever think
they might be talking about us?

Fortunately, however
just as soon as the words had escaped her lips
the young woman realised the absurdity of her
enquiry
&, shaking her head, grabbed a trolley
and returned once more to her labours
on the ward,
happily finding herself able to laugh
& enabled to make light of
the entire unfortunate affair.
Which Rutherford had told
her to try and 'forget all about'.

But did that old Margaret,
yes did that sneaky old naughty
ever-so-sly Sassenach
dine out on that account
of apprehension and uncertainty
patiently savouring her food
in an expensive seafront restaurant
as her dinner companions
laughed, although not unkindly,
attributing such florid indulgences
as 'just another occupational hazard, I suppose'
& which, of course, will ultimately pass, they
concluded.

Just as Margaret Rutherford herself
had suggested.

To The Princess.

But with Connie, in more recent times,
& with depressing regularity,
now dreaming about these things with
a vividness and clarity which had
begun interrupting her sleep.

All the same making a vow
to not so much as open her mouth
about what was happening.
Especially, she promised, to her superior.
Most emphatically, as regards the most recent
and continuing development.
When she had found herself awakened
by the sound of what she took to be rustling
such as that of mice
or grasshoppers, perhaps.

But, on closer inspection of her room
in almost every aspect
had succeeded in finding –
why, nothing actually.

Before returning once more
to her bed
and hearing these words: white,
my dear
is the colour of hope.
You know you can believe me
when I tell you that.
Because Mr Exu always tells the truth.

Not being able to make head nor
tail of it, however
as poor Connie capitulated
in the face of another
bout of sustained imní
breaking into a prolonged and sustained fever
every time she thought about it
that persistent & incomprehensible
sound of *rustling*.

As she lay there
again
with her eyes wide open
recalling the scent of roses
on that Summer's day in the

market square in São Paulo.
& what she'd been taught
all her young life
regarding the so-called 'strength'
that had, supposedly, been
the sole preserve of her father
& which she had believed
wholeheartedly
until the night she had overheard him
in the back room, weeping.
Yes, sniffling the way a little baby would.
And she didn't know why.

She never did get to know the reason.
Before being taken, by her mother, to see him.
Lifeless.
Senhor Papa.
He can't hear you.
The mask of no-more.

Papa Papa
never again.

No wonder that she'd get a dose of
the trimmlins
& worry that she'd never
ever
catch butterflies
by the river
again
with her father
none, that is,
except the black ones
like those which
– she stiffened –
were now
circling
around her pillow.
Féileacháin an bháis,
Auntie Nano used to call them
yes, the butterflies of dread

not even making
a whisper of a sound
as they danced in preparation
for the imminent, final
Great Waltz.

You're mine,
she heard the deep male
baritone voice intone –
as she lay there, ossified,
her mouth sewn up.

& one thing you can be sure of
certainly not singing
any songs by Mott the Hoople
or King Crimson or
Jimi Hendrix
either
no, no 'Stars That Play With Laughing Sam's
Dice'.
Which, as Troy had once explained
was all about the subject
of LSD
to Una
who, of course,
had readily admitted
that she hadn't had the faintest clue
about that
as, safely returned to her post
now, by the library,
which was nothing more
than a little stack of books
on a wooden shelf
just inside the door,
Una was sighing as she picked at
the threads of her cardigan
remembering it all so fondly
as she sat there
bathed in a shaft of light
that came slanting through
the big high window.

Thinking about her Scotsman
lover, who else
& that day they'd spent
together in Watertown.
Troy & me,
she was writing on her forearm
then went & scribbled all over it,
laughing,
preparing to deny it completely
if anyone asked her
anything about it,
shy as a teenage girl she was,
sometimes,
regarding things like that.

Hat, shades,
head somewhere
away with the fairies.
Yes, there goes McClory,
she muses.
Because that's the way
she tends to remember
him now
just as he was
back in those good early days
when she had first arrived to become
a tenant in
Brondesbury Gardens
yes that is the way
our Una prefers to think of him now
Troy McClory
exactly as he had been
in the June of that year
when the two of them had arrived
home from their day trip to Margate
lying there soaking and singing in the bath,
with Troy engaging in what he
called his 'naval manoeuvres'
all those little toy boats he
had collected since childhood
moving them around between the

lolling, drifting islands of foam
as she wielded these two great big sudsy
mittens, light-heartedly massaging his
back.

While the circus band in
nearby Queen's Park
played the popular hit
of the moment 'Welcome Home'.

Sitting alongside him
there on the edge of the bath,
Una Fogarty realised just how she
had never been happier
which was why the beating
heart in her chest
turned around and
'gev a bucklep'
as Auntie Nano would have described it.

As Troy looked up with
that mischievous Scottish
grin of his and
removed his shades
pushing back his hat and
shaking his frizzy curls free
& lifting one finger
said: Listen to them, Una,
as the cymbals hissed
& the drums rattletapped
listen to those words.
Welcome home
the place where we all of us
want to be.

And what did he do then
Troy McClory
twined her fingers around his and
grinned
No, he said, he's not home, my love.
We are.

And, right there in that moment
what did Una see
only the two of them
already far away from The Mahavishnu Temple
lying on the banks
of the Currib river
in Currabawn
the place that she'd been missing
for so long she couldn't remember
even though she'd never been there
at least not physically

Home, Troy had said, that's what you and me both crave,
& what we now,
at long last, have.

But then he turned away again
&
she knew she could feel the tension
wire – right
palpable in his
shoulders,
as he clutched her hand,
clearly struggling to find the words.
It's just that I wanted you to know the truth
to be aware of everything
there is to know about me
before we pledge our commitment
to one another.
I live with my mother
my parents are long divorced
& I once did a bad thing
that I would like you to know
about before the two of us
get together properly

What thing, my love?
she heard herself say
filled with imní at the
prospect of his answer.
But she need not have worried.
Suicide might be attractive,
ending as it does
the sorrow & guilt

but no one is more aware than
I of the pain that such an act can
bring.
The hurt, I mean, it can cause to
those who are close
I stole money from them
five hundred pounds
to buy bennies
O God I'm so ashamed
if only you'd asked
I would have given it to you
my mother said
because we're your parents
we adore the ground you walk on
you don't have to steal or
deceive us, Troy.
Do you think, my love, in time you might
be able
to forgive someone who has divulged
such a thing to you – even spend a
considerable part of your life with them?
Come here, my love! she heard
him cry out,
& had wept as he
pulled her into the water
where together
they conjoined.

Every bit as beautifully
&
transcendently
as they had done
in their undersea kingdom
earlier on that very same day.

In the place that is known
as the City Of Shells
deep underground
among the quavering
aquamarine shadows
of Margate,
Watertown's own
primordial light.

&

which made it all the more difficult
when she discovered what she did
just a few days later
when, in fact, she wasn't supposed
to be anywhere near Brondesbury Gardens
but cleaning offices in the town of Newcastle, in fact
or had it been Scunthorpe
she couldn't rightly remember.

But then the agency
had informed her
told her the firm concerned
had cancelled at the very last
minute
so she could take the day off
& pretty much do whatever she liked.

With her finding herself then
in the position
of being able to give her lover a
surprise,
closing the door of
The Temple behind her
and then hearing the loveliest happy
laughter
wafting towards her down the
stairs.

But not only laughter,
happy or otherwise,
but bouts of excited cries too,
yelps indeed.
O man! moaned Jo.
O Christ! cried Tanith.
As on it went.

Do it, Troy
yeah come on, lover
Troy
Mc

Clory
you
&
your
fucking
hammer, bleated
Tanith
hysterically
as Joanne Kaplan
cried
give
it
to
me,
baby,
fuck your honey
like motherfucking
crazy!
Because that, you know, is
what she wants,
she giggled.

Yes, it really had proved
something of a shock –
looking in to see
Tanith with those
shapely brown dancer's legs
doing the mickey-jump-jubbly
with such delirious & salacious
abandonment
over & over.
But not only that
with it actually turning out
which Una didn't, at first,
realise
that Iris Matchstick-Montgomery
was there as well
chomping away goodo
at the groaning Scotsman's bellybutton
pausing every so often to turn around
and administer a little affectionate *pogue*
to Joanne Kaplan's livid, upthrusting
faighne, vagina.

O, that poor old Fudge
she was saying
or, at least, Una
thought she was
as they all joined in
singing 'A Song Of Fudge'
fresh from Margate with her hooves
in a bucket like a donkey
ha ha.

But Fudge decided she didn't care
about any of them
why should she
I mean why should she ought to,
not now hee hee
not after believing so much
& then what happens
as she lay there alone
on a tatty old mattress
with them being so stoned
that they hadn't even heard her
come in
didn't, as a matter of fact,
even know that she was there
against the odds praying that
her eaglaí, as Nano called them
her worst fears, in otherwords
that they'd remain in secret
& wouldn't ever make an appearance.
But caithfidh duit cuir stad dosna n'éin
you might as well try and mute the songs of
those winged treetop legions.

Aye, squeeze out their vigorous life
as they full-throat it gloriously
high among the oaks and the
the pines and the sycamores
getting ready
to shred their
          brittle
                    spinning
                              blades,

both in Queen's Park
and in all the lush green glades
& forests of the world.

Troy was asleep when he saw
The Professor.
With his spectacles dangling,
seeming gravely concerned.
What could possibly be wrong with him,
wondered Troy.
Perhaps I had too much to dream last night,
he laughed,
still deep within the dream itself.
As I really don't think I've ever seen him like
this.
No, I definitely haven't, he agreed with himself.

Then who did he happen to see but his father
wandering around abstractedly in the forest
& keeping on asking The Professor
did you find it.
Have you found it, Professor, his father
kept on asking.
Och aye, ah hev,
replied Douglas McVittie,
so dinnae be worrying yeer head, for
here it is.
Then rooting among some brushwood
& leaves
& holding up, at first, what seemed
like a chunky wee piece 'ae bark',
as Douglas put it.
But with it actually turning out to be
his, Troy's father's, mildewed penis.
Och ah didnae know! exclaimed Douglas
ah genuinely didnae expect—!
Naw this, swear tae Chr…!

But when he looked
Troy's father was gone
& there was someone
else
entirely different

the voice was old, muffled but yet
clear
measured but firm
a voice which he knew
for he'd heard it
before
gnarled, rattling
as it repeated in
a gravelled whisper:
A bad auld mistake
to be making surely
plunging
your bud into
colleens as you're not betrothed to
bad
oh aye
not good
at all
olc
an-olc

So, Mr McClory,
be aware that you've made
your bed.
I've warned you before, said
the gruagach, retreating,
so you can be expecting
another phone call
so bí ag fanacht ar ar maidin
aye, ye fornicating Scottish bastard –
just be aware –
be awaiting it on the morn.
With the specified phone call,
as had been predicted, arriving
at three minutes past seven
a.m.
Hello! said Troy, picking up
the receiver,
Troy McClory here.
'Your father has been found in a hotel
room in Ayr.
I regret to say he took his own life.'
Then it went dead.

But Troy McClory was destined
never to forget that voice
whoever it was,
whoever they were.
Because he never did find out –
how could they have known?
&
they were always full of surprises,
those voices – unbidden, entering
his mind,
without ceremony,
but with cool assuredness
& a certainty born of ageless
experience.
As he was to discover, yet again,
many years afterwards,
to his horror & disappointment
one dismal grey day in the nineties,
sitting in a panelled snug of
The Crown Select Bar, in Cricklewood,
not long after the episode with
the digger
when he'd been placed in charge
of the site excavator
& then, quite innocently,
had looked down,
with his attention having been
captured
by what he'd, initially,
assumed was a rat or a mouse
moving inside the
bucket
but it was only then that he saw it
just a fleeting grimace
but staring right at him
a disfigured *thing*
attired in a hussar's uniform
with a red scarf tied around his head,
curtseying flamboyantly and
quoting, in a smooth American
man's accent
the stars that play
yes, the stars that play
the stars

that

play

with
Laughing
Sam's

Dice

Ah bejapers

do you remember
the auld times
that we used to have
up
in Killiburn
it said,

& then was gone,
just as dramatically
as he'd appeared,

leaving Troy McClory
trapped
in the claypit
lying underneath the rotating
wheels of
the enormous yellow machine.

With it being
said at the time
that it was only
by the grace and mercy of
Christ
that three or four of the
site workers
hadn't been killed
when 'that fucking prick'
– 'that smart-alec Scottish fucking
would-be intellectual' – had gone

and lost control of the digger.
He never did any labouring
work again after that;
as a matter of fact
he didn't do anything.

Shuffling along the Cricklewood Broadway
every day, snug in the corners of
each and every pub
that he could find
&
wasn't barred from
poor Troy
his generation's brightest hope
The Undersea King of Brondesbury Gardens
who found
he couldn't hack it any longer
& just went back to the hostel
in Quex Road,
with a fresh bottle in his pocket
& already with his mind made up.

So how do you like him now,
Mr Death?
Tell me how you like him, Troy
you sweet and beautiful blue-eyed boy?

And which it's *crua*
yes, it's hard
there is no doubt about it
none at all
that it's hard
yes, very hard
indeed

& none would have acknowledged
that
anymore than Una Fogarty.
Hard, surely, she would readily have admitted –
crueller, maybe, than any man or woman
had a right to expect.

But then, of course,
there had been good times too,
Una would often think –
gathering up all her notes and bits
of paper,
exactly as she was doing now,
standing by the library in the
lobby of the Cliftonville Bay Hotel
while preparing to address her cast
because, after all, time is short
but this time around, as she knows
only too well
now, in the aftermath of her exciting trip
Up West
& having, against all the odds, managed
to secure
her precious silver medal
her lifelong treasure
why would she not be buoyed-up
& supremely confident
here in the home from home
where all systems are go for
the imminent *Cliftonville Capers.*
Hurray! she cries
& pulls out another great big bulging
Capers folder
one with her nickname written
all over it.

Although you wouldn't
be calling her 'Fudge',
not these days –
what with all the weight
she's lost
especially since
her 'scarpering expedition'.

No, in recent times Miss Streep
is looking much more
like Iris Matchstick-Montgomery
as off she wanders again with her walker
going about her business in the
'Dream Hotel'

which is how, of late, she's been
describing Cliftonville Bay,
Margate's 'home from home' care institution.

Sticking up more photos &
times for rehearsal
& handing out bits of paper
to everyone.

Not that anyone pays much heed
as regards At Home With The Fogartys
purportedly the show they'd been working on
all Winter
having long since gone and completely forgotten
all about it, however,
just as she knew she would,
to be honest
which is why she keeps
moving
& repeating, incessantly,
under her breath:
Danger UXB
Danger UXB
Danger UXB,

& doing her level best – and
I have to say I admire her courage,
not to hear the whistles
of the incoming V-1
rockets, silently
obliterating yet another
section of her soul
– one which had once meant so much,
essence of Una,
I suppose you might say
adding to the mounting quota of
obliterated bomb-voids
gradually reclaimed by
a plethora of strange grasses &
assorted wild herbs
like Murphy's patched little bald bits
of fur
hee hee, she said when she thought of
that,

insouciantly looping
a gleaming long string of saliva
around her finger
& replacing it deftly in her mouth
where it belongs
she laughs,
ha ha hee hee.

Before Butley Henderson
stops her near the fireplace.
I was wondering if you'd
seen Mike Yarwood, he quizzically murmurs,
& before receiving any answer
just shrugs his shoulders &
returns to the telly.

Whatever happened to The Likely Lads?
I heard one of the cast enquiring
just now,
before wandering off, apparently satisfied,
however humming the theme from
an entirely different series.

& there are regular, heated arguments
as to where it is
Mike Yarwood has *actually* gone.
With residents making all these
reasonable & seemingly
plausible suggestions –
before realising they're talking
about someone completely different
born forty years before Mike Yarwood
was ever heard tell of
& hasn't, in all likelihood, got anything
to do with television at all.
Bob Monkhouse had a great game yesterday,
one of them remarked, with considerable authority,
only this morning, to Una,
meaning the rugby.

& to which she'd replied:
The library at seven, we'll do a complete
run-through.

There can even be arguments
about the blameless iguana hatchling
with some of the cast cheering unequivocally
for the snakes
& others almost coming to
blows
so attached have they become to
David Attenborough's plucky star pupil.

The Killiburn Brae
is Una's latest suggestion – for the name of the
Autumn production, I mean.

It's going to be great
she's been going around telling
everyone
we're scheduled to headline at
The Margate Seafront Apollo
& are certain to sell
out the entire season
that's what my managers
have been telling me anyway, she
beams.

It's just a pity that Bonnie's not
here to play for us, she says.
Aye, Bonnie Sugrue –
Red Jack's daughter.
Then what does she do
starts this imaginary sawing on a fiddle
with great big sweeps of a would-be bow
before heading off laughing
nearly knocking over this old
chap in a dressing gown
who looks the image of Steptoe,
I swear to God.

They say that the women are worse than the men
Riteful titeful tiddy-fol-day! –

you can hear her coming all the way down
from the bottom of the corridor.

Motherfucking freaking diamondback assholes!
Todd Creedence bellows from
the television room –
go, iguana!

For a while Una'd been considering
taking on one of the sadder
roles in the show herself,
like Rita Tushingham
I remember her saying
in the garden
to Connie.
Yes, Rita Tushingham
or perhaps Rachel Roberts
– with those awful crushed eyes
the very same as I used to have
myself
around the time
it all, inevitably, came
to an end between me and Troy
as I knew it would
& I found myself
completely distracted
wandering the streets of London
would you believe it was a Sunday
well whether you do or not it was
and yes, it was in fact raining,
aye, & heavily
as I sat there on the top deck
of that old Routemaster
plashing through the
puddles of Killburn
until the vast panoply
of slated red roofs appeared
before me
& there I
was flying around
the drab & anonymous
outer London suburb

where Moody Alex
lived with his wife
or had done once
upon a time
yes, like a spirit bird
fluttering through the window
of the Gordons'
modest terraced house
to find myself confronted
by the irregular shapes of
household
furniture all draped in
sheets
of the drabbest linen
where stood a figure
before a mirror
evidently only recently
dead
clothesless entirely
with skin the colour of
pale blue ice
hi I'm Mary Millington
she said to me
soon you are going to
be the same as me
the star of Playmates
Mary Millington
come play with me
Moody Alex
I used to keep him company
as a matter of fact
I would go so far as to say
that, in fact, I might have been
the only love he had
in the end
isn't that sad,
Una dear.
Poor Alex
with the gulf that opened
up between not only
Vonnie, his wife of
almost twenty-five years & him
but the entire world
that he knew

his past and present
& indeed the future that
now wouldn't ever be
cor look at the bristols
on that he used to say
cor look at the bristols
on that
he liked my cleavage
you see
such a silly
liking
my bristols
I mean they're just little
milkies
for babogues
really
babogues that he'll
now never have
because it wasn't, you see,
to be
I'm sorry dear
but are you all right pet
are you all right darling
Una love can you hear me
dear?
and with the imní then returning
with a vengeance
as she retraced her journey
from Killiburn to Northolt
away out there on London's western outer ring
establishing how it was she got there
being in a state of fugue
with all the passengers
on the upper deck of the
Routemaster bus
staring straight ahead
of themselves
until the driver
looked out from his cab
pushing back his London
Transport cap
& revealing a face
that you really did not want to see
no you did not want

to see

       it

          at

            all.

&, indeed, would much rather
be looking into the eyes of
Troy McClory
on that momentous occasion
the morning of their very first day trip
to Watertown
that day when he had laid her gently
upon on the altar
flat out on the ornate mosaic
like his own personal human sacrifice
in the City Of Shells,
yes their own private kingdom
those magic Margate subterranean chambers
which had,
astonishingly,
been uncovered
by a gardener in an unremarkable
suburb
many years before,
in the very same place
where she'd lain
that day
looking up as
she stroked his long hair
and Troy had educated her all
about its history
excavated quite by chance
in the mid-nineteenth century
& which shouldn't,
couldn't,
have possibly been there
& yet, there it was
a real & true proper
genuine stone Temple
vastly superior to the one
they all had dreamed of
in Brondesbury,
containing gleaming passageways

so rich in design
with ornate geometrics
decorated in mussels
cockles, whelks
and oysters
along curving walls
& overarching vaults,
inner chambers & domes
with symbols of the sun
& moon
& that great big Rotunda
through which a silvery light
now made it way
& where, united, they moaned
as one, in ecstasy,
fusing with the universe
& Troy McClory said
forever you will be my
Queen
plunging deep within her
body & soul
Amphitrite
my
i
r
r
e
p
l
a
c
e
a
b
l
e

s
u
b
m
a
r
i
n
e

q
u   ʃ
e
e
n

& which is why
she keeps repeating
the same thing every day
whether in the kitchen or the
library
or just standing there at the
high window,
gazing out –
yes,
shells
shells
shells
shells
shells
shells

enough to drive the poor
Brazilian Princess mad
as if Una's much put-upon nurse
the long-suffering Connie
– yes, as if she didn't have
enough troubles of
her own.

Because she takes Una out
into the orchard, most days,

in her wheelchair.
Hoping the sun will
see them cease temporarily,
those endless incantations
which continue, remorselessly,
every single day:
shells
shells
shells
yes,
shells
shells
&
more *shells*
with the saintlike staff nurse
making Herculean attempts not to
abandon that admirable restraint,
instinctively understanding *imní*
as profoundly as she does.

Especially since her own attendance
to her expected duties in Cliftonville
has become somewhat erratic, to say the least.
With Margaret Rutherford, as she herself
will readily admit,
having been more or less constantly
on the younger woman's 'case'.
& missing few opportunities
to inform her as to how, regrettably,
she's not 'best pleased'.

With Una, still sequestered
under the boughs of an apple tree
in the orchard,
shaking her head
in a manner most
disturbing – even more distressing
than usual.

As though she's attempting
to communicate something of significance
to Connie
something of gravest importance
a matter of life and death, even.

But is too intimidated to
proceed with her quest for the words –
before eventually capitulating
& surrendering hopelessly to
unrestrained laughter,
lifting her pathetic form up
and down,
as she clutches frantically at
the green rubber grips,
as tears of helplessness come
coursing down her cheeks.

As Connie then, in her turn,
begins sobbing
& pouring
out her own private
troubles –
worst of all
the continuing difficulties
she'd been experiencing
with her boyfriend Celso.
Whom I love, Miss Una,
don't think that I don't,
but it cannot,
it cannot,
it cannot, you see, go on!

But Una Fogarty, however,
she wasn't listening
to a word the girl said,
smiling to herself as she commenced
a soft, distant lilt,
scarcely aware she was
doing it at all:
They say that the
women
are
worse than
the
men,
riteful, titeful,
titty folday!

With the trouble,
Connie continued,
oblivious of the fact that
she was in possession of
no identifiable audience,
being that Celso,
her live-in lover of three years,
not only was he in serious
trouble with the authorities,
having embezzled a significant sum
of money from
the online gambling firm
by whom he was employed
for the purposes of funding
his own betting addiction
but there were also other things.
Of comparable seriousness,
she elaborated,
although not availing of those actual words,
– including those associated with
her adored, ageing mother
now living all alone in São Paulo
& who, being a prodigious
smoker all her life,
had recently been admitted
to hospital
to undergo tests
where they had told her it
would probably be OK
it was just routine.
But Connie, nonetheless,
finding she couldn't sleep at all,
kept pacing her apartment,
waking up in the wee small hours –
endeavouring, with little success,
to eradicate apprehensions
of being intimately observed,
combined with suspicions
none of which was true
that certain other residents
in the building were
having meetings about her
& organising subtle & clever
stratagems

by which they, blamelessly,
might
undermine her.
& which was why,
only two nights previously,
she had ended up beating on the
door of the downstairs flat,
insisting that they suspend the music
they'd been playing
demanding, in fact, that
they take it off
immediately,
that they were only playing it
to keep her awake
to get at her
upset her
even more than she was already
that was why they were doing it
the very exact reason
she told them.
Before, eventually, after some
persuasion, realising
just how absurd
the contention had been –
as her elderly neighbour
a grey-haired man in his sixties,
stood there in his dressing gown,
seeming immensely shocked.

I'm sorry – it's my mother! Connie had
tendered by way of apology,
before returning, somewhat dazedly, to
her apartment.
It's my mother, she kept on repeating,
walking the floor the whole night
long.

None of which Una – now the
intended audience,
cared so much as a fig about,
being entirely subsumed in

her own personal, private world,
resting there in the wheelchair
beneath the apple tree,
pulling her fluffy woolly
cardigan tight around her
shoulders
& returning to yet another special day
in Brondesbury,
one representing what had to
be the most memorable,
& proudest day of her life.
When the investigating officer
a sniffy type for sure,
& not at all old-fashioned and gentlemanly
like Inspector Cockrill from *Green For Danger*,
he had arrived in The Temple
& within minutes
had already made
a number of less-than-magnanimous
asides not only as regards the appearance
of Una Fogarty
but also the reputation of her country, background
& family
& just what it was one might
be inclined to expect
from 'them' – meaning
the Irish
the Gaels –
those 'bog-trotters',
as he described them,
who come over here
to live off the community
– make me sick, they do,
he said as he prepared to leave.

Only to find his way barred
by none other than
Troy McClory
who had emerged from the middle of
the shamefully cowed assembly
& stood right there on the threshold,
in an unmistakable attitude of defiance.
Suggesting, in fact, that the officer
concerned,

he might consider having a modicum of decency
& withdraw, unreservedly, the remarks he had
just, & quite disgracefully, made.
Which Troy further categorised as 'wholly racist' &
'entirely despicable'
& beneath the office of
someone who described himself as
'a servant of the people'.

& just watching him do that,
utter those few simple sentences
not only on her behalf
but that of her countrymen
had amounted to nothing other
than the single most uplifting moment
of Una Fogarty's life.
Almost sacred, she thought.
Especially when she heard him
repeat later on
that he didn't give a damn
what anyone thought,
the police or anyone else.
'Because what's right is right,
& people are people,
whether Catholic or Protestant,
Gentile or Jew,
English or fucking Irish!'

That is all, he concluded, there is to it.

Yes, that was what he had done,
without prompting,
& with no prospect of any personal
gain,
proudly, & on her behalf,
stood his ground.
Simply because that was the type
Troy McClory was
&, deep down she knew that,
always had.

Which was why she began trembling
uncontrollably,
& which also was why Connie Gomes
she began waving frantically,
signalling across
to Margaret Rutherford.
Who arrived quite flustered and
out of breath – only to discover that
Una's mood had, once again, radically altered,
& she found herself greeted with the
heartiest of Irish welcomes.
'Begawpers, Maggie Rutherford,
you're the jewel of Cliftonville Bay
so you are!' Una bawled hysterically,
a white ribbon of froth already gathering
on her upper lip.

With the exasperated matron doing her
best to contain herself,
glaring intemperately over at Connie,
clearly considering, privately, to herself:
will I ever in my life
come to understand these people?

Especially when Una
looked up & gave her
a wink.

Before tugging her sleeve
& whispering intimately: *Would you like
to know a secret?*
Maybe the greatest secret of
them all, she explained,
the one about me, Una Fogarty –
turning into Dots.
Yes, becoming in the end,
the very exact same
as my own dear mother
& having a leanbh –
a baby not properly born,

that is,
& who was conceived
in a
City Of Shells beneath the sea.
Where Troy had taken off his
famous blue 'whistling' trousers
& together they'd performed the
most blissful *mickey-jump-jubbly*
in the world together,
right there on that 'great big sacred slab of stone'.

With
all these
wonderful
shadows
enveloping
us, Una continued,
& she'd heard him
whisper: my love, my Lady Ocean,
in your saintlike face
I read the love of ages.

& from which had resulted
the frailest, palest,
loveliest little infant ever.

My precious,
he had said,
Triton,
we'll call it,
our own little
leanbh
yes,
Triton,
born of love
here beneath the ocean.
Baby Triton McClory-Fogarty
conceived in Watertown on this day
In
The
Wake
Of

Poseidon,
when the planets
aligned.

Only for Una to arrive, unexpectedly,
into a bedroom of ruinous
fornication a mere two days later.

After which she had renounced
her job as a contract cleaner
&, like so many before her,
commenced her *via dolorosa*
of wandering.
Aye, rambling
here, there & yonder
up & down the length of the
Albin roads
as some poor old homeless navvy of old
consuming no end of bars of fudge
& performing songs by Mott the Hoople,
screeching them, faith,
at the top of her voice
&
taking
any old
drug
she could happen to lay
her hands on
& taking them
yes, & keeping on taking them
until one day all of them
together,
didn't they meld as one
into a great big ball of slaters
finally exploding inside of her
in the middle of a supermarket
one fine day
where she was standing in an overlit aisle
& which was where they found her
shrieking
as she pointed out all the various different
woodlice

like small meteors
plummeting from the sky.
Look! she cried,
&

look   look &

&   hey

look!

                    TANITH
EGBERT   POLTERGEIST
                              DEFEATS
        THE GREAT
        PLAGUE
                        OF   KAPLAN
        WALKING STICKS
    JOANNE   &
                                        KLUTE
        REACHES TRUE
MATURITY
            *THE OLD GREY WHISTLE TEST

        *UNATTENDED LUGGAGE MAY BE DESTROYED
                        URGENT!
    MC
            *UNATTENDED LUGGAGE MAY BE-
                CLORY   *LUGGAGE

    *DESTROYED
                    *MAY

                        *BE

*FRITZ THE CAT   *IN THE WAKE OF POSEIDON

*ATOMIC ROOSTER   *UPSTAIRS DOWNSTAIRS

*COMPANY OF WOLVES

*EDWARD HEATH

*ALL THE YOUNG

*FUJI

*GORDON'S GIN   *TROUT MASK REPLICA

*THE MAGIC TOYSHOP   *LOVECRAFT
*ANGELA DAVIS

*THE ANGRY BRIGADE

*PROVISIONAL IRA

*DUDES

*PLAYMATES

*MOTT   *DUDES
*ACID   *STONE THE

CROWS
*21ST CENTURY SCHIZOID MAN

*MIDDLE-EAST

*OIL CRISIS

*MAN ABOUT THE HOUSE

*GOODYEAR BLIMP

*HYPER-INFLATION
*CAN

*BAADER-MEINHOF   *SANYO

*WORLD OF ISLAM

until, eventually, they succeeded
in leading her away
& giving her leave to pretend,
just as she'd requested,
that she was, in fact,
all along at home by the fireside.
Yes, there at last,

in the old house in Currabawn
the only place
where she
could ease
her aching head –
at least
until
the day
Baby Triton
was due to arrive.

Except, of course
that ha ha
he
didn't,
I'm sorry to have to say,
even as she drifted
in & out of dead-end
jobs & institutions
with her life
now black-and-white
forever
she knew

as if she were caught
inside a loop of shadow
in a spin of archive-reel material
a grey wintry cine-poem with herself
as the sole performing actress
in a feature
where it always rains on Sunday
but of course it does,
a Rachel Roberts
for our time
the Rita Tushingham
of old Currabawn
in a juddering landscape
jerky & discontinuous
where it was always night
& where
the sky was filled
with wails that went eerily silent

not at all unreminiscent
of certain birds of prey
performing their strange
'war dance',
tracing in the sky
the wide aerial festoon
symbol of their mastery
of their kingdom
first the slow gliding
in the air,
the oblique dive toward
the ground,
V
V
V
V
V
V,
then the short, terrible
dart on the imagined victim,
as she asked herself
repeatedly
why on Sunday
why o why o why
does it always rai...

Trying not to hear
Troy McClory
calling her name
coming out of the fog
doing his level best to reach her
saying Una Una you never gave me a chance
why did you never give me just one
because that screwing meant nothing
I don't even remember
& that bit about the suicide
you imagined that
because you were afraid it might
all go wrong
so you broke it
you imagined it all
on purpose
& ruined what chance we might
have had,

you
&
me
&
our
lovely
baby.

Boy
Prince
of
our
perfect
S
u
b
m
a
r
i
n
e

E
m
p
i
r
e.

Because those were
the films
that she always
watched –
hundreds of them,
in overheated rooms,
hundreds
&
thousands
day after day
circling on a loop

afternoon after afternoon
night after night

Margaret Rutherford,
Googie Withers,
Irene Handl,
Rita Tushingham,
On the Buses
Mike Yarwood
Top Of The Pops
It Always Rains On Sunday.

Yes it does,
it does indeed,
matinee after matinee
always the same
in yet another grey institution
so many of which
all over London
she'd been in
but most of which she had long since
disremembered
with the assistance of
the Luftwaffe &
Baron Von Richthofen
not to mention
so many V-1 rockets.

& which is why,
rocking back and forth in
the wheelchair as Margaret Rutherford
patiently & sympathetically
brushed her hair,
Una – quite exhausted now
by all her exertions,
at last was showing signs of,
at least a little, slowing
down,
smiling as she saw
herself in the front
room in Brondesbury

waiting there smiling
as she sewed the little canvas sack
what, in Currabawn long ago,
they used to call a
mawla bag.

Before quietly informing
her Scrabble-playing flatmates
that she had a casual visit to make
to Limehouse Basin in East London

not that any of them were
listening of course
being way too stoned

as off she went on the bus
with the bag and its contents
safely tucked underneath her arm.
Attired not as some
hippy
who might like King Crimson
in a milkmaid's frock
but a simple cape coat and little pixie hat
the very exact same as her mother before her.

Humming softly to herself
val-de-ree, val-de-raa!,
as she leaned across,
releasing a long-suppressed sigh of
satisfaction
gazing down on the slopes of the
grey stony bank
now forever to be known
as the graveyard of
The Killiburn Brae.

Reflecting how she never
had been so happy
&, for the life of her,
could see no reason
why, right at that moment,
she ought not to
perform a jig

& which was exactly
what Una Fogarty did –
as she laughed, God help us,
her heart out as she did so
yelping as she high-stepped

just
how stupid & a downright
unrealistic
she had been
to, at any time, have imagined that
she and Troy
could ever possibly have
been
husband
&
wife
never mind
live
together
under
the
sea.

& which was why
she was still laughing hysterically
as she raised the snug, embroidered
little *mawla bag*
& fired it high as she could,
away over her head
& let out what could only be
described as an unmerciful cry of triumph
as the bag and its contents
went skittering along the
wet concrete slope
of The Killiburn Brae,
coming to rest on the foreshore
where so many
down the years
had fetched up in the dawn.

Not that there, to tell the truth, was
a great deal inside of it
with its contents consisting
principally of myself.
Aye wee unborn Dan
which didn't amount
to a great deal more
than a biteen of flesh and
a few little drops of fuil

which was all
in the end
she had succeeded in giving
birth to,
ploc
& then ploc ploc ploc
forever inside a bag.

With her relief being immense
as she folded her umbrella
and, dabbing one last wee gallyogue of a deoir
one final thin tear of sadness
from her eye,
gave a last high kick and
shouted out to the capacious darkness
of The Brae:
Mo chroí, lán-briste.

My heart, heavily broken.

And went off then about her business.

With Una, at long last,
finishing her story
& being wheeled back
inside the building by Rutherford.
Smiling ruefully as she
crossed her legs on the window seat
gazing fondly beyond the

high window
at a pair of little childre
robustly playing together among the
trees.
As the little ten-year-old,
complete with baby-pink *Peanuts*
backpack,
yapped away impatiently into her phone:
omg omg I do not believe it!
I cannot believe that she likes mini-pizzas!

With Una's script lying discarded
where she had
gone and completely forgotten
all about it
as over came Todd
leading Murphy the dog
immediately recognising
the kind of mood my sister was in
arguing with herself
whether or not it was 'The Birdie Song'
or 'The Seaside Shuffle'
which was going to close the show,
invoking the ululations
of the winged legions
in tones of varying quality & timbre,
accompanied by a wide variety of
impressively agile facial expressions.

Not that Todd Creedence or Murphy
seem to mind very much,
settling themselves in as they wait for
David Attenborough,
with Murphy glaring at a gull
through the glass –
one whom he appears to know, in fact.
Before giving a sudden, unexpected leap
& knocking a carton of yogurt all
over the carpet.

'Motherfucking dumb fucking mutt!' howls Todd –
just as the television aquatic expert
makes his appearance, quieting everyone
with his trademark dulcet tones.
'I'm sorry!' the baleful eyes of Murphy
seem to be suggesting,
as he rests his great big boxy head
on the lap of the hopelessly
discommoded, yogurt-splattered ex-Marine.

To which laughter, really, is
the only appropriate response.
Particularly when you look at Connie,
minha princesa,
standing out there
again in the garden
underneath a sycamore
glazed with rain,
surreptitiously – *I know it!* –
shredding a piece of
tissue in her pocket.

Of late she seems so *fraught*
– especially when you consider
that she's only just turned twenty-five.
which is no age at all
to be finding yourself fearing
that you might be getting sick
never mind dreading the
onset of early Alzheimer's –
which is her latest concern.

But it's all just that old imní, she'll
perhaps eventually succeed in persuading herself.
Or *ansiedade*, as they call it in Portuguese.

These continuing altercations with her
boyfriend, of course, don't help.
With her just this minute having received

another call from Celso,
requesting that she give him money.

More money, of course.

No wonder she'll often call Rutherford,
ringing in to say
she's sick.

Doing what she can to cure herself,
lying awake half the night,
endeavouring as best she can
to divert her thoughts
by concentrating
on the various people she
has come to
know in Cliftonville Bay,
ever since arriving in the UK.

The nursing staff, in particular,
I suppose,
who she has always admired for giving 100%.
But also, many of her wonderful patients –
in particular, Todd Creedence, who
she took to right from the beginning.
Yes, she likes him immensely –
very affectionate.
& Roystone Oames – who, regrettably,
eventually – inevitably,
succumbed to cancer.

& who, in his time,
had never been remiss about programming
the channel for David Attenborough
arranging all the chairs in a circle in
recreation,
getting everyone ready to cheer on the hatchling.
Yes, she thought,
that indomitable little newborn lizard
who never failed to rouse a cheer of admiration
and solidarity
as it ascended the ridge
& then turned defiantly
to face its pursuers.

What fun they all were.

& then, of course, there was the Irish lady
who Todd insisted looked the spit of
Ho Chi Minh, left way too long in the sun
ha ha.
Una Fogarty was her name, spending a lot
of her time beneath a tree
in her high-backed nursing-home
chair, her hands clenched arthritically, sipping
milky tea from the spout of a plastic training
mug.
She often brought her on trips down to Margate
or maybe, if it was open, to Dreamland.

And would, as a matter of fact, be doing so tomorrow.
She was already looking forward to it.
That is, of course, if her boss didn't summon her
once again into her office.
Matron Irwin, the superior that the lady
in question kept referring to as *Margaret Rutherford*,
whoever she was.
'Just another little birdie,' Matron explained
meaning, apparently, 'fib', *uma mentira*.

With a bit of luck, however,
hopefully it wouldn't come to that,
another of Rutherford's stern office
dressing-downs.

With her retiring particularly early to bed
that same night,
enjoying some silly little film
on Netflix.
& maybe that was what did it, I don't know.
Somehow, obliquely, invoked that unfortunate
dream,
the one in which she envisaged
herself as a twelve-year-old teenager,
hearing the faint distant toll of the
convent bell
in all its poignancy

wandering among the market stalls
where, in spite of the mounds of
bones & discarded fish-heads,
moist innards in filthy water,
she felt herself
transfixed by the fragrance
of the most beautiful roses
borne along on warm
currents of air.
In exactly the same way
as it had been when
she had walked there, after school,
transcendent in the company
of her long-dead father.

Whose voice she could hear so precisely
now, calling out her name:
Consuela! Consuela, meu preciosa!
as he stood there alone,
in a different place now –
silhouetted on the brow of a hill,
shading his eyes as he gazed, implacably, down.
Towards what she had taken to be the city of
São Paulo
but then realised that it was, in fact, Jerusalem.
With drifting clouds passing gleaming domes and
copper minarets, under a red sunset
high over distant hills.
& it was then that she heard them –
three lilting notes
in waltz time, rendered on an accordion,
where do you go to my lovely?
she heard the faint, gathering voice of crushed
velvet beginning to croon,

& she found herself instinctively,
trepidatiously, looking upwards
to observe it forming –
gradually, remorselessly directly above her
on the ceiling –
widening in an ever-increasing circle
seeping into the plasterwork
bordering the light bulb,

until – *at last!* – the very first drop,
mercifully, became detached:

ploc!
she heard,
& then that very soft whispering
sound,
those thin stridulations,
a susurration.

With her initial thought being
that she ought to call Celso –
before realising
that they had only just agreed,
at long last,
to part.

Because I just can't take it anymore!
she had told him.

A course of action which
she was already beginning to
suspect she was regretting.

Because it isn't very nice being lonely, is it?

No – because uaigneas, after a while,
it can be hard.
Especially when it runs the risk of developing into
full-blown imní.

That is to say, anxiety and depression – as,
given her experience, Consuela knew very
well it could.

And which was why she wished with
all her heart that it hadn't recurred.

The susurration, that is –
the noise that one associates with
grasshoppers.

With the beads of perspiration, exactly as on
previous occasions,
lining themselves up
one two three
one two three,
patiently,
methodically,
across her forehead.

As she donned her slippers and, with increasing
disquiet, commenced her journey
across the floor of the room.
Making the sign of the Cross in the process,
just as her mother had taught her to do,
slowly sinking to one knee, craning her neck to inspect
the interior of the pleated white metal grid.

With the immensity of her relief being incalculable
when she realised that,
once again,
as so often before
it had been nothing more threatening than a
simple stray gust of wind,
her sense of relief
acknowledged by the soft cooing melody
of the tireless voyager
who had appeared
perched on the ledge outside her window,
wings & tail stirring ceaselessly
with abrupt movements,
surveying her through the
living pearl of its eye.

Bye bye blackbird, Connie heard herself sigh
as she smiled and stood up,
knotting her dressing-gown cord as she did
so.
Almost laughing, in fact, by this stage –
stiffening sharply, however, the moment
she heard what sounded
like the wind-driven noise of a
V-1 missile,
not that she could possibly have

been aware of such a thing.
But with the sense of dread that
it, unmistakably, induced,
being more than validated,
it is regrettable to have to say,
by the sight which met her eyes
when, eventually, she turned
& saw the smiling figure waiting there
patiently,
hunkered discreetly in a corner,
with that fluted, disconcerting whistle
of admiration finally abating,
not making a sound.

'I've only just arrived from São Paulo,'
she heard herself being
flatly informed,
'there's an important piece of news
concerning your mother, I'm afraid.'

As her visitor began gradually emerging
as though from a mass of foliage
where the light no longer
penetrates
before proceeding calmly,
inexorably towards her –
then performing a skittish little
two-step as he clapped his hands and,
with a suddenness truly startling,
initiated a spirited, lusty lilt:
There was an auld man down by Killiburn Brae
Riteful, titeful, titty folday
There was an auld man down by Killiburn Brae
Had a curse of a wife with him most of his days
      With me foldoarol dol, titty fol ol
      Foldol dol dolda dolder olday

The divil he says I have come for your wife
Riteful titeful titty folday
The divil he says I have come for your wife
For I hear she's the curse and the bane of your life
      With me foldoraol dol, titty fol ol
      Foldol dol dolda dolder olday

So the divil he hoisted her up on his back
Riteful, titeful titty folday
So the divil he hoisted her up on his back
And away off to hell with her he did pack
      With me foldoraol dol, titty fol ol
      Foldol dol dolda dolder olday

And when they came back to Killiburn Brae
Riteful, titeful, titty folday
And when they came back to Killiburn Brae
Well the divil he capered and shouted hooray!

'Dan Fogarty, ma'am, at your service,
if you playze, although there's them that
call me Senhor Exu –
inveterate collector of blue-eyed
boys & girls.
So, let you be getting your bits and pieces together
and the pair of us we'll be on our way –
for we've a long road to travel
& there's plenty we have to say,
in the words of Ginsberg,
McGowan, and Pablo
di mierda
motherfucking Neruda
in soaring circles
shed our triumphant stanzas
scrolling them with abandon
up amongst the drifting clouds,
in the faraway yonder
atwixt the sun and golden moon.

So then, give me your hand
& maybe, if you're willing,
just the smallest *biteen* of a *pogue*
– aye, right here on the swell of your
pearly, undulating *tóin*.
The better, maybe, to seal the bargain,
& reassure Her Ladyship
that divil the bit of harm from this out
will befall her –
whether from Dan or his counterpart
Senhor Exu

this day, me darling princess,
or tomorrow,
or, faith, in the times that are yet to come,
now & for—

ha   !

                                                          ha

          ha   ha   !

                                                                          ha

                    ha

  ha   !

        ha   !   ha

!   ha

    !   ha   !

ha   ha

      !   ha

f—

ha   *   !

              —   *   ha

                  *   r

ha !

                        eve   !

                                              ha

              ! ha ha!

        f—

ha

                        f—   *

ha   *

              ha

                    ha

                                        ha

      *   ha

          ha ha !

      Ha   !

                                              ha

!

    for   !

        *

          ha   ha   *

              *   !

[601]

–ever!

May God forgive me this night should I play you false.

THE END.

unbound

Unbound is the world's first crowdfunding publisher, established in 2011.

We believe that wonderful things can happen when you clear a path for people who share a passion. That's why we've built a platform that brings together readers and authors to crowdfund books they believe in – and give fresh ideas that don't fit the traditional mould the chance they deserve.

This book is in your hands because readers made it possible. Everyone who pledged their support is listed below. Join them by visiting unbound.com and supporting a book today.

Supporters

Jude Abbott
Ellen Adair Glassie
Ashley Allen
Edward Allen
Lulu Allison
Lucy V W Armstrong
Claire Back
Stefan Bainbridge
Gordon Baird
Alan Baldwin
Graham Ball
Julian Ball
Ciara Banks
Pierre Barel
Sebastian Barry
Catharine Benson
Steve Berrington

Neil Best
Graham Blenkin
Dermot Bolger
Alessia Borri
Don Boyd
Richard Brady
Catherine Brand
John Brannigan
Richard W H Bray
Damien Brennan
Damien Brennan
Stephanie Bretherton
Christian Brett
Michael Brooke
Andrew R Brown
John Brown
Caroline Butler
Michael Cahill
June Caldwell
Paul Callaghan
Paul Carlyle
Fiona Carpenter
Team Carr
Cavan County Council Arts Office
Andy Charman
Dolly Claridge
Anne Clarke
Joe Clarke
Victoria Clarke
Brandon Clauser
Charlie Clements
Shari Cohen
Pat Collins
Martin Connolly
Philip Connor
Rebecca Connor
Joe Cooney
Midie Corcoran
Ray Cornwall
Eileen Corroon
Pauine Cotter
Cathal Coughlan
Robert Cox
Therese Cox

Matthew Craig
M. Crawford
Jessa Crispin
Julia Croyden
Daniel Cullen
David Cummings
Kevin Cunniffe
Peter Cunningham
Matt Curran
Paul Curran
John Darnielle
Natasha Davis
Terry Deegan
Paul Dembina
Stanislaus Dempsey
Tony Dempsey
Andy Denton
Luan Denton-Bradbury
Ronnie Dewhurst
John Dineen
Philip Doherty
Jennifer Doig
Damian Donnelly
Maura Dooley
Joe Dotts
Susan Doyle
Daniel Drozdzewski
Paul Duane
Jessica Duchen
James Duffy
Adrian Dunbar
Adrian Duncan
Lindsay Duncan
Philip Dundas
Karl Easley
Bilge Ebiri
Michelle Eiffe
Hugh Elliott
Nathan Erickson
Avril Erskine
Martina Evans
Elaine Feeney
Steven Feeney
Chris Finnegan

Noreen Fitzgerald
Steven Fitzroy Reid
Anne Fleming
Muriel & John Fleming
Joanna Fortune
Martine Frampton
John Francis Cooney
Adrian Frazier
Jacqueline Fry
Nicola Furey
Joe Gannon
Elizabeth Garner
Nick Garrard
Noreen Gavin
Justin Gayner
Lynn Genevieve
Vanessa Gildea
Rina Gill
Helen Gillard Healy
Séamus Given
Henry Glassie
Conor Gogarty
Gerry Gogarty
Giles Goodland
Grainne Goodwin
Bruce Gordon
Declan Gorman
Michael Gorman
Louis Gouzerh
Amber Graci
Andy Green
Jonathon Green
Majella Greene
Sarah Greene
Mike Griffin
Patricia Groome
Dylan Gunn
Elaine Gunn
Seamus Gunn
Marianne Gunn O'Connor
Ian Hagues
Thom Hammond
Tim Hanna
Fionan Hanvey

Michael Harding
Alan Hardy
Dermot Hargaden
Tricia Harrington
Neil Harrison
Barry Hasler
David Hayden
Nigel Heather
David Hebblethwaite
Justyn Hegreberg
Mox Henderson
Nick Hennegan
Carmel Hennigan
Susie Henry
Gina Herold
Alex Hewins
Jason Hewitt
Margaret Hickey
Tony Histed
Thomas Hodgins
Phil Hodgson
James Edward Hodkinson
Keith Hopper
Bridget Houlton
Bob Howell
Maureen Hughes
Richard Hughes
Nick Hunter
Jessica Hurtgen
Jim Hynes
Gary Ilsley
Jenny Ireland
Ruth Irvine
Caz "FunkyRabbitArt" Jackson
Bruce Jacobs
Michael Janes
Dan Jenkins
Lisa Jenkins
Mandy Jenkinson
Alice Jolly
Eddy Jones
Margaret Jones
Rhodri Jones
Jennifer Jordan

Neil Jordan
Andres Kabel
Heiko Kammerhoff
Ciaran Kane
Molly Kavanagh
Jennifer Keating
Joe Keenan
Bob Kelly
John Kelly
Al Kenny
John Kenny
Rachael Kerr
Tim Kerr
Dan Kieran
Alan Kilcoyne
Geoffrey King
Gabrielle Kubicek
Jacqui Lacey
Mit Lahiri
Michael Lally
John Lancaster
Pete Langman
Cara Lari
Fion Lau
Mary Lavan
Eric J. Lawrence
Ewan Lawrie
Abigail Lawson
Alison Layland
Janice Leagra
Enda Leaney
Paul Leharne
Liliana
Amy Lloyd
Jim Lockhart
Rachael Loftus
Kelly Loughlin
Catriona M. Low
Andy Luckett
Ingrid Lyons
Seamas Mac Annaidh
Jonathan Macartney
Colin MacCabe
Paul Mackle

Johnny Madden
Laura Madden
The Madden's
John Maher
Brian Mahoney
Chloe Mahony
Rachel Malik
Doug Mann
Ruth Martin
Steve Matthews
Tim Mawe
Aaron McAdam
Daniel McAdam
John McArdle
Mark McAvoy
Barney McCabe
Ben McCabe
Ellen McCabe
Eugene (Houdi) McCabe
Katie McCabe
Benedict McCaffrey
Eugene McCague
Ciaran McCarthy
Ted McCarthy
Dara McCluskey
Michele McCluskey
Edel Mcconnell
Mike McCormack
Una McCormack
Kevin McDermott
Alex McDonnell
John McDwyer
Collette Doreen McEntee
Paddy McEntee
Kevin McGahern
Bernie McGrath
Jane McGrath
Mary McGuirk
Carole McIntosh
Padraig McIntyre
Gregory McKenna
Shane McKenna
Brian McKeon
Gary McKeone

Catriona McLister
Brendan McLoughlin
Francis McLoughlin
John McMahon
Seamie McMahon
John McManus
Alan McMonagle
Stephen McNamara
Eoin McNamee
James McParland
Dermot McPartland
Jim McQuaid
Garry McQuinn
David McRedmond
Harry Meadows
Paula Meehan
Mary Megarry
Bob Mehr
Sé Merry Doyle
Haverty Michael
Roger Miles
Andy Miller
Christopher Milroy
George Mitchinson
John Mitchinson
Alan Moloney
Aaron Monaghan
Patrick Mongoven
Patrick Mooney
Jac Moore
Mary Morgan
Orla Morgan
Jackie Morris
Danny Morrison
Bernard Moxham
Paul Muldoon
Síne Mullin
Cillian Murphy
Lindsay Murphy
Shane Murphy
Laura Murray
Tiffany Murray
Sally Murrey
Stephen Musgrave

Deen Mutch
Markus Naegele
Carlo Navato
Mark Nevin
Ciara Ni Chuirc
Bláthnaid Ní Oistín
Dearbháil Ní Oistín
Sean Nolan
Georgina Nugent-Folan
Gerry O Boyle
Donnchadh O Briain
Emmet O Brien
Tomás O hOistín
Darach O Tuairisg
Bla O'Brien
Dermot O'Brien
Joe O'Byrne
Alan O'Donnell
Fiona O'Dwyer
Timothy O'Grady
Peter O'Hanlon
David O'Leary
Pat O'Loughlin
Michael J. O'Neil
Mark O'Neill
Geraldine O'Reilly
Karen O'Sullivan
Ryan O'Connor
Ruth O'Rourke-Jones
Thaddeus O'Sullivan
Kevin Offer
Molly Oldfield
Petra Oorthuijs
Inken Ostendorf
Huigenia Ostik
Christopher Owens
Daragh Owens
Eamonn Owens
Marc Pacitti
Jack Page
Jan Page
Michael Paley
Lev Parikian
Steph Parker

Rose Parkinson
Richard Peace
Paul Perry
Neil Philip
Tara Physick
Mae Physioc
Basil Pieroni
Justin Pollard
Alison Collison Powell
Jay Powell
Mandy Powell
Dameon Priestly
Glenaduff Productions
Morag Prunty
Bob Quinn
Catherine Quinn
Dearbhla Quinn
Margot Quinn
Sinead Quinn
Terry Quinn
Simon Ray
Marcella Reardon
Michael Regan
Mick Reilly
Piers Ricketts
Nick Riddle
Laurel Rivera
Anthea Robertson
Lynne Robinson
Abigail Rose
Maurice Roycroft
Jonathan Ruppin
Rita Ryan
Keith Salmon
Grant Samphier
Grant Samphier
Christoph Sander
Garret Scally
Alan Scanlan (Harolds Cross)
Ann Scanlon
Arthur Schiller
Ronald Scott
Bill Scott-Kerr
James Scudamore